# Understanding the Mind of Your Bipolar Child

# Understanding the Mind of Your Bipolar Child

# Understanding the Mind of Your Bipolar Child

**The Complete Guide to the Development, Treatment, and Parenting of Children with Bipolar Disorder**

Gregory T. Lombardo, M.D., Ph.D.

ST. MARTIN'S PRESS ✖ NEW YORK

www.stmartins.com

Brain illustrations by Debra Welling

Kind permission has been granted to use material from the following:

*Diagnostic Criteria for Conduct Disorder, ADHD, ADD, Oppositional Defiant Dis-
order, Panic Disorder, Obsessive Compulsive Disorder, and Social Anxiety Disorder*
from the *Diagnostic and Statistical Manual of Mental Disorders,* Fourth Edition,
Text Revision (copyright 2000) in *Pediatric Hospital Medicine.* Reprinted with
permission from the *Diagnostic and Statistical Manual of Mental Disorders,* copyright 2000. American Psychiatric Association.

Library of Congress Cataloging-in-Publication Data

Lombardo, Gregory T.
    Understanding the mind of your bipolar child : the complete guide to the
development, treatment, and parenting of children with bipolar disorder /
Gregory T. Lombardo.—1st ed.
        p. cm.
    Includes index.
    ISBN-13: 978-0-312-35889-1
    ISBN-10: 0-312-35889-X
    1. Manic depressive illness in children—Popular works.  2. Child
rearing—Popular works.  I. Title.

RJ506.D4L66 2006
618.92'895—dc22                        2006047284

First Edition: November 2006

10  9  8  7  6  5  4  3  2  1

FOR JOANNE

# Contents

## PART I

# Diagnosis

## PART II

# Development

PART III

# Treatment

# ACKNOWLEDGMENTS

This book would not have been written without the urging, encouragement, and forbearance of my wife, Dr. Joanne Intrator. Dr. Christa Balzert's encouragement as a colleague and mentor was also crucial. I am specifically indebted for advice from Dr. Ava Siegler, Dr. Ralph Lopez, Dr. Francis Mas, and Dr. Peter Neubauer. I am grateful as well to the patients and families whose work with me and trust taught me much of what I know about bipolar disorder. My editor, Sheila Oakes, saved me from many careless or inarticulate phrases. Anything I write is indebted to Professor Edward Tayler.

There is a Catskill eagle in some souls that can alike dive down into the blackest gorges, and soar out of them again and become invisible in the sunny spaces. And even if he forever flies within the gorge, that gorge is in the mountains; so that even in his lowest swoop, the mountain eagle is still higher than other birds upon the plain, even though they soar.

—HERMAN MELVILLE

O the mind, mind has mountains; cliffs of fall
Frightful, sheer, no-man-fathomed. Hold them cheap
May who ne'er hung there.

—GERARD MANLEY HOPKINS

# Understanding the Mind
# of Your Bipolar Child

# Introduction

Bipolar disorder is a manageable condition, one that is more manageable the earlier it is recognized and the more comprehensively it is treated. The better parents understand how bipolar disorder affects their child's mind, affects how a child takes in the world, and affects how a child reacts to its complex demands, the better parents can help their child.

I have been diagnosing and treating children with bipolar disorder for many years and have seen a great many of these children go on to live happy and productive lives—not just children who were bright and personable but also those who struggled with learning disorders, intense anxiety, isolation from peers, substance abuse, enormous irritability, and overwhelming anger. Despite their many difficulties, most of these children also have powerful gifts for empathy, imagination, inventiveness, and productivity that they have learned to use to their best advantage.

In my treatment of these children, I have worked both pharmacologically and psychotherapeutically, using play therapy for younger children and talk with adolescents. I have worked individually, with groups (ones that talked and ones that didn't), and with a wide range of families, including those that were intact, those split by divorce, single-parent families, and families in which a child was being raised by grandparents. I have had the opportunity to work with these children and families over the course of as many as twelve years, allowing me to see bipolar disorder as a condition that affects not only mood and behavior but also development: development from one set of developmental tasks on to the next and the next.

Before I became a psychiatrist I was a teacher, at both the college and secondary levels. This experience has given me a special understanding of the problems a bipolar child encounters at school—not only problems with behavior but also challenges with thinking and writing. Bipolar disorder has an effect not only on a child's mood and behavior but also on the way he experiences the world and consequently on the way he thinks. The unusual intensity and fluidity with which a bipolar child senses the world and perceives his own emotions and those of people around him can be a source of inventiveness, leadership, and artistic talent. People with bipolar disorder see things in unusual ways, they make unusual associations, they have a powerful impact on other people, and they see the world with an intensity that can be inspiring. However, a bipolar person's intensity, his quickly shifting emotions, racing thoughts, and distraction by this intense inner world can also be a source of confusion and disorganization. This disorganization can extend subtly into basic tasks like reading and writing. Even a verbally gifted child can have difficulties with reading and writing that don't affect other children. These problems, especially in a gifted child, can cause frustration and discouragement with academic work. A bipolar child's quick intuitive thought can be an asset, but it can emerge as a problem when it comes to paying attention to details. These characteristic qualities of the mind of a bipolar child are easily misunderstood both by teachers and parents.

Over the years I have become increasingly optimistic about my ability to help children and adolescents with bipolar disorder. I am also convinced, however, that the role of loving and well-informed parents cannot be overstated. The greatest gift you can give your child is understanding. Yet a child with a bipolar disposition is sometimes very difficult to understand. My goal in writing this book is to increase your knowledge of the disorder, its treatments, and how you as a parent can be most helpful to your child. I'll explain both the biological and developmental aspects of the disease, because if you can grasp the link between your child's biology and her development, you can help her cope with the impact the condition has on the growth of her personality and her mind.

Unfortunately, in the time I have been working with bipolar children and their families, a separation has emerged between the professionals responsible for a child's care—increasingly psychiatrists simply prescribe medication, and other professionals (psychologists, social workers, psychiatric nurses, substance abuse counselors) carry on the day-to-day, week-to-week work of psychotherapy. Communication between psychiatrists and these other professionals with whom they collaborate is often infrequent and difficult to arrange. Economic forces drive this separation, because most families can't afford to see a psychiatrist regularly. Insurance companies have also contributed to this change—more in mental health care than in other areas of medicine—because they typically place tight restrictions on psychotherapy, both on the number of sessions allowed and on the compensation given for the time-consuming work of psychotherapy. There is an unstated pressure to treat mental illness with medication alone. A medical model of infrequent brief checkups with a psychiatrist is being fostered.

Additionally, there have been changes in support for medical education, so that residency programs have less opportunity to teach psychotherapy. For example, when I trained as a child psychiatrist, the average hospital stay for severely ill adolescents was six months; now it is two weeks. With this brief length of stay, the opportunity for young psychiatrists to learn individual and group psychotherapy in a hospital setting is virtually eliminated. Whether in a hospital or as an outpatient, it is all too common for a child to see a psychiatrist infrequently and then only for brief med-checks. These limits on a psychiatrist's role in the treatment of patients are creating a separation between the biology of bipolar disorder and its impact on a person and on a personality. This book will bridge that divide.

The book is organized into three parts: "Diagnosis," "Development," and "Treatment."

Part I, "Diagnosis," explains how a doctor arrives at a formal diagnosis of bipolar disorder. Chapter 1 introduces the symptoms of bipolar disorder and explains how a physician makes the diagnosis. Chapter 2 describes the behavior, anxiety, and/or personality disorders that can complicate that diagnosis.

In Part II, "Development," you'll learn what bipolarity looks like at different ages. Chapters 3–10 are arranged according to a child's developmental tasks, comparing and contrasting bipolarity with average development, showing how it affects a child's ability to move through crucial developmental tasks, and explaining how it impacts your job as a parent. You'll learn how you can help your child handle the more manageable problems early on, such as self-regulation or accepting limits, before these problems become serious difficulties (such as oppositional behavior, social isolation, substance abuse, or school refusal). In Chapter 9, you'll learn about the consumption disorders that frequently accompany bipolar disorder (alcohol and drug abuse, eating disorders, promiscuity, compulsive shopping, and stealing) and how they can arise from or complicate earlier problems. Chapter 11 also describes the overlap of behavioral, anxiety, and personality disorders with bipolar disorder.

What happens at one stage of development crucially affects later developmental tasks. In order to illustrate how this happens, the clinical vignettes in this section are sometimes quite lengthy—spanning years—so that you can see both how one developmental difficulty can lead to another and how different interventions by parents or therapists help over time.

Part III, "Treatment," examines how the different kinds of psychotherapy work: play therapy, behavioral therapy, individual talk therapy, and group therapy. Bipolar disorder often has a devastating effect on a child's relationships with other children, particularly groups of children. Activity-group therapy, discussed in Chapter 12, is particularly effective for children between the ages of eight to twelve who have severe disturbances in their peer relationships. (Indeed, in most cases these problems cannot be treated *except* with group therapy.) For adolescents who have difficulty with peers, more traditional group therapy, also discussed, is more appropriate.

Appendix A will teach you about the medicines used to treat bipolar disorder and related conditions. You'll find detailed descriptions of the different classes of medications, what these medicines do, their potential side effects, and when their use is appropriate.

Appendix B is dedicated to fighting weight gain in children, a problem that can be fostered by some of the medications used to treat bipolar disorder and complicated by the effects of blood sugar on mood. The Glossary defines terms associated with bipolar disorder.

When you have finished reading this book, you will have a complete picture of bipolar disorder, ranging from infancy through adolescence, including the impact of bipolar disorder on your child's development, as well as the need for professional diagnosis and psychiatric and psychotherapeutic treatment. This book will enable you to better understand your child and provide effective support every step of the way.

Finally, although the inspiration for this book grew principally from my work as a child psychiatrist, some of it comes from my own experience, which has helped me understand from within what it means to be bipolar. I have not suffered from classic manic depression but from the more subtle and clinically confusing bipolar II, a form of bipolar disorder that consists of recurrent depressions alternating with periods of irritability and elation. This form of bipolar disorder typically begins with depression and often at an early age, which was the case with me. For myself, as for many children, my awareness of the condition (and its relation to my own family history) did not occur for many years, until I was in my forties.

Like many of the children I see, I had to contend with subtle learning difficulties affecting my ability to read and to write clearly. I also exhibited a classic symptom of attention-deficit/hyperactivity disorder (ADHD)—impulsivity. My earliest memory of reckless impulsivity was at the age of four when I raced my tricycle down a hill and out into the street. That was only the first of many incidents. In those days, no one recognized ADHD, but I remember often being scolded for "hand trouble" (touching or playing with things I was supposed to stay away from), for losing my keys, or for being "off in the clouds." I enjoyed some of the positive sides of bipolarity as well, having a good imagination, an ear (if not an eye) for language, precocious empathy, and a way of looking at things more deeply and from a slightly different angle.

The hardest aspects of my bipolarity were the depressions and the irritability, which went untreated until I was in my forties. Like many other people who suffer from bipolar depression, however, I sometimes found in the depths of my depressions perceptions, strength, and wisdom I otherwise would have lacked. I have been fortunate ultimately to receive good treatment and master the dangerous intensities of this condition. Without such treatment I would never have succeeded as a psychiatrist, and this book would never have been written.

# PART I

## Diagnosis

# CHAPTER ONE

# Understanding Bipolar Disorder

The following portraits will give you a vivid illustration of how differently bipolar disorder can appear in different children and at different ages. I will then go on to explain what connects these very different children to a single diagnosis of bipolar disorder.

> RALPH, age eleven, was an excellent student and a creative, talented artist. He was also impulsive, overly excited in groups, often silly and goofy, and subject to sudden aggression. Ralph's inappropriate behavior made him a target for teasing at school, while at home his difficulty in accepting limits was causing his relationship with his parents to deteriorate. His mother brought him to me primarily because he seemed depressed and had difficulty sleeping.
>
> JEAN was first seen at the age of twelve, because of complaints of depression. She cried frequently, had great difficulty sleeping, imagined herself dying, and had recently begun deliberately scratching herself superficially, enough to break the skin but not penetrate it. Jean also had periods of intense energy and high spirits during which she had unrealistically grand ideas. When I saw her, her speech was rapid and her thinking was scattered. While her developmental history was largely normal, she had experienced great

difficulty with the word *no* when she was a toddler and had an episode of depression as early as the fourth grade.

**KLAUS** was a handsome, sweet, blond six-year-old who was brought to me because of severe tantrums, as well as oppositional and bizarre behavior. He was also highly activated—becoming hyperactive and silly—when he ate sugar. Klaus had been started on Ritalin at age five for what was thought to be ADHD, but when I first saw him he was frankly psychotic: hyperactive, silly, grimacing, and talking incessantly. He drew several pictures in rapid succession in a wild and scribbling style. He had cut up his clothes with scissors after a dream in which he found himself in a "paper world" where a paper tiger had bitten off his head. He told me he cut up his clothes while trying to cut up the tiger that was attacking him. His reaction to the stimulant (and to sugar) made clear to me that his hyperactivity and inattention were symptoms of early onset bipolar disorder.

Each of these children suffers from bipolar disorder, a psychiatric condition characterized by dramatic movements between two poles or extremes of mood. As you may already know, a child with bipolar disorder can go from periods of being overly high or irritable (hypomania) to periods of despair and hopelessness (depression) and back again— sometimes within the space of just a few minutes. These mood changes (oscillations) can be startling and confusing, both to the child and those around him. He may feel happy and content one minute, then suddenly plunge into deep despair or intense rage. He may ricochet between a sense of well-being and personal power and a sense of hopelessness and depression, between feelings of creativity and energy and feelings of frustration and inertia. A manic silliness or an explosive irritability can suddenly be replaced by an anxious withdrawal from the world.

Mood swings can be triggered by stress, monthly or daily hormonal cycles, seasonal changes, variations in blood sugar, or the ups and downs of life. Although mood swings affect all children to some extent, they can be disabling for a child with bipolar disorder. Once set in motion, these swings can develop a life of their own—they can build up a biological head of steam, a momentum that carries well beyond the original insult and cannot be quelled by typical parenting.

Bipolar disorder is also characterized by intensity: intense energy, activity, imagination, anxiety, anger, stubbornness, irritability, shyness, sensitivity, silliness, or restlessness. These two traits—oscillation and intensity—may be present very early in life, appear at a particular developmental stage, or occur in response to certain stressors.

Because of their intense energy, creativity, and perceptiveness, bipolar kids can be wonderfully engaging, inspiring joy and pride in you as a parent. But their intensity and changeability can also make them unpredictable, oppositional, and at times inconsolable. Tasks that are routine for other children—making friends, obeying rules, staying asleep at night, performing well at school, and feeling comfortable in the world—can be very difficult for them, and for you as a parent.

## SOME BASIC TERMS

**attention deficit disorder (ADD).** A condition in which a person has unusual difficulty staying focused on a subject or an activity. A person with ADD often loses track of what she is asked to do or where she has put things, or what she meant to do a moment ago.

**attention-deficit/hyperactivity disorder (ADHD).** A person with ADHD has the same problems as a person with ADD but is also restless, impulsive, talkative, and in constant motion.

**bipolar I.** This is classic manic depression with episodes of both highly elevated and depressed mood. It must include at least one episode of full-blown mania (defined below) and usually more frequent depressions. Although manic episodes and depressions can be extremely disabling, this condition is also often characterized by unusual imagination, productivity, artistic talent, or inventiveness.

**bipolar II.** This is a less flagrant (although no less dangerous) condition. It consists of hypomanic episodes and recurrent depressions. The hypomanic episodes may be more irritable than elated and may appear as explosions of temper as well as an increase in activity. The hypomanic episodes may also be characterized by a driven pursuit of some goal, real or imaginary. Although bipolar II is not characterized by the extreme moods seen in bipolar I, it can disable a person's ability to function personally or professionally, and it carries a significant risk for suicide.

**bipolar III.** This is a more recent term (not yet accepted by all psychiatrists), which refers to a person who appears to be normal or simply depressed but has a manic or hypomanic response to an antidepressant. In children it can include a child who appears to have ADHD but becomes manic, hypomanic, or depressed when treated with a stimulant.

**depression.** The central feature of depression is an inability to experience pleasure. It is usually accompanied by negative and self-critical or self-destructive thoughts. Depression can also cause crying; irritability; rage; anxiety; fatigue; and disturbances in sleep, appetite, thinking, and movement (usually a slowing but sometimes agitation).

**grandiosity.** Thinking or behavior that is based on a grossly exaggerated sense of one's power, importance, intelligence, or ability to succeed.

**hypomania.** A state of arousal with some of the characteristics of mania but not to a degree that is necessarily disabling: increased energy, imagination, productivity, grandiosity, silliness or wittiness, pressured speech, increased motor activity, or irritability. People who are hypomanic may or may not have impaired judgment (if they do, it is less severe than with mania). Some bipolar I patients, when they are hypomanic, seem larger than life or infectiously amusing. Bipolar II patients when they are hypomanic can be frighteningly irritable or destructive.

**mania.** True mania is a disabling condition of arousal that usually requires hospitalization. It consists of rapid pressured speech, racing thoughts, extreme impulsivity (usually a form of pleasure seeking but sometimes an attempt to escape an irrational danger), hypersexuality, decreased sleep, increased energy, decreased appetite, grandiose thinking, hallucinations, and delusions. Mania is always accompanied by gross deficits in judgment.

**oscillation.** A movement up and down, as with the movement of a wave or a spring. One can talk of mood oscillations, hormonal oscillations, oscillations of blood sugar, or seasonal oscillations.

## WHAT CAUSES BIPOLAR DISORDER?

Bipolar disorder is an inherited condition, like hair color or intelligence. There are almost certainly several genes involved, and a child can inherit some from one parent and some from the other. Probably some bipolar patients have a different set of inherited genes than others. In some children I have seen, I don't recognize the disorder in either parent, although there are traces of it in grandparents, uncles, aunts, or cousins. As with other medical conditions, such as cardiovascular disease or emphysema, what is probably inherited is a biological vulnerability that appears more or less severely depending on the influence of environmental stress or biological risk factors.

The first sign of the disorder is often depression, unaccompanied by mood elevation, appearing before or during puberty. The depression may come about in response to a personal loss or a social setback (an environmental stress), or it can begin in response to a recreational or prescribed drug (a biological risk factor). In younger children, however, the disorder can appear in forms of increased arousal: severe temper tantrums, unusual anxiety, intense silliness, or an early sleep disturbance.

## How Do I Know If My Child Is Bipolar?

A reliable diagnosis of bipolar disorder requires a thorough psychiatric evaluation, including an examination of the child, a description of current symptoms, history of symptoms, developmental history, and family history. Even then a diagnosis may be tentative, depending on a child's course over time. There are, however, things you can look for.

Contrary to what many people think, bipolar disorder is not just another name for manic depression—although the concept arose from earlier understandings of manic depression, and bipolar disorder includes manic depression. What unites other forms of bipolar disorder with manic depression is the characteristic movements between depression and a state of arousal—irritability, silliness, anxiety, a driven or obsessive pursuit of a particular goal, hypersexuality, or other kinds of compulsive pleasure seeking. Like manic depression, other forms of bipolar disorder also can react unpredictably to some medications used for depression or ADHD. What separates these other forms of bipolar disorder from classic manic depression is the variety and subtlety with which the symptoms can appear.

Surprisingly, bipolar disorder isn't a specific diagnosis: it is not, like other medical diagnoses, the result of a single underlying physical condition. Rather, it is a syndrome, a recognizable group of symptoms that can arise as a result of different underlying physical (in this case neurological) conditions. We know that the underlying biology of various patients must be different because bipolar patients with similar symptoms can react differently to the same medication. In fact, two people can react oppositely to the same medication.

Although our recognition of the disorder is based on a recognizable pattern of symptoms, there isn't one particular disposition or behavioral pattern that immediately pinpoints this disorder. That's because there can be a variety of symptoms in different combinations appearing at different ages. Nor is there yet any blood test or brain scan that confirms the disorder. The term *bipolar* can be applied to a large number of children, including some who appear to be normal and high functioning and others who are more seriously affected. An accurate assessment of a child ultimately rests on three sources of information: current symptoms, developmental history going back to infancy, and family history.

Although no single characteristic in the checklists below is by itself an absolute sign of bipolar disorder, a number of them *occurring together with particular severity* should serve as a red flag warning that a child may be disposed to developing bipolar disorder. Notice also that some of these indicators can be recognized only in retrospect. There is no way a parent could appreciate their significance at the time they first appear.

## CURRENT SYMPTOMS

*Current Symptoms*
    _____ extreme anxiety
    _____ marked irritability
    _____ marked impulsivity
    _____ high level of activity
    _____ grandiosity
    _____ excessive talkativeness
    _____ rapid speech
    _____ racing or rapidly changing thoughts

_____ auditory or visual hallucinations

_____ intense oppositional behavior (trouble accepting the
word *no*)

_____ deliberate destructiveness

_____ extreme silliness

_____ shyness

_____ separation anxiety

_____ sensory hypersensitivity

_____ florid imagination and prominent creativity

_____ an early or prolonged sleep disturbance

_____ vivid nightmares that include violence and death

_____ frequent night terrors

_____ movement between depression and an elevated mood

_____ a prominent rebound reaction, or a sleep disturbance during
treatment with any medication used for ADD or ADHD

_____ a worsening of symptoms in response to treatment with
an antidepressant

_____ hypersexuality in the absence of sexual abuse

The symptoms that bring a child to psychiatric attention may be obvious, such as a depression or a manic episode, or they may be less definitive, such as a behavioral disturbance, an anxiety attack, hyperactivity at home or in school, or problems with peer relationships. It is also true that in toddlers and latency-age children (ages eight to twelve), symptoms of mania and depression often occur simultaneously. Even when there are no clear signs of mania or depression, severe irritability or anxiety can be a marker for the increased arousal typical of this disorder. It often takes an experienced clinician to recognize a significant pattern.

## DEVELOPMENTAL HISTORY

*Developmental History*

_____ difficulty being soothed as an infant, not due to
some obvious physical problem such as gastrointestinal
distress

_____ difficulty sleeping through the night for more than six months

_____ a tendency toward sensory hypersensitivity or overarousal

_____ severe oppositional behavior and difficulty accepting *no*

_____ onset of depression before or near puberty

_____ seasonal mood changes

_____ hyperarousal, increased anxiety, or mood changes in the evening and marked difficulty falling asleep

_____ mood changes with fluctuations in blood sugar

_____ severe social anxiety

In some children, certain constitutional traits, apparent from infancy or early childhood, are the first signs of bipolar disorder. These traits include prolonged difficulty sleeping through the night, difficulty being soothed, hypersensitivity or a tendency toward sensory overload, a high level of activity, unusual irritability, pronounced oppositional behavior, marked silliness, frequent nightmares or night terrors, or an unusually florid imagination.

Severely oppositional behavior can be intensified by one of the important symptoms of the disorder—grandiosity—in a form more difficult to recognize than in an adult. The child with bipolar disorder may believe that her ideas or desires are not just more urgent, but are all-important, certainly much more important than rules or what her parents say. She may do what she wants, regardless of the rules, or she may insist fiercely on having something wildly extravagant—an expensive toy or a completely unmanageable pet. Such a child may also have a sense of omnipotence that minimizes danger or the warnings of parents. Grandiosity and omnipotence are normal for a toddler, but the bipolar child continues to exhibit this kind of thinking at a much later age and with unusual intensity.

A bipolar child also often has a history of difficulty getting along with other children. However, this difficulty can take different forms: intense bossiness and inflexibility, intense shyness and sensitivity to insults or aggression, or an overly ardent desire for contact but with a poor sense of boundaries.

## FAMILY HISTORY

*Family History*

_____ manic depression

_____ psychotic depression or depression requiring
electroconvulsive therapy (ECT)

_____ severe recurrent depressions

_____ postpartum depression

_____ women who experience prominent mood changes with
hormonal fluctuations: the onset of menarche, in the
premenstrual period, during pregnancy, following
delivery, or following menopause

_____ relatives with prominent mood swings, irritability, or
anxiety

_____ relatives with marked creativity, inventiveness, intense
energy and productivity, or grandiose thinking

_____ alcohol or substance abuse

_____ domestic violence

_____ sexual or physical abuse

The family history may include members with obvious bipolar disorder, but various relatives may have one or two traits or behaviors that go along with the disorder: anxiety, creativity, marked success, irritability, impulsivity and violence, physical abuse, hypersexuality or sexual abuse, recurrent depression (especially psychotic depression), suicide, marked mood changes with hormonal flux (in women), substance abuse, a disregard for rules and lawbreaking. Especially when a child's symptoms and developmental history are not definitive, it is important to examine family history.

It is also important to bear in mind that in psychiatry, diagnosis is sometimes clarified only over time and not with a single evaluation. Even when diagnosis is made accurately, the child's future course cannot be predicted: it will depend on the severity of the condition, the timeliness with which treatment is begun, the comprehensiveness of the treatment, and sometimes on good fortune. The best assurance of comprehensive and effective treatment is a family that is well informed and open to help.

## Diagnosis and Treatment

Once again, there is no single trait or item in the current symptoms, family history, or developmental history, nor any particular combination of them, that definitively establishes the presence of bipolarity in a child. But if

- you've marked several of them
- they have persisted over a period of time
- *and* your child is off track developmentally

you should consult with a child psychiatrist *before any medicine is started.* This is important because in psychiatry, bipolar disorder is a great masquerader, often appearing at first like other less serious conditions, such as ADHD, simple depression, or an uncomplicated anxiety disorder. However, the medicines commonly used to treat these other conditions can aggravate bipolar disorder.

This is not to say, however, that medication is to be avoided in bipolar disorder. The importance of appropriate medications cannot be overstated. Without appropriate medical treatment, bipolar disorder tends to worsen over time, with episodes becoming more frequent and severe. It can seriously impair a child's ability to manage specific developmental tasks, leading to increasing developmental as well as biological difficulties over time. Children and families can also suffer from confusion and misunderstandings that have lasting effects on everyone. Indeed, it is common that a parent has undiagnosed or unacknowledged bipolar disorder and needs pharmacologic treatment too. Bipolar disorder carries a high risk for suicide, and an even higher risk for complicating conditions such as substance abuse, eating disorders, social isolation, or academic failure. Early effective treatment, which includes pharmacologic care, can avoid these complications.

The good news is that there have been enormous advances in recognizing and treating bipolar disorder over the past twenty years. This progress is comparable to the improvement in treating infectious diseases since the introduction of penicillin. Today, we can be much more precise when assessing and treating children who were formerly labeled difficult, anxious, or hyperactive. We also have an array of new medicines and increasing experience in using those medications.

Initially, treatment of bipolar disorder consists of pharmacologic intervention—with mood stabilizers such as Trileptal, Lamictal, lithium, or Depakote; with minor tranquilizers such as Klonopin, Ativan, or Xanax; or with major tranquilizers such as Seroquel, Risperdal, Geodon, or Abilify. The developing standard of care usually involves using more than one of these medications to treat different aspects of the condition: mood instability, anxiety, a sleep disturbance, or problems with attention. The correct medication or combination of medications is particularly important because it not only helps ease current symptoms but also helps prevent future episodes and the development of more severe illness. Parents are often, appropriately, quite worried about the long-term effects of medication on their child. Against such concerns, however, it is important to weigh the long-term effects of the untreated condition. A child cannot develop normally or benefit from competent psychotherapy if he is subject to constant, unpredictable emotional storms. (See Appendix A for detailed information about medications.)

However, pharmacologic treatment, especially in a child, should be combined with appropriate psychotherapeutic treatment—individual, family, group therapy, and sometimes a combination of these. Once the biological storms have been quelled, an adequate understanding of your child usually requires psychotherapeutic care. Early treatment of bipolar disorder is a powerful force in improving the affected child's developmental course. Yet without the proper diagnosis, there can be no effective treatment. Although diagnostic methods have greatly improved, determining whether a child has bipolar disorder continues to be a complicated problem.

# CHAPTER TWO

# Difficulties with Diagnosis

Not many years ago, bipolar disorder was seldom diagnosed in children. While working at a foster care home in 1991, I realized that many of the children who were thought to have attention deficit disorder (ADD) were actually bipolar. When I mentioned this to a colleague, he said, "You see bipolar everywhere!" Today, however, psychiatrists and psychologists are recognizing bipolar disorder in so many children that it's beginning to feel like an epidemic. What happened? Have children suddenly become more troubled than ever before?

We aren't sure. Thanks to an explosion in the knowledge and understanding of both the brain and the medications used for emotional and behavioral problems, we can recognize and treat bipolar disorder in new ways. This increased recognition increases the number of children diagnosed with the disorder. Yet experts still wonder if the number of children suffering from the condition is actually rising. Experts also have trouble confirming the diagnosis because the disorder manifests differently in different children and can appear in different ways at different ages. What is more, *all* kids go through difficult phases, and, particularly during adolescence, it is common to have heightened emotions and extreme mood swings. Complicating accurate diagnosis even further is the fact that bipolar disorder is often *accompanied* by panic attacks, obsessive-compulsive symptoms, ADD or ADHD, a learning or language disorder, substance abuse, eating disorders, or a personality disorder. This means that bipolar disorder must often be recognized as a complicating condition or as a force contributing to other conditions.

In addition, the disturbing impact a bipolar child has on his family can increase family conflict, which then becomes another contributing factor to the child's symptoms. It is not uncommon for family discord *caused* by a child's disorder to be blamed as the source of the child's problems. When such family conflict is identified as the cause of a child's difficulties, parents find themselves not only confronted with undeserved blame but their child's biological problem also goes undetected.

However, because bipolar disorder is an inherited condition, problems in the family may come from both sources—from the bipolar child and from a bipolar parent. Finally, the effect of this illness on a child's development entangles biological symptoms with consequences of developmental failure: misbehavior, school failure, problems with peers, substance abuse, eating disorders, and school refusal.

Recognizing bipolar disorder can be a lengthy and confusing task for both parents and doctors.

## A COMPLICATED DIAGNOSIS

The diagnosis of bipolar disorder can be complicated by a number of factors:

- · the several sources of information contributing to the diagnosis
- · the varying spectrum of symptoms
- · the varying age of onset
- · overlapping or complicating conditions

Until recently, most psychiatric diagnoses, including bipolar disorder, were made on the basis of a recognizable cluster of symptoms that had been present for a certain period of time. For example, depression was diagnosed as a set of symptoms—depressed mood, difficulty enjoying activities that are usually pleasant, negative thinking, changes in sleep or appetite, fatigue, irritability, or difficulty concentrating—that had been present for at least two weeks. Increasingly, however, we have realized that it is important to know the patient's developmental history and family history. Among other reasons, it is important to have this information in order to choose the right medication.

The diagnosis of bipolar disorder, and the treatment of different patients with bipolar disorder, is often shaped not only by a patient's symptoms but also by her response to medication. Today's new psychotropic medications often function not only as treatments for various conditions but also as biological probes, telling us something about complex neurological relationships that cannot be known through other methods. For example, a negative response to antidepressants or stimulants (increased agitation, mood instability, or a sleep disturbance) can help us distinguish among uncomplicated depression, ADHD, and bipolar disorder. Similarly, even among patients with bipolar disorder, a positive or negative response to a medication separates one patient from another. There are patients who respond well to lithium, alone or in combination; others do poorly on lithium but respond better to other mood stabilizers; some children respond only to a major tranquilizer.

It has also become clear that certain medications—especially antidepressants and stimulants—can have unintended consequences. For example, prior to the use of antidepressants we rarely saw the rapid-cycling bipolar patient (one whose changes of mood can take place on a daily or hourly basis rather than over a course of months). We also see depressed patients who cannot tolerate antidepressants (these patients become more irritable, more impulsive, manic or hypomanic, or even suicidal). I have also seen many patients with panic disorder whose symptoms become worse when given an antidepressant (the medications considered first-line for this disorder). Similarly, I frequently see children diagnosed with ADD who become more unmanageable (with episodes of uncontrollable rage and even psychosis) when treated with stimulants.

By contrast, the use of some medications has enabled us to accurately diagnose and help patients whose conditions formerly were misunderstood: patients once regarded as schizophrenic who respond to mood stabilizers or electroconvulsive therapy are now understood to be bipolar and are often more responsive to treatment. Today, the diagnosis of bipolar disorder is sometimes arrived at by the recognition of symptoms, sometimes by family and developmental history, and sometimes by a response (positive or negative) to a medication. Even when the diagnosis has been confidently made on the basis of symptoms, the appropriate pharmacologic treatment is often reached by trials of different medications.

## Varying Spectrum of Symptoms

Whereas formerly bipolar disorder was diagnosed only by the presence of mania along with depression, we now recognize—especially in children—a number of other symptoms as indicating the disorder. In some children, a high level of anxiety, problems with sleep, stubbornness, and irritability are the principal symptoms. In other children, hyperactivity, racing thoughts, rapid speech, a florid imagination, and psychotic thinking are more prominent.

The character of a depression can also be markedly different. There can be decreased appetite, weight loss, and agitation; there can also be an increase in appetite, increased sleep, and a slowing of movement and thought. Psychotic symptoms—hallucinations, delusions, or a thought disorder—may be present or absent. In a child, a psychotic thought process may be detected in drawings as well as in speech. A depression can last months on end or cycle rapidly into mania or hypomania and back again. There can be a mixed state with symptoms of both depression and mania.

A depression may come on characteristically in the fall or winter, or in the springtime. In women, mood changes can be brought on by hormonal changes, especially fluctuations in the levels of estrogen and progesterone in the monthly cycle, in pregnancy, and postpartum.

Mood changes can also be brought on by rapid changes in blood sugar—a sugar high or irritability with low blood sugar.

## Varying Age of Onset

Research clarifying the course of bipolar disorder has helped us understand that it can become manifest at different times in life and appear differently at different ages.

· In some infants and toddlers, early symptoms can be a severe sleep disturbance, difficulty being soothed, or marked oppositional behavior and a violent temper. (By themselves these traits do not constitute bipolar disorder, but in a child who is later definitively diagnosed they can be seen as early harbingers of the disorder.)

· At an early age, children with bipolar disorder may not have distinct periods of mania or depression; they may cycle rapidly between elation and irritability.

· Depression occurring before or at the time of puberty is frequently—some say almost always—a sign of bipolar disorder. (Strangely, this circumstance has not been widely connected with the reports of an increased rate of suicide in children treated with antidepressants. We know, however, that in adults with bipolar disorder, antidepressants can worsen the condition, causing suicidal thoughts and a greater risk of acting on those thoughts. Consequently, it is reasonable to conclude that since a large portion of depressed children are in the early stages of bipolar disorder, they are at greater risk when treated with an antidepressant, especially if their bipolar disorder is unrecognized.)

· Bipolar disorder can appear as a consequence of hormonal changes at puberty (in both boys and girls). At this time, it can appear either as depression or as mania and is likely to be complicated by other problems, such as substance abuse, eating disorders, social withdrawal, conduct disorder, and academic failure.

· Substance abuse, which commonly begins in adolescence, can also trigger bipolar disorder in a genetically vulnerable child. (Like the negative effect of a prescribed medication—a stimulant or an antidepressant—alcohol or cocaine can deliver a destabilizing chemical insult.)

· Bipolar disorder in women may appear as marked changes of mood or anxiety, sometimes with bizarre thoughts, during the premenstrual period.

· For similar reasons, in pregnancy, bipolar disorder can appear as depression during the first trimester (when there are high levels of progesterone) and a buoyant or hypomanic mood during the second and third trimesters (when estrogen levels are high).

· After childbirth, when the placenta is shed, estrogen levels drop precipitously. In vulnerable women, this hormonal change can cause a postpartum depression, sometimes with psychosis. A postpartum depression can mark the onset of more severe bipolar disorder.

· Onset of bipolar disorder after menopause is less common than before, but not unseen.

Bipolar disorder presents differently at different ages and looks somewhat different in children than in adults. What in an adult might appear as hypomania, in a child may appear as hyperactivity or excessive silliness; what in an adult might appear as depression, in a child may appear as an inordinate need to have fun coupled with an intolerance of routine activities; what in an adult might appear as explosive irritability can in a child be taken for a temper tantrum; what in an adolescent or adult may appear as an eating disorder complicating bipolar disorder, may appear in a child as sugar craving or a childish struggle about eating. Some psychiatrists believe that juvenile onset bipolar disorder should be considered a separate condition. Because the diagnosis of bipolar disorder in children is fairly recent, we don't have long-term studies to settle the question. There is agreement, however, that in *all* bipolar disorder, appropriate early intervention lessens the severity of the condition.

## OVERLAPPING OR COMPLICATING CONDITIONS

Diagnosis of bipolar disorder is also made difficult by the presence of other accompanying problems—panic attacks, obsessive-compulsive symptoms, ADD or ADHD, substance abuse, or an eating, a learning, or a personality disorder. Bipolar disorder must sometimes be recognized as hiding behind or underlying these conditions and complicating their treatment. The additional problems these complicating disorders pose are discussed in depth in Chapter 12.

## THE DIFFERENT TYPES OF BIPOLAR DISORDER

At present, two forms of bipolar disorder are described in the official listing of psychiatric diagnoses—the *Diagnostic and Statistical Manual of Mental Disorders,* 4th edition (*DSM-IV*)—bipolar I and bipolar II. Bipolar I is what most people think of as manic depression. It always includes at least one manic episode and most times also includes episodes of major depression, often just before or after a manic episode. A person with bipolar I may also have hypomanic episodes or episodes of mild depression. Over time, a person suffering with bipolar I usually moves toward more frequent depressive episodes and fewer, if any, manic episodes.

Bipolar II disorder consists in recurrent episodes of depression alternating with hypomanic mood states: that is, states in which a person has symptoms resembling mania that are not as disruptive of normal activity and may possibly enhance it. Although a hypomanic person may have decreased judgment, he does not become psychotic. A patient with bipolar II can often display an intense, obsessive preoccupation with a certain task, a nasty disposition, or an explosive irritability in the hypomanic episodes. When alcohol is added to the mix, severe and dangerous impulsivity can appear, the proverbial mean drunk.

It's also important to remember that *this disorder occurs along a spectrum,* so someone can be slightly bipolar. A child's (or adult's) symptoms may be more subtle and may not fulfill the criteria for mania, hypomania, or major depression. Present symptoms may be harbingers of later, more serious ones, or they may be a condition called cyclothymia (cycling moods). We aren't sure whether this more subtle condition is a milder, less dangerous form of bipolar disorder or an earlier stage that can become worse over time.

In summary, bipolar disorder is a developing concept, evolving with our understanding of the brain and the medicines we use to temper its moods. The disorder is recognized as a pattern of symptoms occurring over time. Bipolar disorder is transmitted genetically, but it probably results from the combined effects of several genes, which can skip generations or appear in various family members. Like other medical conditions, its severity is influenced by genetic vulnerability, environment, and the presence or absence of biological risk factors. It is a disorder that can appear differently at different ages and occurs along a spectrum. That spectrum varies in severity and in the character of its mood swings—the degree to which mania or depression is present. The usefulness of the concept of bipolar disorder is its ability to inform treatment and to explain complex sets of feelings and behaviors.

# PART II

## Development

# CHAPTER THREE

# The Bipolar Infant

## *Trouble Settling In*

Bipolar disorder is not, and cannot be, diagnosed in infancy. However, by examining the developmental histories of children who are later diagnosed as bipolar, we can understand some of the problems that may confront bipolar children and their mothers during their first developmental tasks. Your child almost certainly passed this stage of development long ago, and there would have been *no way* for you to have recognized these developmental difficulties as symptoms. It is helpful for you to know about them, however, because these developmental difficulties—especially when they have not been mastered—persist into later stages of development. Your understanding of their origin will help you have more accurate expectations for your child and for yourself. Your understanding will help you recognize what kinds of help your child needs.

## LIVING INSIDE A MEMBRANE

All life, whether it's a single cell, a fetus, or a full-grown person, takes place inside a membrane, a crucial boundary protecting life. In some ways the purpose of the membrane is obvious: to keep the outside out and the inside in. However, in order to live, we must take some things in and let some things out. So the membrane is not a wall but a filter—a filter that maintains a certain balance, or homeostasis, within a living thing.

The first complete membrane for an infant is the mother's amniotic sac. When that sac breaks and the infant is born, however, she cannot regulate herself to keep warm, to sleep, to eat, or to burp. Consequently, many of the functions of the membrane must be assumed for the infant by her mother. During infancy, adequate regulation feels like safety; inadequate regulation feels like danger or anxiety. Thus, an infant's sense of safety or anxiety comes to her through crucial channels: skin contact, oral contact, eye contact, and smell.

A mother's most important skill at this developmental stage is *attunement,* an ability to anticipate the infant's needs. The infant's most important skill is *attachment,* forming an emotional bond to the mother. If this stage of settling in goes well enough, the infant gradually begins the next crucial process of separating from the mother, while at the same time maintaining psychological connection together with physical and psychological balance (homeostasis).

## THE SECURITY BLANKET

An infant achieves psychological balance by forming an emotional membrane, at first in a concrete way. As a child begins to separate physically from his mother, to crawl and to walk, he adopts and becomes attached to an object—a blanket, a stuffed animal, or a piece of cloth. He brings this object with him into any situation that threatens his tenuous emotional balance: separation from mother, separation from home, separation from consciousness in sleep, movement into any unfamiliar emotional space.

Whatever object the child settles on, it will have four necessary qualities: it must be selected by the child; it must be soft to the touch; it must be chewable or suckable; and it must have a certain smell. The smell, however, is *the child's,* not the mother's, for the child is moving from a sense of regulation and safety received from the mother to a safety coming from within.

As development continues, what began as a blanket—a vital boundary pulled around the self—is transformed into a psychological membrane that helps maintain *emotional* balance. The child begins to provide himself with an inner security that had formerly been provided solely by the mother: the smell, the taste, and the feel of safety, the beginnings of self-regulation. As Donald Winnicott taught us, the child's ability to achieve self-regulation hinges on having received "good enough" maternal regulation in the first place. Never perfect, but good enough. If something stands in the way of a mother's ability to soothe her child, an infant's ability to self-regulate can be derailed.

A problem affecting many bipolar infants is sensory hyperacuity: an increased sensitivity to light, sound, and other bodily sensations—present at the outset and often continuing into adulthood. When this is the case, an infant has trouble filtering stimuli and achieving sensory equilibrium, making him colicky, restless, and difficult to settle down. Changes and intensities in his environment bother him more; he is less capable of soothing himself and harder for the mother to soothe. These difficulties affect both the child's ability to attach to the mother and the mother's ability to become attuned to the child. Their relationship can get off on the wrong footing from day one.

## PROBLEMS WITH SLEEP

Another common problem for a bipolar infant is sleeping through the night. Normally, during the first two years of life, a child develops an increasing ability to soothe herself, feel comfortable in the world, and feel comfortable in her own skin. Unfortunately, many bipolar children do not follow this path. Indeed, one marker for bipolar disorder in an infant is the inability to sleep through the night, sometimes for as long as two years or more.

As mothers know, disruption of sleep in a child disrupts mood. In a child with bipolar disorder, a disruption of sleep causes a particularly severe disturbance in mood. What is more, when an infant doesn't sleep, her mother doesn't either. When *both* the mother and infant suffer from sleep disturbances, both their moods are affected: attunement, attachment, and the infant's task of establishing emotional equilibrium are all threatened. This upheaval can become particularly unmanageable when (as is often the case) both mother and child suffer from bipolar disorder. Psychiatrists familiar with treating bipolar adults know that a lack of sleep aggravates this condition. In the case of an infant and mother who both suffer from bipolar disorder, a destructive cycle can develop between the infant's problem sleeping and the mother's, resulting in a deterioration in both their moods. The infant's first developmental task, internal self-regulation—feeling comfortable in her own skin—becomes even harder to accomplish.

To make matters more difficult, some bipolar children are born to bipolar mothers who suffer a postpartum depression. The dramatic drop in estrogen that follows delivery can have a destabilizing effect on the mood of a vulnerable mother. Maternal depression constitutes a serious risk for depression in any child. But the bipolar child is at greater risk. Self-regulation, regulation of sleep, and regulation of mood are all at risk.

Problems with sleep can be divided into two parts: getting to sleep and staying asleep.

## GETTING TO SLEEP

Adults often regard sleep as a welcome refuge from a day's work and activity. For infants and young children, however, sleep can mean a loss of control and separation from the parent's protection. The infant or young child with a bipolar disposition can have a particularly hard time at bedtime because his level of anxiety is naturally higher than that of other children, his sensations more acute, and his daily cycle moves toward increased arousal in the evening. The drop in cortisol—a biologic shock absorber—that takes place for everyone in the evening affects a bipolar child more powerfully. This decrease in cortisol may be experienced as an increase in stimulation or as anxiety. Typically both are managed by increased activity. The bipolar child may have just barely mastered the task of feeling safe and comfortable while awake. Entering into sleep, he may often have intense fantasies, which amplify his anxieties and make it more difficult to fall asleep.

## STAYING ASLEEP

The bipolar infant also reacts more intensely than other infants to daily hormonal rhythms and to the rise and fall of blood sugar, bringing about increased restlessness, difficulty sleeping during the night, and early morning awakening.

One of the most important hormonal cycles is that of cortisol, a hormone that acts as a biological cushion during times of stress. Cortisol levels rise in the morning and fall in the evening. In a normal child the rise and fall of cortisol occurs unnoticed, but in the bipolar child the evening drop in cortisol can cause markedly increased anxiety, which often is expressed as hyperactivity. Parents of a child with bipolar disorder are familiar with the intense arousal their child can have in the evening. In more seriously affected children, this arousal can translate into intense and irrational fears, nightmares, night terrors, or hallucinations. The same arousal and anxiety can happen to an infant, but because she can't speak, her restlessness can easily be misinterpreted as an immaturity she needs to get over by toughing it out.

The hormonal activity that precedes the morning rise in cortisol—just like the evening drop-off—can also create problems. In the early morning hours (at about 4 A.M.) the body produces a burst of ACTH (adrenocorticotropic hormone) to stimulate the production of cortisol. This burst of ACTH can cause spontaneous early morning awakenings in adults as well as infants. (In hospitals, fevers rise and heart attacks or panic attacks often occur at this time.) It's not hard to see how this hormonal change can affect a vulnerable infant, disturbing sleep, mood, and the most basic types of self-regulation.

Sleep can also be disrupted by fluctuations in blood sugar. An infant whose blood sugar drops quickly during the night wakes up more frequently. (During the day, a drop in blood sugar can trigger storms of irritability or anxiety.) Unusual weight gain during pregnancy, gestational diabetes, or an unusually high birth weight in the infant are markers for an instability in the mother's glucose metabolism. This instability of blood sugar can often be inherited by the child, adding another variable affecting physical and emotional equilibrium and interrupting sleep. An instability of glucose (blood sugar) is not part of bipolar disorder, but when the two coincide, marked fluctuations in blood sugar drive fluctuations in mood and anxiety.

## GETTING HELP TO GET SOME SLEEP

*What do I do when my infant can't fall asleep or stay asleep and I am exhausted?*

The first thing to do is to calm yourself as much as possible. Then determine what is disturbing your child. Is it gastrointestinal distress? An earache? Low blood sugar? Hyperarousal without discomfort? Overtiredness? There are different ways of approaching each of these problems, and a pediatrician (or a dula) can help you understand how to approach them. Your presence, when you can manage it, is a precious resource to your infant, but it needs to be well informed. Explore possibilities for helping with your child's sleep problems before you are at the end of your rope.

Remember, your presence is not a limitless commodity! If you can, alternate nights with a spouse, grandparent, or dula: take advantage of whatever resources you have. Also, if you can, get help during the day, so you can catch up on your rest.

Above all, don't let your child tough it out! During infancy (and for some bipolar children well beyond infancy), your task is to help your child settle in, not to set limits or build character.

## Look at Me, Mommy!

One of the first steps in the formation of a child's emotional membrane is the experience of being seen approvingly by the mother. Indeed, the earliest source of an infant's self-esteem is his mother's regard for him—literally *being seen* by his mother. Put simply, *an infant's mirror is the mother's face,* and the way she regards him is the way he may come to regard himself.

Young children have an inexhaustible need to be *seen* by their parents, especially their mother. Their conversations are filled with requests for a parent's gaze: "Look, Mommy! Look, look!" Whether playing, attempting something new, or simply watching television, their experience is more complete and their actions more skillful when seen by their mother. The familiar phrase, "Look, Ma! No hands!" reminds us that a child's ability to move into the world with poise and daring depends on the experience of being *seen approvingly* by his mother. The opposite experience, a failure to be seen, causes anxiety. The experience of being seen disapprovingly is felt as shame: a fear of being seen, a fear of the evil eye.

Later a child also acquires the experience of being *spoken to approvingly*. The innumerable times parents say such things as, "How pretty you look!" "I'm so proud of you!" "Let me see." "Oh, what a fine job you have done!" "Don't worry, you'll be all right," become a voice with which the child speaks to himself, an internalization of the parent's soothing voice. That voice also comes to include prohibitions and values, which at their best also help a child negotiate social boundaries and feel safe within certain behavioral limits. The voice can, however, become critical or persecutory, depending on both the quality of the parent's voice and the child's sensitivity. (In a vulnerable child or in the face of an abusive parent, the voice can become a persecutory auditory hallucination.) A bipolar infant or toddler can provoke more than his share of negative responses from his parents, eventually leading to problems with self-esteem and developing an internal soothing voice.

Troubles in the developmental task of settling in—attachment, attunement, and self-regulation—can also result in an intense dependency of the infant on the mother, a dependency that can later become increasingly burdensome, evoking hostility in both mother and child. The infant feels more and more helpless and frustrated, and the mother becomes more depleted and resentful of the infant's demands. The mirror of self-esteem can become clouded. You can't avoid an intense dependency with an infant who has great difficulty settling in. In such a circumstance, a mother may need help to avoid becoming angry at her infant or at herself.

## IN A NUTSHELL . . .

The crucial concept to remember is that the *intensity* and the *oscillations* of a bipolar infant profoundly affect her ability to achieve biological and emotional stability, and this not only affects her sense of herself but also can disrupt the connection between a parent and child. An injury to that connection can cause lasting developmental difficulty.

## WITHIN YOU AND WITHOUT YOU

While an infant is developing the ability to feel comfortable in his own skin, he must also begin to distinguish between what is inside himself and what is outside. He gradually learns to perceive the presence of another person, first in a fragmentary and later in a more integrated way. From this first perception of one other person he proceeds toward a perception of other people and the world beyond.

Perception, however, is only the beginning. Ultimately the infant has to venture out into that world. To do this, he must actively move away from his mother and develop a sense of himself as separate from her, in both space and power. The psychological consequences of separation are enormous, complex, and fraught with danger, even in the best of situations. In a child with a bipolar disposition, these tasks can be overwhelming and may not be fully achieved far into childhood and adolescence. In future chapters I will explain how continuing problems with separation affect a child's movement through later developmental stages.

## BALANCE AND SEPARATION

The tasks of achieving emotional equilibrium and of achieving separation are entwined: as in the task of walking, separation without *internal* balance becomes dangerous. A satisfactory early rapport between mother and child establishes what Erik Erikson called "basic trust," which allows a child to be curious about and tolerate the presence of the unknown. Basic trust also allows a child to separate physically from her mother and explore the world. The child's confidence in herself and in her attachment to her mother actually creates a transitional space, in which the child is at once separate and connected to her mother. There the child draws on the experience of being seen by her mother, and there the mother is her crucial audience. As the famous child analyst Donald Winnicott taught us, it is in this transitional space that a child *plays,* and it is out of this space that creativity and art emerge.

In contrast, a child whose early experience has been permeated with frustration and anxiety lacks basic trust and reacts anxiously to the presence of a stranger or in a new situation. She may have unusual difficulty separating from her mother. On the other hand, some children who have an inadequate attachment make a premature separation from their mother, rushing impulsively into dangerous situations. (It may have been such impulsivity that launched my own reckless ride on my tricycle into the street at about the age of four.) Premature separation is characterized by counterphobic risk taking. Despite their apparent independence, such children experience enormous anxiety, which interferes with their ability to perceive, much less negotiate, the external world. Whether holding on or running away, the anxiety such children feel can drive them further into their own internal world where fantasy and reality become more and more difficult to distinguish from one another. Their play, their relationships with adults and with other children, and their tolerance for being alone suffer from confusion between reality and fantasy.

## Characteristics of the Infant with Bipolar Tendencies

· **Heightened sensory awareness.** This is the most important characteristic, to which many other features can be traced. It leads to difficulty achieving emotional and physical balance (homeostasis), increased anxiety, sleep disturbance, excessive motor activity, or frightening fantasies. It can also negatively affect the relationship between infant and mother.

· **Pronounced biological ups and downs.** In infancy, this is seen as a greater response to fluctuations in blood sugar, normal stress, and the daily hormonal rhythms, causing increased restlessness, irritability, and difficulty sleeping at night and in the early morning hours.

· **Intense reactions to normal stress.** Intolerance of change, separation, and the onset of sleep.

· **Difficulties with basic developmental tasks, leading to a problematic relationship with the mother.** These difficulties manifest as problems with attachment, self-regulation, and separation. These difficulties are not, however, particular to children with bipolar disorder and also are seen in children who suffer different kinds of stress—neglect or abuse, for example.

Below are practical suggestions for parents of a bipolar infant. They are meant to help you recognize fundamental developmental difficulties that you need to help your child master. They are also meant to help you realize that these difficulties may be ongoing for your child beyond the time that other children have mastered them. (Even if your child is long past infancy, you may recognize the persistence of these difficulties in an older child, and you may need to draw on some of the same parenting strategies.) Although it is difficult, it is important not to become discouraged by or impatient with your child or yourself. His particular biology determines a different developmental pace from that of his peers.

## BEAR IN MIND

· Be especially attentive to the task of self-regulation—sleeping, eating, exercise, and breathing, beginning with infancy and continuing beyond childhood. The bipolar child (and adolescent and adult) needs to be taught the importance of rest—sleep begets sleep, whereas fatigue produces restlessness. The bipolar child (like the bipolar adult) also has a tendency to eat irregularly: at times going too long without eating and at times bingeing on sugar. Regular exercise and proper breathing are also important tools in managing your child's ever-present anxiety. Self-regulation is the first line of care for bipolar disorder and never stops being important.

· Protect your infant (or child) from excessive stimulation (hunger, fatigue, skin irritations, too much light, heat, cold, noise).

· Give your infant plenty of skin contact, eye contact, and rhythmic rocking. This is especially important in helping your child to make a secure attachment and to begin feeling safe within himself. However, watch for signs that he is having difficulty tolerating contact, which may mean that he needs relief from excessive stimulation.

· Your child may need an unusual amount of soothing, so don't make her tough it out when she awakens during the night. Follow your instincts to soothe your child rather than someone else's idea of good parenting.

· If your child is troubled with an unstable blood sugar and you are nursing him, when he is ready consider giving him formula at night. Formula is digested more slowly than breast milk and helps keep his blood sugar up longer, helping him and you get more rest.

· Understand that your child may need a night-light, television, or a parent in order to get to sleep long after other children have learned to fall asleep alone.

· Be on the alert for problems with separation, and don't enforce it prematurely. Instead, help your child achieve it gradually.

· As much as possible, give yourself a break. Hire a helper; when available, enlist family members. Try not to be indispensable. Your rest is crucial in helping you stay attuned to your child.

· Watch for signs of maternal depression—excessive fatigue, irritability, crying, feeling overwhelmed by everything, a loss of pleasure in your child—and treat it aggressively.

· Be patient with your child's difficulties and your own. Bipolar children (and adults) are almost always impatient, but your child needs your patience as a source of calm and as a model in order to tolerate frustration.

· Finally, don't compare your child's rate of development with that of other children. No matter what other parents say or do, your child needs to go at her own pace.

# CHAPTER FOUR

# The Bipolar Toddler

## *Learning to Accept* No

Learning to accept *no* is perhaps the most important developmental task of all. It carries with it profound benefits, while failure to master this task can cause lasting deficits. Don't be discouraged if your child has passed well beyond the age described in this chapter: the same fundamental difficulties and opportunities apply throughout development. Your understanding of the ins and outs of this task will be just as important to your child at twelve or at twenty as it was at two. There are few people who don't need help and a better understanding of how to manage conflict, to accept *no* in their closest relationships.

At about the age of two, several things combine to trigger a profound change in your child's emotional equilibrium—and in his relationship to you.

· He develops the capacity to keep track of people and things that are not immediately in view (so parents can't use the trick of distraction as easily as before).

· He becomes more mobile and can go places that are dangerous or inconvenient.

· He begins to understand and use the word *no*.

Up until now, your principal task has been to give your child whatever he wants and needs: nourishment, warmth, love, and shelter. But now, with increasing frequency, you must stand between your child and what he wants, firmly saying *no*.

## ACCEPTING *No*—A CRUCIAL DEVELOPMENTAL TASK

Learning to accept *no* helps a child to integrate her personality, stabilize her emotional life, see you more clearly, feel more deeply connected to you, develop a sense of time, and begin healthy moral development. How can one little word make such a difference? Saying *no* and sticking with it brings about a cascade of reactions in a child that challenge you but are necessary to help her develop psychologically in a healthy way.

When you say *no,* a child's response is always the same: rage! This rage transforms you from a figure of fond attachment to a horrible adversary. At the same time, it alters the child's sense of herself from that of a beloved or lovable child to a bad or hateful one. When such a change takes place, the child loses contact with her former secure sense of her parent and herself. No child can tolerate this loss; she must do something to escape. If she feels safe enough in her relationship with you, she will try to get rid of this horrible feeling by projecting her rage on to you. If she can get you enraged she can, in effect, say, "You see! It's *you* who's horrible, not me!" This gives her a partial victory, an escape from a toxic sense of self.

Your task, in the face of this projected rage, is complex and requires at least three kinds of restraint, known as holding the situation:

· **You must not give up the *no*.** Don't get blown away by your child's rage.

· **You must not become contaminated by your child's rage.** Do not accept, much less act out, your child's perception of you as horrible *or* of herself as bad. Put differently, you must survive your child's attack unharmed.

· **You must not leave the situation or allow the child to leave.** Your child's ability to accomplish the task of impulse control (her ability to say *no* to herself) depends on her being able to reestablish a connection with you. So you need to be there.

These three kinds of restraint need to be maintained over an extended period time. They provide a psychological holding environment in which a child has time to master this developmental task. The time it takes for mastery to be achieved varies depending on a child's temperament and on the difficulty of the demand.

### Anger over Moving

**CHARLES** was eight when his parents decided to move from the home he'd lived in all his life to a more prosperous neighborhood. This meant leaving his bedroom and playroom, his treasured backyard, his wonderful tree fort, and his very best friend. Furious and heartbroken, he hurled devastating insults at his parents, topping them off with, "I will never do to my child what you are doing to me!" His parents didn't become intimidated or guilty. They knew enough not to try to talk Charles out of his distress. Instead, they stayed with him, remaining silent for a long time and allowing him to talk. When they did speak, they didn't try to point out the advantages of the new house or the new neighborhood. Instead, they validated his loss, saying things like, "It's terrible to have to leave your best friend and your tree fort behind. We wish you could bring them with you. It just won't be the same."

They didn't surrender the limit—Charles still had to move—but they tolerated his rage and grief, staying with him until he saw that his rage had not destroyed either them or his connection to them.

> After a very long hour, Charles began to acknowledge their presence fondly and allow them to comfort him. It was a year, however, before he allowed himself to accept the new home.

The importance of restraining yourself in the face of your child's rage—whether she's a toddler or a teenager—cannot be overstated. Your restraint and composure combined with your actual presence help your child know that her impulses are not overwhelming—first for you and later for herself. You will be able to see the effects of your restraint (or lack of it) in children of all ages, but they will become more and more apparent as your child gets older.

## LEARNING TO SEE THE GOOD AND THE BAD TOGETHER

No parent accomplishes such restraint perfectly, nor does any child learn to bear such containment in a single try—or even in several successive tries. But if you manage to contain your child *well enough* to hold the situation, there will come a time when your child realizes that her rage may have damaged you, or damaged her connection with you. The thought that she may have destroyed this connection is extremely uncomfortable for her—which is why the perception of this potential loss is so hard for her to achieve.

The emotional consequence of this perception of loss is depression—a normal, healthy kind of depression that comes from an acceptance of loss or the possibility of loss. In order to reach this state of mind, your child needs to surrender her sense of omnipotence and a grandiose sense of herself. She needs to acknowledge that you, her parent, are of crucial importance to her. However, when a child surrenders these defenses and tolerates this depression, the benefits are enormous.

When your child realizes that the person she hates is also the person she needs, she'll start to see you as both the person who says *no and* the person to whom she's fondly attached. At the same time, she'll see herself as both enraged *and* lovable. As she brings together these contradictory perceptions, your child begins to integrate her sense of self and her sense of you: she is beginning to form a more complex and realistic view of herself, of you, and ultimately of other people.

Until your child accomplishes this emotional feat, her sense of people (and of herself) will be split into opposite versions: the good and the bad, the loved and the hated. She won't be able to connect these opposite pictures of you, the parent, or of herself. Instead, she will move back and forth between the two with an emotional volatility that we recognize as the terrible twos—because such volatility is normal for a two-year-old. It is also normal for most people some of the time. A measure of maturity, however, is a person's ability to exchange such absolute perceptions and such volatility for ambivalent feelings and reflection.

## Learning to Perceive Time

When a child's perception of people and events is divided into opposites—good or bad, loved or hated—his splitting disrupts his ability to perceive *time*. One event (or one perception) cannot be connected to another when it has an opposite emotional value. The good feeling of yesterday or of five minutes ago can't be connected to now. The child who cannot connect one event with another cannot perceive time. A child who can't perceive time can't wait, can't connect the past with the present or the future, and can't learn. An inability to perceive time leads to impulsivity and intense impatience. These qualities are normal at the age of two but not at the age of twelve. However, many children with bipolar disorder still struggle with these difficulties at twelve and for some time after.

When a child learns to see his parent and himself at the same time in opposite ways, he has begun to integrate his personality, stabilize his emotional life, and live in time.

## LEARNING TO FEEL EMPATHY

There is another momentous accomplishment connected with the ability to accept *no*. When your child sees that his rage may have hurt you, he begins to realize that your emotional life is separate from his own. That is, if my rage can hurt you, then your feelings are separate from mine—you are hurt when I am enraged. This is the earliest form of empathy—the capacity to understand that other people's feelings are distinct from our own and to imagine their inner life as separate although connected to our own. The connection consists in mutual perception and emotional exchange. Without empathy, aggression turns into violence and people are seen as things to be used or discarded.

Following closely on empathy comes remorse: your child's rejection of his own behavior because it has hurt someone else, someone he wants to be connected with, is the earliest form of remorse. A healthy morality develops from empathy and remorse, a morality based on the desire to stay in contact with other people rather than the urge to have one's own way or a desire to escape punishment. This is not only a matter of treating other people as you want them to treat you—the Golden Rule does not require empathy or remorse. Remorse and empathy mean treating other people as if they *were* you, while understanding that they have a separate emotional life.          •

## LEARNING TO REPAIR RELATIONSHIPS

As these perceptions occur (however long they may take) your child will be well on her way to quelling her rage, limiting her impulses, and accepting *no*. Her next step is to attempt *reparation*. This may be a small, almost imperceptible gesture such as a toss of the head, a shuffling of feet, or a fleeting glance. Your task as a parent is to recognize this attempt, accept it, and move on. You don't give up the *no*, but you reestablish connection. The entire process—which can take hours or years—moves from rage into a deepening of contact and intimacy.

When you set limits with your child, when you say *no* and hold the situation, you are beginning to teach your child how to tolerate conflict with someone she wants to stay close to without hurting that person, without getting hurt herself, and without leaving the situation. This ability to metabolize conflict within a relationship without giving up one's own boundaries or fleeing the relationship is the sine qua non, the essential skill in achieving intimacy at any age.

## THE BIPOLAR CHILD'S EMOTIONAL RESPONSE TO *NO*

Accepting *no* is particularly difficult for the bipolar child because bipolarity carries with it such an intensity of feeling. The rage, the anxiety, the sense of loss, and the defenses against loss are all more powerfully felt. Melanie Klein (perhaps the first person to describe the emotions infants feel) described an infant's defenses against loss in terms we still use to describe behavior in bipolar disorder. For example, she described the manic defense, in which a child (or adult) denies a loss and engages in frantic pleasure seeking, sometimes silliness, to escape feelings of depression. Parents of a bipolar child encounter this defense often when their child, in the face of a difficult task or a disappointment, demands a new toy. Consider also the humorous—and too often true—statement about certain infantile adults: "When the going gets tough, the tough go shopping." Parents also repeatedly face a child who revs up and demands more time to play when it is time for bed. These manic responses are found in all children, but in the bipolar child they are extremely intense and last well beyond the toddler stage.

Another part of the manic defense is displaying contempt for the one who disappoints the child, blending it with a manic grandiosity that can lead to aggressive and destructive behavior: "You can't make me!" or "I don't care!" or the child who breaks things, even his own toys, in defiance. Indeed, deliberate destructiveness—driven by contempt, rage, and grandiosity—is a common feature in a child with bipolar disorder.

Klein also described the defense of paranoid thinking: a projection of an infant's rage onto the parent and the outside world, followed by a retreat from that rage now perceived as coming back at the child. "You hate me, you never want me to have fun!" The parent parries this paranoid defense by not becoming contaminated with the child's rage—in other words, not becoming enraged herself and shouting back at the child or, worse, hitting him. The adult with paranoid thinking may have an enemies list, or think that people are talking about him as he enters a room; the bipolar child may have frightening hallucinations, waking fantasies that seem real, or an inarticulate rage that obliterates thinking and erupts into uncontrolled destructive behavior.

The many emotional tasks included in accepting *no* are made more difficult by the *intensity* of a bipolar child. This intensity makes it especially hard for him to move from rage to empathy, remorse, and connection, and to put feelings into words rather than acting them out. The bipolar child's *hypersensitivity* also makes these tasks more of a struggle. Because it is so difficult for many bipolar children even to feel comfortable in their own skin, because they have to work so hard at this earlier task, any interruption, the slightest *no,* unsettles them. Their anxiety and sense of helplessness can then emerge as explosive irritability. It is common for such a child to perceive his own rage as coming from you, so that *he* feels under attack. The bipolar child's intense imaginative involvement with his inner world, even when he is playing happily, makes an intrusion more difficult to bear. Finally, the world comes at many bipolar children so intensely and from so many different directions that it is hard for them to choose between opposing demands—external ones and internal ones. It is because of this extreme intensity that some bipolar children need the help of medication in order to succeed at this and other developmental tasks.

The most obvious features of bipolar disorder between the ages of two and five include

· an inability to accept the word *no*
· intense stubbornness

- an inability to tolerate transitions
- intense and extended tantrums
- deliberate destructiveness
- a preoccupation with revenge
- intense destructive fantasies appearing in play or in deliberate aggression
- heightened anxiety about being alone, being in the dark, or going to sleep
- hallucinations (visual or auditory)
- excessive silliness
- acting provocatively
- an ability to needle or get under other people's skin
- episodes of intense hyperactivity, sometimes induced by large amounts of sugar
- nightmares or night terrors

While some of these patterns can be seen at times in just about all young children, they are often the *primary* way of thinking and reacting for a bipolar child. And while this behavior is considered normal at age two, it often persists in a bipolar child to the age of eight or even fourteen.

## ACTIVE PARENTING WHILE SAYING *No*

In setting limits, you should *not* give up the *no*, become contaminated with your child's rage, or leave the situation. But what should you be doing in this situation? When setting limits, the active parenting task—what you need to do—is to get your child *to talk to you,* to put the worst of feelings into the worst of words. Most parents get this backward. They think their task is to get the child to *listen* to them. When their child ignores what they say and talks back angrily, they think they have failed. In fact, when your child begins to *tell* you how angry he is, you are on the right track. The child who can *say,* "I hate you, Mommy!" has less need to hit his parent, kick a wall, or turn the anger against himself. This ability to articulate rage allows your child to turn a corner, moving from rage to connection.

One reason this is true is that *language attenuates feeling*—rage that can be put into words is calmed by that very act. (In part this is because in talking, the cortex—the most developed and flexible part of the brain—is brought to bear on the raw emotions of the deep brain.) Verbally expressing rage also gives your child more room to maneuver in the presence of overwhelming emotion. In action, a child can either comply or protest; in language, he can say, "I hate you, but I need you." Language can move in two directions at once, integrating opposite feelings. The task of active parenting is to deliver your child into language, to help your child to articulate rage and move on to the more complicated feelings that follow it.

A parent can deliver a child into language first *by listening*, by making the child feel heard. Your task is not to get your child to give up his feelings but to help him articulate them. The next step is to validate your child's feelings (without giving up the *no*). In some cases this means (tentatively) articulating his feelings: "I can imagine how angry you must feel" or "I guess it does feel unfair to you." By putting into words how a child may feel, you give your child a model for expressing negative feelings *and* an emotional ground to stand on. When your child feels heard and when he has an emotional ground to stand on, he can begin to see you and, eventually, listen to you. Validating a child's feelings is not, however, the same as saying he is right. A child's feelings can be valid when his judgment is wrong.

## WHERE YOUR CHILD SLEEPS

One of the more important limits to set at this age—between three and five—is the boundary of the bedroom. The question of whether or not your child is allowed to sleep in your bed can be an area of great contention. It is also a conflict that can occur more frequently with a bipolar child. Because of her heightened anxiety and her more intense imagination, the transition from consciousness to sleep can be much more difficult. You may be tempted to let her sleep with you at an age when other children manage the task alone. However, the boundary between your bedroom and your child's needs to be maintained—and can be quite difficult to restore once it is breached. This separation becomes particularly important at about the age of three, when your child starts to move around freely and understands that she is excluded from the special relationship between her parents. At this age she will attempt to insinuate herself between the two of you to try to regain the exclusive attention of one parent. If she sleeps in your bed, there is no way to figure out if she's trying to get between the two of you or if she just needs help getting to sleep.

Sometimes parents encourage this behavior. Anxious parents may take comfort in the child's presence in their bed, confusing their own needs with the child's. This can be particularly true of single mothers, or a woman whose husband has begun to distance himself from her and their difficult child. The child's coming into the parent's bed is then met with relief rather than alarm. In other cases a parent's exhaustion may perpetuate the problem: getting up, taking the child back to her room, and helping her fall asleep in her own bed just seems too exhausting at the end of a long day.

If your child has trouble falling asleep in her own bed, take her to her bed and stay with her until she falls asleep. If she awakens and comes into your bedroom, one parent should take her back to her bed and stay with her until she falls asleep. (If possible, this task should be shared by the parents, alternating on different nights.) This can be a trying interruption, but it is also a precious opportunity to deepen your relationship with your child: read stories, sing a lullaby, or simply lie quietly together. Lying down next to your child *on* (not in) her bed is very different from allowing her in yours. The connections formed at this time will carry forward into distant stages of development. Most important, this practice will help develop your child's ability to surrender consciousness in an untroubled way. Like other limits, this one may take time to master.

## When a Parent's Response Goes Awry

Clearly, when a child learns to accept *no,* he also learns several lessons crucial to his development. But what happens when he doesn't learn to accept *no?* The process can go awry for many reasons:

- the parent failing to hold the limit
- the parent giving in to rage
- the parent breaking off contact with the child
- the parent setting limits that are too forbidding
- the parent letting go of active parenting

### Giving Up on the *No*

When you don't hold to a limit that you have set—when you give up the *no*—you validate your child's sense that he *must* have what he wants. Your retreat confirms that his desire is so powerful that even you are helpless in the face of it. In a subtle way, this idea that his own desire is too powerful to be denied erodes his sense of his own power and self-esteem—he will feel unable to say *no* to himself. The idea also erodes his sense of your power and thus his sense of safety. His belief that he *must* have what he wants disrupts his sense of time by undermining his ability to tolerate, or even conceive of, time's passage. He can imagine only now.

Another consequence of the failure to hold on to the *no* is that your child isn't required to change his initial perception of you or of himself. He doesn't question his idea of you or himself as horrible. Nor does he connect his rage-filled image of you with the opposite experience of being loved and cared for by you. Opposing perceptions continue to exist in his mind, but they are disconnected, split off from each other. He moves unpredictably from one sense of you (or himself) to another. His sense of himself and of time is then profoundly disrupted.

When events charged with opposite feelings cannot be assigned to the same person (or the same sense of self), they cannot be linked in time. So your child remains impulsive and impatient: for example, when a child, reminded of his bad behavior on a previous day, replies—as if it were a self-evident rebuttal—"That was yesterday!"

## GIVING IN TO THE RAGE

Becoming contaminated by your child's rage and acting out her vision of you as horrible confirms her polarized vision of you—and of herself—as either wholly bad or wholly good. She may conform to your limits, but she does so out of a desire to get away from you, the bad parent, and escape from her own bad self, rather than out of a desire to preserve her connection with you.

Compliance out of fear can't foster empathy or establish a desire to maintain connection with others. Instead, she thinks of wrong as only what she gets punished for. Right, on the other hand, is what satisfies her and what she gets away with. This externalized sense of right and

*A self-portrait of an eight-year-old bipolar child exhibiting a toxic sense of self, with his rage exhibited as fire. His choice of black and white rather than color is purposeful, an expression of his darkened sense of himself.*

wrong encourages deception, both of the self and of others. Compliance driven by fear doesn't deepen intimacy: rather, it leads to an accumulation of rage.

## When a Parent Becomes Enraged

ROGER and his parents were referred to me by the military's preventative services when Roger was four and a half years old. Roger had appeared at nursery school one day with the imprint of a hand on his face. It was easily learned that his father, an officer, had struck Roger in frustration because he refused to control his bowels. The family, who had just been moved to the post, had been told that if Roger was not toilet trained, he could not attend the nursery. Both Roger's parents worked, and this placed them under great stress in a new environment where they had no support system beyond the military facilities. Their move had been a difficult and protracted one, over the course of which Roger had lost his newly acquired control of his bowels. The efforts of the post psychologist to work with Roger had failed; the family was furious at their humiliation, and Roger refused to talk or to control his bowels.

The first time I saw Roger, he came unwillingly and refused to speak to me. I could see that he felt caught between loyalty to his parents, their ambivalent demand that he see me, and his own anger. Roger agreed to draw, however, and produced a Ninja Turtle. My only intervention that day was to tell him that if he would bring his good guy next time, I would bring my bad guy.

At our next session, Roger appeared with Donatello, one of the Ninja Turtles; I had come with Rock Steady, their implacable foe. Roger proceeded to attack my figure savagely throughout the session, which I allowed without protest, encouraging the symbolic expression of his rage. At the end of the session, just as he was ready to leave, he kissed my figure and asked me to keep his.

I worked separately with Roger's parents, learning the history of their family. An important part of that history was to establish that there were no medical reasons why Roger might be incontinent. I also wanted to understand the impact of the move on the family's emotional stability and on Roger. Finally, I was looking to identify the pressures that were acting on the family from without: from the army and from past generations. I reassured them that Roger would ultimately achieve this developmental goal and instructed them to put no pressure on him to control his bowels. They were to show no interest in whether he used the toilet or not.

Meanwhile it had occurred to me, vaguely at first, why Roger and other four-year-olds were so intensely taken with the story of the mutant turtles who lived in the sewer and spent their lives struggling for control with the powerful and sadistic Shredder, a former associate of their gentle master, Splinter. The story managed to weave together these children's unconscious preoccupations with transformations that took place in their bowels, in what went in and came out of them. It contained too the drama of their growing but still uncertain muscular control, and the changes in their relationships to their fathers and to the powerful but alien world into which they moved from time to time. Finally, the story also contained polarized images of authority—the kindly but powerful Splinter and the sadistic, violent Shredder.

Treatment progressed nicely. Roger went from playing with figures of the turtles to drawing them, and I saw that he was quite talented. Meanwhile, I learned that in consequence of his military duties, Roger's father had been isolated from the family and from Roger at a time when the boy needed his father's strength to face the changes in his life. I also made the fortunate discovery that Roger's father was himself a talented artist. This allowed me to involve him in the sessions helping Roger draw. I emphasized the superiority of his drawings to mine and observed the common talent in the father and son. Roger was still not controlling his bowels, and neither he nor I had made direct reference to the

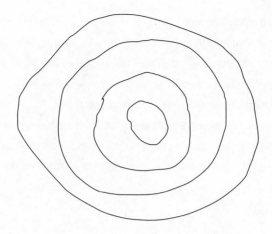

problem. His parents, under my instruction, were ignoring it as well. I encouraged Roger and his father to draw together outside the sessions.

In the family work I clarified how the pressures placed on the family by the military and its nursery school had been unwittingly transmitted by them to Roger and had become focused concretely in the muscular control of Roger's anal sphincter. I validated the sense of shame and violation the family felt and used it to help them sense Roger's own shame and sense of violation.

My last session with Roger and his family, after some two months of treatment, was a memorable one. Early in the session, Roger produced the above drawing without comment.

His parents were by now capable of recognizing Roger's uncanny representation of the concentric circles of pressure he and they felt—from the army to the day care center to the family right down to Roger's anus.

Roger proceeded to play with a mop head that had been modified to resemble an octopus. He dropped the puppet on top of small toys as if it were eating them. At one point he dropped it onto a rather large metal truck, while looking at me somewhat anxiously. I went straight to the central issue, this time in plain talk: "Do you know what will happen if he eats the truck?" Roger listened with heightened anxiety. "He will make an enormous pooh plop!" Roger broke into laughter. The shame and anger that had been so unspeakable for him were now brought into language in a way that left Roger feeling seen in an approving way, enjoyed! Roger needed to feel seen before he could talk or be talked to, but he needed to be seen at his own pace and on his own terms. After that afternoon, Roger began controlling his bowel movements, and the family decided that they no longer needed treatment. I agreed.

## Losing Contact with Your Child

If, in the face of your child's rage, you lose contact with her—whether by isolating her, allowing her to flee the situation, or leaving yourself—you deprive your child of your presence. It is only in the presence of a parent that your child can learn to tolerate the frustration and loss that go along with accepting *no*. It is also only in a parent's presence that your child can develop empathy, remorse, and the skills for repairing a relationship. If you leave, there is an unspoken message that her rage is too terrible to be confronted, even by you. By staying, you allow your child to imitate the model of your restraint, taking strength from your presence.

Giving your child a time-out is a common, useful practice that lets her calm down before proceeding, like letting an overheated engine cool off. But it's important *not* to combine time-out with separation. Your child needs your presence to make the necessary developmental moves. There is also the danger that she will perceive the time-out as a punishment, meant to intimidate her. *The goal is to set a limit, not to punish!* Many bipolar children see a parent's departure as abandonment and the ultimate rejection. Remain in the room with your child and stay neutral; that is, neither punishing nor peacemaking. If you try to make peace before your child becomes remorseful, you risk increasing her contempt or sense of omnipotence.

On the other hand, it is also necessary to be aware when your child needs emotional space. Some bipolar children become so enraged they cannot restrain their destructive impulses or their physical assault on the parent. What is more, your immediate presence can intensify the rage. Giving your child emotional space is not the same as leaving her. Discerning the difference is a matter of tact: sometimes an awareness of how your anxiety or tension can impact your child; sometimes an awareness of your child's need to exhaust her rage before confronting you. In all cases, however, there needs to be a time when you and your child come face-to-face in the presence of your *no*. Paradoxically, your child needs to be able to experience an annihilating rage but have you survive the onslaught.

## SETTING LIMITS THAT ARE TOO FORBIDDING

A different kind of failure can occur from a containment that is premature or too forbidding—when you communicate that your child's rage will not be tolerated and therefore cannot be expressed. Some parents communicate that the child will lose love and connection if he does not comply; others communicate that the child needs to take care of the parent by being good. A parent's intolerance of rage—communicated either by anger or by pleading—prevents a child from challenging his parents' limits at all. Such parental intolerance may stem from poverty, depression, wealth, or other factors, but most parents who expect immediate compliance from their child weren't accommodated in their own childhood. They were emotionally starved and consequently have no true reserve of caring to offer their children.

When a child is not permitted to express rage, he becomes compliant, doing just what he is told—at a cost. Such children, especially the more gifted ones, learn to anticipate their parents' needs, satisfying them at the expense of their own emotional life. Indeed, such a child may have an inability to play or to know what he wants to do when not told what to do. Even more worrisome, he may begin to perceive his authentic desires as dangerous or bad. These children may also have an inability to say no to others and, consequently, harbor an accumulation of hidden rage. As a result, they lose the ability to perceive their own feelings and, ultimately, to know themselves. While they often appear to be models of self-control through their elementary school years, during adolescence, much to their parents' surprise, they tend to explode in rebellion or implode with academic failure, substance abuse, or a sense of aimlessness. In either case, their lack of connection with their own feelings prevents them from formulating an authentic identity.

## You Don't Have to Be Perfect!

When dealing with a bipolar child, your ability to hold the line without becoming enraged, punitive, or distant is difficult. It is even more difficult if you yourself suffer from intense sensitivity, irritability, or depression, or if your parents didn't set limits like this for you. If bipolar dispositions are part of your heredity, a mood disorder has disrupted your family, you're dealing with substance abuse or abandonment, or if you're a single parent, the task of setting and holding limits may sometimes be overwhelming.

However, you don't have to be perfect or succeed all the time. In such circumstances, perfect is the enemy of good. You can be a role model for your child by acknowledging *your* mistakes in the process. When a child sees that you can make a mistake, acknowledge it, show remorse, and maintain connection, she will be encouraged to follow your lead. If you are feeling overwhelmed, don't be critical of yourself or of your child: get help! Consult with a pediatrician, therapist, or psychiatrist. If you are already working with one, draw on that relationship for suggestions of what to do, where to find resources, or how to improve your own mood.

What's most important is that you continue to work at it. In later chapters you will learn about the cumulative consequences of a child's failure to accept *no,* or to metabolize conflict in a crucial relationship. Holding the line the right way and teaching your child to "swallow *no*" is a difficult task, but when successfully completed it avoids more serious problems later on and deepens your connection with your child.

## BEAR IN MIND

· Learning to accept limits is one of the most difficult and most important developmental moves your child must make. Give this task all the time, patience, resolve, and tenderness it demands.

· Realize that while this task is difficult for you, it is even more difficult for your child. A child who is out of control suffers beneath a façade of omnipotence.

· Make eye contact when you are enforcing limits and notice when your child avoids your gaze. Eye contact not only keeps your child from subtly leaving the situation, it gives him the comfort of being *seen* by you.

· Pick your battles. Hold the line on crucial limits and be prepared to carry through to the very end. The crucial developments that accompany this task all depend on you not accommodating your child's demand.

· Be alert to your child's attempt to split people and situations into the good and the bad. This can happen in several ways. Your child may cast you as either a good or a bad parent and then may compare you to yourself at another time, to the other parent, or to other children's parents. So when your child says, "You let me do this before!" you can say, "Yes, sometimes I say yes and sometimes I must say no." Or when your child says, "But Mommy always lets me do this!" you can say, "Mommy and Daddy sometimes allow different things, but we both say no sometimes."

· The mastery of this task will take your child *years,* at least through adolescence. Even when she appears to have mastered it, there is a tendency to move drastically from a healthy sense of the self to a devalued or grandiose posture. She will in another situation find *no* intolerable.

# CHAPTER FIVE

# The Bipolar Child's Effect on the Family

A bipolar child can have a profound effect on a family. Parents often feel uncertain about their abilities to care for a child with this illness; their uncertainty is often compounded by worry about their child's ability to make it in the world. They can be frightened by the diagnosis of bipolar disorder, especially if a relative—a sibling or a parent—has suffered from a severe form of the disease. They may be confused about what the diagnosis means and anxious about medicating the child—particularly if the child has already had a bad experience with medication. Shame and guilt about having a psychiatric illness in the family are also common. Sometimes there is a breach of communication and cooperation between parents, who may blame each other for difficulties that are inevitable in parenting a bipolar child. At times teachers and inexperienced mental health professionals also blame the parents for the child's problems.

Denial is a fundamental part of bipolar disorder—mania and rage, core symptoms of the disorder, are denials of depression and helplessness. Consequently, there can be a family secret about one or another person who has suffered from the condition. There may also be an impulse to keep the child's difficulties a secret. Denial is a way of trying to avoid loss: a loss of self-esteem, a loss of power, or a loss of an idealized sense of the self or of the child. But denial prevents both parents and child from getting help, and it deepens the isolation that both the child and family suffer.

Divorce, already a common occurrence in our society, is more likely to occur in a family with a bipolar child, making everything more difficult to manage.

For these and other reasons, it is important to recognize that a family should also receive treatment. With appropriate help, parents can recognize each other's and their child's difficulties and make use of available resources for treatment.

## Mom and Dad: The Guardians of Life and Limits

The family is the womb within which a child develops. For better or for worse, its atmosphere is the emotional air a child breathes. The good enough home—like Winnicott's "good enough mother"— provides another kind of membrane, *a secure space* where there is a predictable routine, where needs are met, including the need to have appropriate limits set, and where a child feels protected and secure. It is also a place where, because of that security, a child can *play*, developing and elaborating his understanding and imagined control of the world beyond. The controlling and protective presences in the home, the parents, have roles that are necessarily distinct: Mom is typically the guardian of life; Dad is the guardian of limits.

Recognizing a clear distinction between the roles mothers and fathers play in their child's development is not paternalistic. It is quite compatible with mothers who are the professional equals (or betters) of their husbands and with fathers who share in the physical care of their children and maintain the inner world of the home. Women's liberation and redefinitions of masculinity have not changed the importance of the very different gifts fathers and mothers have to give their children.

## MOM'S ROLE: THE GUARDIAN OF LIFE

The mother's primary task is to take care of the child's internal well-being. A mother keeps track of her child in a special way. She is much more aware of the child's whereabouts and his internal life. Whatever she is doing, Mom has an idea of where her child is and what he is up to. She is the one most likely to notice that he is hungry or tired; she is the one most likely to take him to the doctor when he is sick. Mom never quite forgets that her child began inside herself, and, at first, the child actually sees Mom as part of himself. Their internal lives are linked in a profound way.

A mother's attunement is vital to her child's settling in and developing a sense of basic trust, but her attunement also makes it more difficult for her to set limits for her child. In saying no to her child she must go in two directions: she must attend to her child's inner life while upsetting or challenging it.

## DAD'S ROLE: THE GUARDIAN OF LIMITS

As an outsider, Dad performs the crucial task of drawing his child out into the world, away from the fused relationship with Mom. Mom also plays a necessary cooperative role in presenting the child to Dad. For a male child, Dad's presence is important in helping the boy develop a masculine identity. Later, even if he isn't around nearly as much as Mom, Dad will play a crucial role in helping his child to accept limits. Unburdened by an intense sympathy with his child, Dad tends to set limits more abruptly and uncompromisingly. Often children with ADD or an oppositional disposition—kids who have lots of trouble with *no*—accept limits more readily from their fathers. A father's imagined presence can be of crucial help to a mother when she sets limits. (Remember the familiar warning: "Wait until your father gets home!")

Dad should be the quintessential adult: not only physically powerful but powerful also in the role he plays in the family. His presence and his separate relationship with Mom mark a boundary between the child's fantasies of being an adult and an adult's real accomplishments. The stronger and more affectionate their relationship is, the safer a child will feel. As the child surrenders his exclusive relationship with his mother, Dad's power in the world and in the home becomes a goal for the child to reach, one step at a time. As the child makes those steps—in school, in sports, and in work—Dad plays a crucial role in enabling him to move powerfully and honestly into the world.

## DANGERS TO A MARRIAGE

When any child is born, the father is displaced (at least somewhat) from his relationship with the mother. Suddenly, nearly all of Mom's time, energy, and love are directed toward the baby, rather than toward Dad. Not surprisingly, Dad feels the loss and resents it, but these feelings are usually offset by the satisfactions of being a father. However, a bipolar child has extraordinary needs for attention and caring, not just in infancy but at all ages. The child's vulnerability and increased need for her mother further intensify the closeness between the mother and baby. Dad's exclusion becomes more pronounced. What is more, the bipolar child's restlessness and prolonged sleep disturbances disrupt his parents' patterns of sleep and intimacy, which is not good for mood or for marriage.

Caring for a bipolar child is exhausting, and Mom's need for help with the tasks of mothering may not be understood or met by Dad, who may be preoccupied with his profession. Such misunderstanding can make both of them resentful: Mom because she feels abandoned and Dad because he feels his wife is placing an extra burden on him. Alienation can set in.

Dad may also start to feel disappointed with both his wife and his child. Mom's difficulty soothing the child can begin, unfairly, to raise questions in Dad's mind about his wife's competence as a mother—although these questions may not emerge until later when problems with separation or discipline crop up. Similarly, the child's neediness and unmanageability may also be frustrating for Dad, who is less at-tuned to the child to begin with.

Because of these and other stresses, Dad can begin to distance him-self from both Mom and the child. In some cases, depending on Dad's character and vulnerabilities, this withdrawal can appear as excessive involvement in work, an affair, substance abuse, or abandoning his family altogether. But even a subtle separation diminishes Dad's ability to perform his crucial roles of separating the child from Mom and set-ting appropriate limits. A distant father is less available as a goal for his child to strive toward.

## If Dad Withdraws

Dad's withdrawal, if it occurs, allows an excessively close relationship to form between the child and the mother, making separation more difficult for them both. Dad's attachment to his child is also weakened. The loss of Dad's watchful presence makes it more difficult for his child to handle later developmental tasks, such as accepting limits and managing aggression in the peer group. Dad comes to be viewed not only as a distant presence but also as a more frightening one. The child is challenged to see her father as both a source of limits *and* a source of strength. At the same time, because he seems frightening, Dad can have a harder time setting limits in a way that fosters connection with his child. This lack of connection with Dad makes it more difficult for the child to form an independent identity as an adolescent and to move out into the world as a young adult.

Because Dad can't seem to connect with his child, the distance be-tween them increases and conflict builds—a conflict that spills over into Dad's relationship with Mom. Dad may start openly questioning Mom's competence as a parent and criticizing her inability to set appro-priate limits, while Mom accuses Dad of being absent and of terroriz-ing the child. Caught in the middle, the child's feelings of helplessness intensify, affecting her ability to accept limits, function in school, and manage in the peer group.

## If Mom Gets Overly Attached

When Dad withdraws, Mom may fill up the empty emotional space by becoming overly attached to her child. The effects a child (bipolar or otherwise) experiences from being overinvolved with the mother vary. The child may feel intense separation anxiety when being left with a babysitter (if the overinvolved mother even allows this), when going to nursery school or kindergarten, and, of course, when going to bed. Anxiety can also be seen when a child plays or attempts new skills.

The emotional reality of the child's feelings for his mother is different than it appears. Superficially, the child seems to have an intense need for his mother's presence and is relieved when she is close. At a deeper level, however, the child is angered by his mother's intrusiveness and his own dependence on her. He becomes frightened that his anger will hurt her, leaving him alone. When he is separated from her, the child does not fear that something will happen to him but that something will happen to his mom. Magically, and unconsciously, the child imagines his own rage destroying Mom.

The child's anger also appears in intense oppositional behavior when a parent sets limits. In a bipolar child, whose emotional pitch, anxiety, and irritability are already heightened, these difficulties with separation and with limits are each intensified. Sometimes, if the child also has a vulnerability to panic attacks, an attack can occur at times of separation or overwhelming anger. When this is the case, medication may be required, but there also needs to be an adjustment in the child's relationship to Mom and to Dad.

Overinvolvement between mother and child can also lead to the pseudo-adult child. Because he doesn't have to compete with Dad for Mom's attention, the child can develop a false and premature sense of being an adult. Such a child may begin to develop an adultlike self, which shows in his bearing, speech, and preference for adult company. A little adult can have significant difficulty taking on appropriate developmental tasks, in part because he's already received some of the usual rewards for fulfilling those tasks—he is the apple of his mother's eye, the little man of the house, her most important companion. Actually, however, beneath his pseudo-adult self the child feels insecure, incapable of fulfilling his role. He also has difficulty fitting into his peer group because he is less childlike and other children see him as strange. As a result, he has even more trouble separating from his mother and fending off the aggression of his peers. He also has difficulty tolerating the frustration that accompanies true development in any area.

In some cases, an overwhelmed mother, enmeshed in an intense dependency on her child, reverses the parent-child relationship, demanding that the child take care of *her* emotional needs. (This may be the case when a mother is depressed, abandoned by the father—relatively or actually—or abusing alcohol or some other substance.) The child then becomes parentified: he may be left alone for extended periods of time, expected to be responsible for younger siblings, or converted into a supporting companion to his mother. Worse, the child may become his mother's companion in bed, where the child's anxiety and the mother's needs form an unhealthy alliance.

Even if the child manages to settle in well enough, intense dependency needs (unsatisfied because the parental relationship has been reversed), anxiety, and anger accumulate—all of which affect his later development. When the child is allowed to stay in the mother's bed for an extended period of time, there can be severe developmental reversals. (One six-year-old girl was brought to me because, when her father left the household, she began asking to nurse again.) Prolonged presence in a mother's bed also has an effect on the child's developing sexuality. The nature of this effect varies depending on the child's gender and how long it takes for the child to return to his or her own bed.

With a bipolar child it is often impossible to avoid more intense dependency—the child's disability requires an increased dependence. However, the changes that bipolar disorder can cause in a family have the effect of intensifying this dependence. Ultimately, the mother's ability to resist the pull to merge with her child is determined by the quality of her relationship with the father, his availability, and the mother's character. Such difficulties, when they occur, may appear to center in one parent, but it is the family and its function that are impaired.

## The Bipolar Child and Siblings

The bipolar child's effect on the family also affects the relationships between children. This effect differs depending on whether the affected child is older or younger than the other children and depending on the nature of the child's symptoms.

### Differences in Attention

Because the bipolar child needs an excessive amount of attention, other children in the family receive less parenting—especially if they're healthy. A parent may be less available to help with homework, less available to drive a child to friends' houses or to practices for sports or other activities. A more subtle but just as important loss is emotional. The parent of a bipolar child may well have less emotional reserve for other children. They can get the brunt of a parent's exhausted irritability, have to tolerate constant emotional chaos, or simply be left on their own because, by comparison, they should be able to cope. They may also find themselves having to assume household duties to compensate for the other sibling, such as walking the dog or taking out the garbage. At times when their parents (or parent) are not available, they may be asked to assume responsibility for their sibling.

### Envy and Competitiveness

The excessive attention that the bipolar child gets can foster an unhealthy competition between her and her siblings. The sibling or the affected child (depending on who is physically dominant) may engage in merciless bullying (see page 75). Conversely, the bipolar child may envy her sibling's greater success in school, with friends, or in the parents' regard and take revenge by attacking the sibling or destroying his things. The bipolar child's envy may also go underground, emerging as an anxious self-consciousness that intensifies her withdrawal and isolation from family and peers.

It is important to distinguish envy from jealousy. Envy is a more primitive emotion arising at an earlier stage of development. It is a desire for some *thing* another person has, material or personal. It is not competitiveness for a relationship but desire for a *part* of someone. Envy, in other words, does not see a whole person but a fragment.

The longing in envy is, however, also combined with a sense of hopelessness of ever having that thing and, consequently, a determination to destroy it in the other person and in oneself. Jealousy is usually conscious and can be verbalized; envy is more often unconscious, acting beyond a person's awareness or emerging as a feeling that cannot be put into words. Because its intent is destruction and because it is beyond awareness, envy is more dangerous than jealousy and more difficult to control.

## DISRUPTED FAMILY FUNCTIONS

A bipolar child can have a chaotic effect on family function—arguments at mealtime, disrupted vacations, the parents' missing another child's events at school or in sports all can disrupt other children's development. When more profound disturbances occur—such as increasing hostility between parents, abandonment by one parent, or substance abuse in a parent—the healthier child often experiences guilt and resentment, as well as helplessness to do anything about these feelings. The healthier child can sometimes be placed in the role of parent to his struggling sibling, fostering anxiety and feelings of being overwhelmed. At the very least, these disruptions can instill a profound fear of mental illness in other siblings, which can prevent them from acknowledging their own more subtle difficulties and seeking help for them. Usually these children also experience a chronic sense of neediness made more confusing by their comparative success.

## Repairing a Family Function

Eight-year-old Sidney was anxious about unpredictable situations and extremely oppositional. It was hard enough to get him into the car for the trip to his uncle's Thanksgiving dinner, but when the family arrived he refused to get out of the car. His younger sister who was always well behaved went on ahead easily, but Sid not only wouldn't leave the car, he also protested being left alone. His mother felt caught between her concern about her child's anxiety and her husband's mounting anger and impatience. She and Sid's father had already disagreed many times about how to handle Sid's tantrums. What could she do?

· The first requirement is for Sid's parents to be on the same side. This may not at this very moment be possible. But their best chance is to make the extended family gathering a distant second priority. Helping Sid out of his bind must come first. Sid's mom may first need to calm down Sid's father—they need to manage *their* conflict before they can help Sid manage his.

· Because there is a sibling who needs some accompaniment, it is necessary to divide parenting responsibilities. In view of Sid's anxiety and irritability, his mother is best suited to work with him; his father needs to support her role—"You stay with Sid, while I look after Lisa"— rather than express anger at Sid's misbehavior. Dad needs to remember that it is Sid who has the problem and that Mom is his (Dad's) ally.

· Mom needs patience, looking for a chance to get Sid to talk about what is bothering him. She may also have to decode his response for him—anger and entitlement may cover anxiety or hurt.

· Ultimately Sid can't call the shots and cancel the family gathering. That limit must be held. The task is to not become enraged, not leave Sid, and to deliver him into language. It won't happen if his parents can't work together.

## Bullying

A child with bipolar disorder often is excessively aggressive, but under that surface he feels at a distinct disadvantage in comparison to his sibling. He may try to even the score by bullying. Difficulties setting limits with the bipolar child can allow the situation to become unusually abusive. Conversely, an older sibling's resentment may be expressed as bullying of the bipolar child. These difficulties can prevent the normal bonding that occurs between siblings, adding to division in the family.

### Bullying in the Family

Matthew is bullying his brother Steven again.

> **STEVEN** is eleven but acts more like eight most of the time. He has an essentially sweet disposition, but he has suffered terribly from bipolar I disorder, having had two hospitalizations, a long list of different medications, and side effects of bed-wetting and weight gain. Their father left the family years ago and doesn't see the boys or contribute to their support. Mom, who struggles with bipolar depression herself, has hung on (just barely) through a long economic slump that has cut her income in half. She must work and take care of the boys without help. Often she must rely on Matthew to care for his younger brother or to do chores Steven isn't up to doing.

> **MATTHEW** is bright and handsome. He has ADD and a touch of depression. He is really a good kid, although he has his defiant side. He also has lots of reasons to be angry—his absent father, the

poverty that has surrounded him in the last few years, his mother's intermittent irritability and shouting, and his having to cross boundaries and act as his brother's keeper.

Today Matthew is waling hard on Steven, who is crying loudly to Mom. The house is a wreck, and the boys won't cooperate and stay apart. It looks like a completely unprovoked attack. What's a mother to do?

· First, don't assume it's an unprovoked attack. Nothing may have set it off here and now, but there is a long history. Besides, both boys need to learn to manage aggression.

· Mom needs to keep as calm as possible. She needs to see that both boys are in trouble, but both are also basically good kids. She can't accept their descriptions of each other *or* of her as horrible.

· She needs to separate them. In this case, the best way is to take Steven out with her, telling Matthew to stay home for the time being. She runs the risk that Matthew will leave, but he can take care of himself better than Steven can. Out of the house, she can calm Steven, but without blaming Matthew. "Steven, it's so hard for you and your brother! Of course it doesn't feel fair." (She should *not* say, "It isn't fair for me either!" She needs to be the parent, not one of the victims.)

· When things are calmed down, she can speak with Matthew. She needs to get him to talk about what was bothering him, listening first. She needs to validate those parts of Matthew's feelings that are justified. Then she needs to set a limit with him verbally. (She has already done it in action by taking Steven out.)

· It is important that she not blame one boy or even both of them. They are learning to get along under very tough conditions. She needs to have compassion.

· She also needs to have compassion for herself—accept that she might not always get it right, keep in mind what ought to be, and do her best to approach from where things are now.

· Probably in order to do all these things she will need some help from a therapist or from the psychiatrist who treats Steven.

**P.S.** This mom is an unsung hero.

## DIVORCE AND THE BIPOLAR CHILD

A marriage is put at increased risk by the stress a bipolar child exerts. The difficulties such a child innocently brings to a family promote alienation, disappointment, and conflict between parents. The conflict such a child can provoke between herself and her siblings, or between her siblings and her parents, makes it even harder for Mom and Dad to cooperate with one another. It is not surprising, then, that the bipolar child often enough finds herself in a broken home.

A child with bipolar disorder has all the difficulties other children normally suffer in divorce, and then some. Any divorce results in a loss of parenting, and bipolar children need more parenting than other children. A bipolar child can also have particular difficulty moving between households, especially when the rules change from place to place. Bipolar children have trouble accepting limits in the first place, but it's harder when the limits change—especially if one parent suggests that the other parent doesn't set appropriate limits. The bipolar child's tendency to split—to see one parent as good and the other as bad—and to switch these perceptions back and forth in rapid succession, plays havoc with her ability to accept authority.

When there is intense animosity in the divorce—which can more easily happen when Mom or Dad (or both) suffer from the intense anger that accompanies bipolar disorder—the child's difficulties are even more severe. Studies show that the single most destructive factor affecting children in a divorce is hostility between parents. The children in bitter divorces are often quite guarded, because they're afraid that anything they say may anger or betray one of their parents. This guardedness about their feelings affects the child's ability to put her feelings into words and makes it even more difficult for her to accept limits in a healthy way. These problems are amplified for the bipolar child. Even if she does not become oppositional, accepting limits without comment exacts an internal price: a child's capacity for trust and intimacy is often damaged. These children can sometimes be helped to talk about their predicament in groups for children of divorce, such as the Banana Splits groups that some schools offer. Individual therapy is also important to help restore basic trust and a capacity for intimacy.

## Help for Families of Bipolar Children

The disruptions that bipolar disorder causes in a child and in family function may make different kinds of psychotherapy—individual, group, and family—necessary at different phases in treatment. There are, however, a number of factors that keep families from seeking treatment. Many families are worried about the cost. Because psychiatric coverage by insurance companies is scandalously meager, families sometimes try to minimize treatment—especially psychotherapeutic treatment, which commonly has poorer coverage than drugs. Because of cost, there is an understandable temptation to depend mostly on medication. Many families also feel shame about the problems they suffer. There may be an unacknowledged assumption that their difficulties are the result of their failure as parents—as if they should be able to get it just right and their children wouldn't suffer. If there is any kind of abuse in the family— emotional, physical, sexual, substance—a culture of secrecy develops, keeping people from seeking the help they need.

Although there have been spectacular advances in psychopharmacology in recent years, medication (even when it successfully controls the illness) doesn't treat the person, much less the family. Bipolar disorder, especially when it begins in childhood, profoundly affects a person's development and sense of himself. It also injures families in ways that can be hard to understand when you are in the middle of the disruption, and especially when you are a child. These problems cannot be addressed merely by medicating the affected child. (See Chapter 12 for a discussion of different kinds of psychotherapy.)

## BEAR IN MIND

· No matter what the stresses are, Mom and Dad need to maintain their relationship as parents and as companions. One way to do this is for Mom and Dad to take a periodic day off together away from the children. While the children are in school or day care, Mom and Dad should have an outing: lunch at a nice restaurant, a hike together, a movie, an afternoon alone.

· Make sure the psychiatrist treating your child is aware of difficulties you are having as parents. If the psychiatrist limits herself to considerations regarding medication, make sure she also provides referrals for appropriate psychotherapeutic help. Also, once the psychotherapy has begun, make sure there is good communication between the therapist and the psychiatrist.

· Finding a therapist—for your child, for yourself, or for the family—can be difficult. It is hard to know who is good, and the letters after their names—M.D., Ph.D., M.S.W.—are not a reliable indication. One approach is to go to a leading clinician (someone you might not be able to see on a regular basis) and have a consultation with the purpose of getting a referral to a well-qualified professional (see pages 251–253).

· Managing aggression between siblings is a tricky problem. Avoid the trap of deciding whose fault it is. Children usually want to be together more than they want to fight. Take advantage of this when they can't keep from fighting by separating them, without blaming either child, for a limited period of time. Do this not as a punishment but as a cooling-off period, after which they can try being together again.

· Avoid keeping secrets, especially between one parent and a child. Children need to know that parents talk to each other and share information. They need to know that they can't split one from another. Secret keeping in a family is almost always a sign of trouble.

· Help children notice their feelings. Envy is particularly hard for a child (or even an adult) to notice in himself. When you notice it, help your child to see it without being punitive. Your help is crucial for your children to be able to talk about uncomfortable feelings like resentment, anger, loneliness, or being overwhelmed.

· Have regular family councils that encourage children to express their difficulties or point out yours.

· If abuse occurs—physical, emotional, sexual, or substance—get help *now*. Don't look to assign blame but take responsibility for changing the situation. The factors contributing to abuse are always complex and go back generations. The important thing is not to keep it secret; it is in secrecy that it proliferates.

# CHAPTER SIX

# Going Out into the World

## *School, Separation* Again, *and Functioning in a Group*

Most children have already accomplished several milestones before beginning elementary school. They have attached securely to their parents, have separated from them, sleep comfortably on their own, and have learned to negotiate certain social expectations—accepting limits, basic interaction with peers and adults, and toilet training. Then the bar is raised again: the child must learn to separate from home (at least temporarily), attach to teachers, conform to a new set of social expectations, and begin to manage peer relationships in a wider arena.

A child with bipolar disorder embarking on elementary school can have an additional set of problems: severe separation anxiety, panic attacks, difficulty with peer relationships, and trouble functioning in group situations—trouble keeping still and concentrating. Difficulty adjusting to school is especially true for a child who has had problems with earlier developmental tasks such as feeling comfortable in her own skin or accepting limits. While many children have some of these problems as they make the transition from home to school, the bipolar child experiences them more intensely and may experience multiple challenges.

## Separation Anxiety and Panic Attacks

A panic attack is a sudden overwhelming flood of anxiety that is usually experienced physically as well as emotionally. For adults and children, it is usually confusing and disabling, but a child typically can't describe or even identify the feelings as unusual. What is more, a panic attack can appear differently in a child than in an adult, so it sometimes goes unrecognized. In an adult, a panic attack is most frequently experienced as overwhelming anxiety, rapid heartbeat, shortness of breath, a cold sweat, and chest discomfort. In early school-age children, panic attacks may take the form of severe separation anxiety or a recurrent complaint of an upset stomach before school or at school. Children are also less able to describe their symptoms and may complain only of anxiety and an intensely uncomfortable feeling in the region of the stomach or diaphragm, which they call a stomachache.

A history of panic attacks in a family member can help parents or a physician recognize the problem. When panic attacks are present in a child with bipolar disorder, medication may be necessary to prevent an aggravation of bipolar symptoms—sleep disturbance, depression, irritability, additional anxiety—to help avoid school refusal, and to keep the child on track developmentally. In a bipolar child, however, the standard treatment for panic disorder with an SSRI or another antidepressant can make matters worse. (See the discussion of panic disorder in Chapter 11.)

## Bipolar Intensity from the Inside

Maintaining an inner sense of calm or an external focus can be a constant challenge for a bipolar child, who has heightened sensory awareness, a high level of anxiety, and an intense internal life. When he plays, he becomes intensely absorbed; when he becomes engaged in fantasy, he is captured intensely; and when he is disturbed from any activity, he reacts intensely—with anger, defiance, or distress. What's more, a child with a bipolar disposition often has a tenuous state of inner equilibrium, which makes him particularly intolerant of its disruption. It is also true that some children with bipolar disorder experience external and internal demands from several directions with unsettling intensity—they freeze, lose focus, or explode when they are asked to move in one direction or another.

One consequence of this inner intensity and tension is that *approaching* a child with bipolar disorder can be particularly difficult. The child may demand that a parent, teacher, or another child approach him in an exact way. In soothing or talking to such a child, there is a good chance that the other person will be rejected or attacked for not getting it just right.

The intensity of a bipolar child of this age (six to eight, or even twelve) often appears in the form of fervent desires and impassioned demands. Harrowing struggles triggered by visits to a toy store, concerning food, or over electronic games are especially common. The child's extreme overvaluation of a desired object—a toy, an ice cream cone, a ride in an amusement park—couples with an enormous sense of entitlement, and the distress a child feels at being denied can be overwhelming, as can the child's response to the frustration. For this reason it is particularly important that you be ready to hold a limit *and* help your child with his distress. The same techniques of limit setting discussed in the last chapter still apply, but now they are needed in increasingly public situations. In these situations it is important to remember that the child is in distress. It is not the child's job to protect the parent from embarrassment; it is the parent's job to help the child tolerate frustration.

## Time Squeeze

Seven-year-old **TAMMY,** who has a diagnosis of early bipolar disorder, has difficulty getting up in the morning, and when she does she is irritable and uncooperative. Dressing, eating, and brushing her teeth are all a struggle. On an especially difficult morning, the school bus is due to arrive in a half hour and Tammy is screaming, unwilling to get dressed or sit down to breakfast. Dad left an hour ago for work and Mom is due at her part-time job in an hour. What does she do?

· Right now, Mom needs to prioritize. Yes, Tammy is being opposi-tional and uncooperative, but she is also in some kind of distress. She needs help the most now.

· It may be some time before Tammy's distress can be relieved, and in order to help her daughter, Mom needs to reduce other demands on herself. She should probably call in and let work know that she will be late or absent that day and accept as a given that Tammy will miss the bus. This gives her some breathing room and relieves the pressure to get Tammy to do what she's told.

· Another short-term goal is to get Tammy to *talk* about what is wrong, which is easier if the immediate pressure is off both her and her mom.

· Ultimately it is important to determine why Tammy is so irritable and uncooperative each morning. Is her mood unstable, tending to-ward depression early in the day? Is Tammy getting enough rest? Is this problem aggravated by seasonal change? Are there problems at school that she doesn't feel able to cope with? Does she suffer from low blood sugar in the morning? Is it some combination of these or other problems?

· Depending on the answer to these questions, a plan needs to be formulated to deal with each part of the problem *ahead of time:* mood stability, nutrition, or contact with the school. A problem with mood may need to be addressed pharmacologically; low blood sugar may respond to an eye-opener of orange juice; problems at school can be complex and require a different approach depending on the source.

· It may also be that Mom needs more help from Dad, if that is workable. However, this may be one of those problems Mom has to face alone, at least in the immediate situation. In the larger picture, however, she needs *not* to be alone.

## Sleep Problems

Bedtime can be extremely difficult for children with bipolar disorder because they have vivid imaginings as they approach sleep, resulting from heightened sensory awareness, anxiety, and (sometimes) depression. The bipolar child is prone to nightmares, night terrors, and a more pronounced response to the normal rising and falling cycles of sleep—the transitions back and forth between REM or dream sleep and the deeper stage-four sleep in which night terrors occur. It is more common for such a child to awaken in the middle of the night as sleep cycles rise and fall. It is also not uncommon for a bipolar child's dreams to involve things that would be considered psychotic in an adult, such as extreme violence and visions of his own death.

The bipolar child's difficulty falling asleep at this and at other ages may be due in part to a heightened response to the normal evening drop in the hormone cortisol, causing increased anxiety and heightened sensory awareness. Rather than becoming tired, a bipolar child can become increasingly active and fight attempts to get him to bed. The combination of heightened sensory awareness and increased anxiety can also intensify fears of the dark and of letting go of mental control in sleep. This struggle against going to bed is more difficult when the child has still not mastered the earlier developmental task of accepting limits. A regular bedtime ritual, which involves a parent accompanying

the child and helping him relax and sleep, is helpful to both the child
and the parent. Establishing a routine and an ability to anticipate what
is coming are in themselves comforting.

At this developmental stage, when the normal barrier between unconscious emotional processes and conscious thought is more perme-
able for all children, a bipolar child can have auditory and visual
hallucinations while awake, and especially as he is approaching sleep. It
is important to note that, although these symptoms shouldn't be ignored, they aren't as worrisome in a child as they would be in an adult.
They aren't necessarily a sign of psychosis. The question of whether
they need to be treated with medication, and with what medication,
needs to be answered by a child psychiatrist.

## Difficulty with Peer Relationships

One of the most important tasks of the early school years is attachment
to the peer group, and this can be extremely difficult for the bipolar
child. Problems with peers continue in later developmental stages but
often make their first appearance in early elementary school. Children
this age are just beginning to use rules of play and observe social
niceties; their impulse control is subject to frequent lapses. Although all
children are occasionally disruptive, a child who is particularly out of
control makes other children anxious, and they can respond by withdrawing or driving the child away. Impulsivity and difficulty with rules
are magnified in a bipolar child. She may be alternately bossy, intolerant, aggressive, excessively needy, or overly silly. (Intense silliness is particularly common when a child experiences anxiety.) It is also common
for a bipolar child to be excessively ardent, with a heightened desire for
contact but a poor sense of personal boundaries and an anxiety that
shows in shyness or awkwardness. These behaviors make it hard for the
bipolar child to enter the peer group. Unfortunately, the bipolar child
can also be highly sensitive to rejection, making her exclusion from the
peer group exquisitely painful.

*A six-year-old bipolar child depicts her rejection by peers who laugh at her distress. In addition to the poignancy of this child's drawing, note the skill with which she renders the rejecting peers smiling together with nastiness!*

## Loss of Bowel or Bladder Control

The stress of starting school or entering any new developmental stage can cause a temporary loss of earlier accomplishments, such as bowel or bladder control. This might not be due to developmental stress alone. When a child doesn't master toilet training by the age of five or six, or when a loss of bowel control involves excessive retention of stool, a pediatrician needs to be consulted. On the other hand, bed-wetting is frequently (about 70 percent of the time) an inherited problem, one that's related to how deeply a child sleeps or how well he can sense the fullness of his bladder or inhibit urination when his bladder is full. Bed-wetting occurs more often in boys than in girls. When a loss of bowel or bladder control occurs together with a change in behavior, however, the possibility of some environmental stress and even sexual trauma needs to be explored.

Some medications used to treat bipolar disorder—lithium and major tranquilizers—can interfere with bladder control. When the problem is particularly severe or socially disabling—preventing the child from participating in sleepovers or embarrassing him in front of siblings—there is a safe medication available. Synthetic antidiuretic hormone acts to decrease the production of urine. When given to a child just before bed, it can often put a stop to bed-wetting.

Whatever the cause—developmental, genetic, or medical—a loss of bowel or bladder control can be socially agonizing for a child. It's important that you be as matter-of-fact as possible. Get your child the help he needs, and remember that control will eventually develop.

## DISTRACTION: THE BIPOLAR CHILD'S PARTICULAR FORM OF ADD

The bipolar child has an intense internal life that competes with whatever is going on around her. Her emotional intensity can make it particularly difficult for her to enter into language, to put her feelings into words, and consequently to understand her feelings, especially when they are strong ones. This difficulty expressing herself also affects her ability to listen to and understand other people's words, which can make her seem spaced out, careless, or simply defiant. These difficulties have a particular impact on her ability to make the transition into the school setting.

In school she needs to give up her private mental life and physical activity to be part of a group and follow the group's agenda. Kindergarten can be particularly tough because it's very hard for the bipolar child to make the transition from her intense emotional and imaginative internal world to the rational worlds of language and learning. She may protect herself by cutting off from things that disrupt either her thought world or her precarious emotional balance. A bipolar child can also be unusually activated by the influence of a group, increasing her impulsivity. She may become intrusive, hyperactive, excessively silly, or withdrawn.

As she goes from one task to another, or from one thought to the next, the bipolar child tends to get stuck in the immediate present and lose the thread of continuity. The abundance and speed of the bipolar child's thought can also cause problems. Sometimes, she can't comprehend what she's reading or what's being said because so many thoughts are careening off each other in her mind. Her intense internal life also affects her ability to manage competing demands. If someone insists that she choose between two tasks that need to be done or to interrupt a task in which she is involved, she just can't handle it. She becomes anxious and explodes in protest or simply cuts off.

One uncommon, but important, explanation for distraction in a child of this age is *dissociation,* which is usually a result of trauma. Some young children, when they find themselves in a situation that is overwhelmingly painful or frightening, have a capacity to leave the situation by cutting themselves off from consciously being there. This defense opens a door in the mind that is then hard to close. Later, in situations of even minor stress, the child will again break off contact with his surroundings and zone out. Substance abuse, high levels of anger and irritability, and physical abuse are often seen in families of a bipolar child. The bipolar child who has been emotionally traumatized can mentally and emotionally check out of a stressful situation for an extended period of time. In such cases, it may be difficult to tell how much of a child's distraction stems from her emotional disposition and how much stems from trauma and consequent dissociation.

It may also be true that shocks from early infancy, which impact more powerfully on an acutely sensitive child, can cause a tendency toward dissociation. Dissociation can occur along a spectrum in addition to occurring massively as a result of overwhelming emotional trauma. Several of the characteristic mental traits of children with bipolar disorder—absorption with internal mental life, hyperfocusing, difficulty with transitions, spacing out, and problems with sensory integration— can also be symptoms of dissociation. The overlap between dissociation and bipolar disorder has not to my knowledge been studied. I work with several bipolar children who have marked dissociative symptoms but no history of trauma. (This subject is discussed further in Chapter 11.)

## DISTINGUISHING BETWEEN BIPOLAR DISORDER AND ADD OR ADHD

Attention deficit disorder (ADD) is characterized by difficulty staying on task—paying attention, following directions, even sustaining some kinds of play. Russell Barkley, a leading expert on ADD, has observed that it can also be thought of as a difficulty *sustaining motivation*. He points out that children with ADD can stay involved in tasks they are interested in or in which their interest is multiply reinforced. For example, a child with ADD can stay focused on a video game, in which interest is encouraged through color, sound, story, and continual movement, but the same child will have difficulty with repetitive, routine tasks that are not particularly pleasurable, such as schoolwork.

Some children with ADD think better when they are moving. Research suggests that an increased level of norepinephrine released as a result of muscular activity contributes to this phenomenon of improved thinking with movement. Norepinephrine is a neurotransmitter known to be deficient in people with ADD. It is also true that ADD is diagnosed largely in highly verbal cultures where desk work abounds, rather than in ones where there is a predominance of farming or hunting and gathering. ADD may be an unanticipated consequence of our civilization. In any case, most children with ADD are at a special disadvantage when they have to sit still and listen or perform routine tasks—they have particular difficulty in the classroom, with homework, or in test taking.

Attention-deficit/hyperactivity disorder (ADHD) has the additional symptoms of physical restlessness (a tendency to move around continually) and impulsive behavior. Children with this disorder have a higher level of unproductive physical activity than their peers. In these children, unfortunately, motion does not improve attention or the capacity to sustain thought. They not only have difficulty listening and staying on task, they also have difficulty sitting still and a tendency to fiddle with objects around them. Their impulsivity also has a verbal dimension: they make spontaneous remarks, interrupt people, and can talk incessantly. They not only have difficulty functioning in a classroom, their impulsive behavior also disrupts other people's ability to work.

Because of a lack of inhibition, children with ADD/ADHD tend to get distracted by the external environment and also have difficulty screening out impulses from the internal environment. They have difficulty *staying on track*. Biologically, these disorders are understood to result from an underactivity in certain regions of the cortex, the outer portion of the brain. The prefrontal cortex and the hippocampus help us focus on one task by inhibiting our attention to irrelevant noise, movement, or thoughts. (PET scans of adults with ADD show decreased blood flow to the prefrontal cortex and the hippocampus when they concentrate.) These areas of the brain are normally rich in inhibitory neurons using the neural transmitters norepinephrine and dopamine. We do know that medicines that increase the activity of either norepinephrine or dopamine—for example, methylphenidate (Ritalin, Concerta, Metadate) and amphetamines (Dexedrine, Adderall)—improve symptoms of ADD/ADHD.

## ADD/ADHD in Bipolar Disorder

Superficially, the behavior of some children with bipolar disorder and one with ADHD are similar: both are impulsive, hyperactive, talk incessantly, and are completely disorganized. However, the hyperactivity and inattention seen in bipolar disorder come from *increased arousal* in the limbic system, the deep brain, rather than decreased activity in the cortex, as in typical ADHD. These deeper portions of the brain regulate the *internal environment* and automatic behaviors, like body temperature, pulse, blood pressure, emotion, and the general level of arousal. When the deeper portions of the brain are overactive, it is difficult to focus because it is harder to inhibit those powerful impulses. (For example, when our bladder is full, a powerful impulse from the bladder stimulates the deep brain, overriding our ability to think or even act.) In bipolar disorder, a child periodically becomes flooded with unusually powerful feelings and impulses to act. A child can also be flooded with an abundance of thoughts that appear as racing thoughts or as a loosening of logical connections between thoughts that then career off one another. An abundance of thought can also appear as rapid, pressured speech. Increased activity in the cortex shows up as hypersensitivity to the external environment. Behaviorally this can appear as irritability, explosiveness, or a complete shutting down to manage the overload. Hyperarousal in the deep brain and in the cortex account for a bipolar child's impulsive behavior and speech and the difficulty he has responding appropriately to the world around him.

Because their internal life is so intense, bipolar children must spend a great deal of effort (inhibition) in order to maintain internal calm. They often appear distracted—and they are—but they're distracted by their internal environment rather than by the external one. While the impulsivity of children with ADHD can seem random and their conversation wandering, bipolar children's impulsivity is driven by anger, silliness, excitement, or sensory overload; their speech also has an emotionally driven quality. Children with bipolar disorder are also able to hyperfocus, to pay extremely close and sustained attention to something that interests them. When their internal world locks on to something, they can powerfully inhibit external interference. What these children have difficulty with is stopping one thing and going on to another. These children are *captured by their internal environment,* and they have difficulty changing tracks.

Although they share some common properties—inattention, hyperactivity, impulsivity, and an abundance of speech—ADD/ADHD and bipolar disorder arise from different problems in different areas of the brain. For this reason, the medicines used to treat ADD/ADHD can be dangerous in children with bipolar disorder. The typical medications used to treat ADD/ADHD are stimulants—methylphenidate (Ritalin) and amphetamines (Adderall and Dexedrine)—which increase the activity of dopamine and norepinephrine. These medicines act on the

# The Brain as a Split-Level Organ

## Cortex

- Scans the external environment (contains all sensory processing)
- Mediates between the internal and the external environment:
  - inhibits impulses from the internal environment
  - initiates and moderates motor activity
  - sustains attention to one thing rather than another
  - language

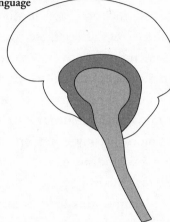

### Limbic System

Controls the internal environment
- reflexes
- pulse
- blood pressure
- pleasure, pain, rage, anxiety
- level of arousal

# Brain Activity in ADD/ADHD and Bipolar Disorder

## Cortex

Decreased arousal in the prefrontal cortex in ADD/ADHD causes

- hyperactivity
- impulsivity of thought and behavior
- difficulty sustaining attention and motivation
- distractability (external)
- talkativeness

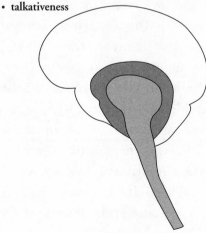

### Limbic System

Increased arousal in the limbic system (deep brain) in bipolar disorder causes

- hyperactivity
- impulsivity of thought and behavior
- distractability (internal)
- hyperfocusing and difficulty changing track
- talkativeness
- irritability and rage
- oppositional behavior
- mood changes
- anxiety

cortex to *increase inhibition,* helping a child to concentrate on one thing by inhibiting his attention to others. This works with ADD/ADHD because these disorders stem from decreased activity in the cortex—the stimulation helps the child stay on track.

However, bipolar disorder is driven (in part) by increased arousal in the deep brain. Stimulants can cause increased activity in those regions. What is confusing is that these drugs affect these two areas of the brain at different rates. Stimulants affect the cortex almost immediately—within a half hour to an hour. The effects of stimulants on the deep brain can take a longer time—weeks to months. Consequently, a bipolar child may initially respond quite well to a stimulant, because it helps him focus more intently. After a period of time, however, this child may develop a sleep disturbance, a rebound reaction (hyperarousal and irritability as the drug wears off), mood instability, and possibly psychosis. Sometimes this kind of reaction happens immediately: one child I treated said, "Mommy, something inside me is making me angry." Sometimes, however, it takes longer for the limbic system to react, and mood instability appears only after a period of time. In either case, the aggravation of bipolar disorder occurs because the deeper areas of the brain have begun to heat up, to kindle.

There are, however, children with bipolar disorder who have a form of ADD (described above) who benefit enormously from stimulants. A few of these children can tolerate a stimulant alone; many more can tolerate a stimulant when it is combined with a mood stabilizer. But some children with bipolar disorder cannot tolerate stimulants at all, or even nonstimulant medications used to treat ADD/ADHD, with or without a mood stabilizer. Because bipolar disorder and ADD/ADHD can resemble each other, and because two children with bipolar disorder can react differently to the same medication, it is important to consult with a child psychiatrist before beginning medication for ADD/ADHD. Unfortunately, a diagnosis of bipolar disorder does not rule out ADD/ADHD, nor does it predict whether a child can benefit from (or tolerate) medications used for ADD/ADHD.

## TO MEDICATE OR NOT TO MEDICATE?

Hyperactivity or difficulty paying attention doesn't necessarily indicate that your child needs to be medicated. All children have this problem to some degree. The key question is, can she stay on track *developmentally*? Can she make the transition into a classroom, accept limits from a teacher, and move with the group *well enough*? Some schools have higher expectations and may not be appropriate for certain children.

Before allowing your child to take medication for hyperactivity, you should consult with a child psychiatrist. Medications that are safe and effective for other children with ADD/ADHD can pose a significant risk for a child with bipolar disorder. Even when medication is appropriate, the correct kind or combination of medications can differ importantly from child to child. Because of the risk of an accompanying bipolar disorder, evaluation for ADD/ADHD should include not only a behavioral rating scale or continuous performance test but also a developmental history and family history.

## THE POSITIVES

There are often positive aspects to a child's bipolar disposition:

· an elaborate and intense fantasy life
· creativity, inventiveness, and artistic talent
· sympathy or empathy for other children
· an infectious good nature
· charismatic leadership

An elaborate and intense fantasy life with an extensive ability to play within that internal world and link that play to perceptions of the external world are basic requirements for creativity and artistic talent. It is not surprising, then, that large numbers of artists, inventors, and powerfully influential people suffered with bipolar disorder. Abraham Lincoln, Herman Melville, Edgar Allan Poe, and Vincent van Gogh are well-known examples. For creativity to flourish, however, there needs to be what Donald Winnicott termed a transitional space between the child and the mother within which, under her appreciative eye, he can imaginatively play. Later the development of talent requires material parental support and the artist's ability to tolerate an apprenticeship, acquire discipline, and make a sustained connection with his audience or culture. Child and parent need to pass through many developmental challenges before the child's creative gifts can bear fruit.

Because of their intense awareness of their own and other people's feelings, many children with bipolar disorder show a heightened sympathy or empathy for other children. In their calmer states of mind, these children may not only be aware of other children's feelings, they will also feel them intensely themselves and can go to unusual lengths to comfort or befriend another child. This heightened awareness of others can then develop into a professional strength, giving the child an extra capacity to act, to direct other people, or to connect with other people's emotional life in other ways. Abraham Lincoln's political genius—his charisma, his personal sense of vision, his compassion, his single-mindedness, and even his ability to tolerate the suffering of the country during the Civil War—may well have owed much to the positive aspects of bipolar disorder.

## BEAR IN MIND

· Choose a school that will work with your child's needs and vulnerabilities, one that will help him feel his strengths and encourage his development. Especially in the beginning, your child needs to experience school as a place to grow, not a set of restrictions.

· Don't undermine the school's authority. Parents who themselves have difficulty with authority may unwittingly communicate their feelings to their child, making it harder for the child to trust or attach to teachers. On the other hand, don't leave your child in an environment that simply doesn't fit her disposition or demands an overly high level of maturity.

· Pay close attention to your child's anxieties with respect to peers and to school. At this age, children can't fully express their worries (much less deal with them) without your help.

· Help your child expand his relationships with peers. This may mean more than arranging playdates, especially in the suburbs where children may not live close to one another. Supervise and facilitate your child's play with peers. If you are working, you may need to find an after-school setting that gives your child a consistent and structured environment in which to develop social skills.

· Encourage your child's changing interests, rather than insisting on mastery of any one of them. A child's interests at this time tend to be fluid. If you push too hard for involvement in or performance of any activity, you can destroy the fun and turn your child off. Be a presence that accompanies your child when necessary. Her growth at this time still depends importantly on being *seen* by you.

· Be aware that old problems you thought had been mastered may suddenly reappear (e.g., bowel or bladder control or sleeping in one's own bed). Have patience, but set limits and stick to them.

· Set clear boundaries between normal aggressive play and victimization or bullying. Let your child know what's acceptable behavior—whether it's his or someone else's.

· Dad's role becomes increasingly important at this time as a companion in play who can help a child feel more comfortable venturing out into the world and managing aggression. He does this less by what he says than by the rhythm of his interactions. Fathers often underestimate their importance at this time in their child's development. Hang in there.

# CHAPTER SEVEN

# The Bipolar Child from Eight to Twelve

## *Entering the Peer Group, Mastering Aggression, and Developing Skills*

I f you observe children during kindergarten and first grade, you will notice that they touch each other freely, walking with arms draped over each other's shoulders and with relatively little attention to gender. By second grade, however, there is noticeably less casual physical contact, and boys and girls are beginning to segregate in their play. What physical contact there is tends to have a prodding, aggressive quality, more noticeable in boys than in girls. Also noticeable in both boys and girls is a manifest anxiety when they see—on television or in a movie, for example—kissing or other physical affection. Children at this age frequently cover their faces or avert their gaze to avoid seeing displays of affection. This is not the result of puritanical social conditioning but the early signs of a transition from the parent-centered years (three to seven) to a peer-oriented period (eight to twelve) called latency, during which sexual interests—for example, the desire to be caressed and held—begin to be submerged and an interest in aggressive play becomes more prominent. A child's earlier interest in sexuality is now charged with negative feelings and suppressed. Just as the toddler's fascination with feces is followed by the idea of bodily wastes as dirty or smelly, the boy who used to be infatuated with his kindergarten teacher now goes out of his way to avoid such feelings.

Some bipolar children contradict this normal set of changes, because hypersexuality can accompany bipolar disorder. Hypersexuality can also be a symptom of sexual abuse. When a child's interest in sex persists prominently at this age, it is necessary to look more closely to understand what is going on. Looking more closely does not mean assuming the worst. Be discreet. If there is confusion or concern, consult with a mental health professional—an M.D., a Ph.D., or a C.S.W.

As he progresses through latency, the child with bipolar disorder will show many of the same symptoms seen in earlier years: high anxiety, irritability, oppositional behavior, increased arousal in the evening, and difficulty getting to sleep. If bipolar disorder is surfacing for the first time, it might appear to be ADD with a trace of irritability accompanied by a sleep disturbance. Depression may also be the harbinger of the developing disorder, although the symptoms—a lack of interest in playing, irritability, whining and crying, and self-blaming—may be different at this age than in an older child. Depression can also surface as a whining insistence on having fun. Although a child may take pleasure in certain activities and insist that he's not depressed, his desperation to have fun together with an intolerance of tasks that are slightly difficult may indicate a problem. It's as if the child is seeking fun to stave off depression—using fun as self-medication.

## SOCIAL MEMBRANES

Children age eight to twelve start to form social circles or groups that may take the form of secret organizations, clubhouses, or pajama parties, but they all have one goal in common: creating a social membrane that makes the members feel safe while excluding nonmembers. For boys, this exclusion of others often takes the form of physical aggression or a defense against it. They play war games or cops and robbers, and build forts. Their aggression can also take the form of baseball, boxing, and flipping baseball cards. Another important part of their aggression—one they share with girls—is verbal, as they one-up each other or engage in verbal duels.

Girls also form social membranes, excluding others and enforcing group boundaries. Their play also is aggressive, although expressed more socially and verbally. (At this age, as at others, girls tend to be more verbal and more social than boys.) Girls erect social barriers by forming cliques; they become verbally cutting by commenting on each other's clothes, appearance, or popularity. They gossip. Like boys, they also compete in sports and other games. For both boys and girls, an important function of such play is to allow them to develop a sense of how to play by the rules, develop a feel for how far he or she can push against someone else's limits, and how far he or she can allow someone else to push against theirs.

At this age, many children with bipolar disorder have difficulty entering the peer group because of their excessive aggression, poor sense of boundaries, oversensitivity to rejection, and social anxiety. Difficulties managing in a classroom can also draw negative attention to a child. Individuals (children and adults) with bipolar disorder often become overstimulated in a group, leading to greater difficulty with social judgment and their ability to stay within the boundaries of the group. When there is also intense family discord or a single parent, opportunities for playdates may be more limited, depriving the child of practice in peer relationships in a more protected, one-on-one setting.

## MASTERING AGGRESSION

During the elementary school years, one of a child's crucial developmental tasks is learning to master aggression—knowing how far to go with someone, putting a spin on it, and doing it with style. Any living thing that moves and competes with other living things for resources needs to be aggressive in order to survive. In intelligent species, however, aggression is mastered first in play.

The function of aggressive play is to develop a child's sense of how far she can push against someone else's limits or how far she can allow someone else to push her. This mastery of pushing and shoving is of crucial importance in later social and professional life, and is best mastered *before* the reemergence of sexuality in adolescence complicates the task. A child who is excluded from the peer group or avoids entering it cannot join in aggressive play and so is at grave risk for developmental failure in the mastery of aggression.

## THE PARENTS' ROLES IN HELPING A CHILD MASTER AGGRESSION

A mother keeps track of where her child is emotionally as well as physically. When approaching an infant, Mom takes notice of *where* her child is (physically and emotionally), approaches gently, makes eye contact, and initiates play or gradually moves him elsewhere. Because of Mom's modulation, the child is able to maintain inner balance and a sense of safety. Later, in interactions with peers, he will be less anxious and more confident in approaching others or being approached by them. A child who has not received Mom's help with modulation and the confidence it inspires will have difficulty tolerating aggression from peers: he is more likely to move psychologically into a primitive, paranoid stance and explode with an impulsive attack.

Fathers, in contrast to mothers, pay relatively little attention to where their child is emotionally—they tend to dive-bomb in. Children usually experience a father's sudden approach as exciting and pleasurable, but they also inevitably become overly excited. When this happens, Dad typically demands an abrupt halt: "Cut it out!"

Both Mom's and Dad's styles of interaction are necessary to a child's development. But it is Dad's abrupt style that teaches a child to make a sudden emotional hockey stop, requiring him aggressively to limit his own behavior. Later, in his peer group, the child draws on this ability to make abrupt emotional and behavioral maneuvers. The child who has learned to be aggressive in limiting himself is less likely to be intimidated by others' aggression and is better able to set limits with them.

## Exclusion from the Group

A child is usually excluded from the peer group for one of two reasons: either he's seen as a wimp who can't limit the aggression of others, or he's seen as a bully who can't limit his own attacks on peers. Children naturally shy away from anyone who is obviously out of control *or* who invites them to lose control.

In working with children of this age, I have found that those who have difficulty setting limits with other children's aggression (wimps) often have an absent or ineffective father and tend to be overinvolved with their mothers; those who have trouble keeping their aggression in check (bullies) tend to have had a lack of both mothering and fathering. A deficit in fathering contributes to difficulty setting limits with one's own and other people's aggression; a deficit in mothering leads to an inability to calm oneself and to contain one's own aggression. However, a child raised by a single parent does not necessarily have trouble in the peer group. Often there is someone who stands in for the missing parent, or the parent who is present manages to impart the necessary emotional skills to his or her child.

A bipolar child can find himself excluded from the peer group even with parenting that would normally be adequate, in part because it is so much harder for Mom to soothe the child and for Dad to set abrupt limits with him. As has already been discussed, the bipolar child is also at risk for having an absent or alienated father or a mother who is depressed and has problems soothing herself, much less him. The child's anxiety also raises the bar in a stressful situation, making him less able to maneuver with his peers. His emotional intensity often adds to these difficulties. For one reason or another, then, the bipolar child often finds himself excluded from the peer group, unable to practice the mastery of aggression, setting him up for further developmental failure.

## Parental Intervention

Early impulse control, learned within the family and enforced by parents, teaches a child not to cross complex, invisible boundaries. During latency, children must learn to observe each other's boundaries *without the intervention of parents.* Indeed, it is a humiliating sign of incompetence if a latency-age child calls upon an adult to defend her against peers, and peers typically respond with an intensification of aggression, either through overt physical or verbal attack or by exclusion.

Yet there are times when it *is* necessary for a parent to intervene. If, for example, your child is being bullied repeatedly by one or more children, avoid direct intervention with your child's peer group. Instead, contact the other child's parents and try to find out what's going on. (Clarifying the situation should always come before more forceful intervention.) When necessary, your forceful intervention with the parents of an abusive child can be a crucial *preliminary* to the child's own resolution of the problem. If the trouble arises at school, talk with the teacher. Some schools don't pay attention to bullying and, moreover, foster a nasty competitive culture. In such a case, you may need to get involved or even consider changing schools. Dad is particularly important at this time as a forceful presence in the world beyond home.

There may be times when your child needs to withdraw temporarily from peers into the safety of her relationship with you, where she can recoup her self-esteem. When this happens, it's most important to *listen* to her while she tells you about her distress, and perhaps briefly share some of your own experiences. You may also want to get her involved in an activity that puts her in contact with peers in a structured situation and bolsters her self-confidence—a sport, martial arts class, dance class, or theater workshop.

Unfortunately, it is usually not possible to help your child through difficulties with peers by simply talking to her—by encouraging more aggressive or less aggressive behavior—or by talking to an offending child's parents. Like riding a bicycle, learning how to push and shove and where to observe limits in the peer group is a skill acquired *practically* and to a large extent nonverbally. Mastering aggression is a complex emotional and behavioral skill and amounts to more than doing or not doing a particular thing. Witnessing the difficulties one's child has with peers is one of the first times parents become acutely aware of the inevitable separation that will take place between their lives and that of their child. The help you give a child in such circumstances comes out of a relationship developed long before the crisis, a relationship the child draws upon during that crisis.

For children who cannot manage (or are unable to try) any interactions with peers, group therapy is a valuable resource. Individual therapy is usually not effective for serious problems in peer relationships. When a group is not available, however, it may be possible to arrange a duo-therapy with a matched peer. Some children who can find neither resource have benefited from therapeutic work with animals, learning in those relationships effective nonverbal rhythms of interaction.

## BUILDING SKILLS

Another major developmental task facing a child at this time is building academic skills such as reading, math, and spelling; physical skills such as jumping rope, skateboarding, or playing ball; artistic skills like drawing, playing a musical instrument, or learning to dance; and skills in games such as checkers, cards, or chess. Mastery of various skills adds to a child's self-esteem in a concrete way, similar to collections—of matchbooks, stamps, coins, baseball cards, Barbie dolls—also characteristic of this period. At this age (eight to twelve), a child's involvement with a particular pursuit may be brief and intense or sustained without indicating particular strength or weakness in the child.

As in earlier stages, a child's ability to master new tasks is influenced by the way his parents regard his efforts. A child needs more than just exposure or opportunities to take up various skills: a continuing interest on the part of the parent is necessary. You must maintain an interest in the child's developing mastery but remain relatively neutral with regard to winning or the child's level of achievement. A parent who becomes involved to the point of demanding a particular level of success may, by that demand, actually preclude success and will certainly prevent the child from having fun. A child who feels compelled to be right cannot risk being wrong, and so cannot learn. Just as the freedom to make mistakes is a requirement for learning, freedom to fail is a requirement of success. The parental task is to pay attention to where the child *is* rather than to where he should be. During latency, although children must make important moves within the peer group, they still very much need the presence of their parents, psychologically and at times in action.

I attended a birthday party of an eight-year-old boy where there were approximately twenty children, most accompanied·by their parents. One boy, who did not know most of the children, was dropped off by his father without so much as an introduction to the host. Later the boys were taking turns jumping from a tree fort (some fifteen feet off the ground), by holding onto a strap attached to a pulley and a cable running to a lower tree. Some of the boys refused, intimidated by the height; some took part, enjoying the daring flight. The boy who had been left alone by his father vacillated and then attempted the jump, but he let go as his weight came down upon the strap, fell, and broke his wrist. It struck me that he had been carelessly dropped off and then had let himself drop. He had been unable either to comfortably refuse, as other children had, or to commit himself to mastery of the skill. When the boy was injured, his father could not be reached, and the host had to take him to a hospital—confirming my sense of the father's distance, so discouraging to his son.

## THE BIPOLAR CHILD AND THE MASTERING OF NEW SKILLS

Whether in school or in an activity, a bipolar child's impatience makes it hard for her to tolerate incremental learning. She has trouble mastering academic, athletic, or social skills. Often enough, the bipolar child has a learning difficulty as well as an emotional one, making acquisition of academic skills more problematic. The difficulty these children have accepting limits and tolerating loss also makes it especially hard for them to play by the rules. Finally, because most athletic and social skills are learned and practiced in the peer group, a child who has problems entering that group will be at a loss in mastering those skills.

Learning new skills also means accepting the idea of starting out as a beginner. A child who hasn't accepted her role as a child—who can't accept authority or who has become her parent's companion—has particular difficulty being a novice. A bipolar child who is excessively shy or has a grandiose sense of self may find it excruciating to be compared to peers. Development takes place, however, step by step and *requires* being compared to other people. For all these reasons, some bipolar children have particular difficulty playing games: they cheat or change the rules rather than lose, causing additional problems with peers or siblings. Indeed, helping your child learn to play games can be an important parental task. However, some bipolar children cannot accept instruction from their parents. They can learn to tolerate competition in play therapy.

In addition to acquiring skills, latency is a time when children explore their world more widely, expanding their sheer mastery of information. The conversation of children this age, whether among themselves or with adults, abounds in sentences that begin, "Did you know . . . ?" They also have an ability to explore areas of experience that when younger they would have found frightening—for example, death and physical mutilation. At this age, children are fascinated with ghost stories, macabre news reports in tabloids, and fantastic lies. Lying, used not for calculated deception but as an exploration of the limits of credibility, can be just another area of play. Lying of this kind blends seamlessly into storytelling, which is more intensely enjoyed at this age than any other.

The latency-age child gathers collections of objects, heroes, skills, information, political and moral positions, and jokes with an unabashed derivativeness. The child has neither the capacity nor the need to unify these fragments into a coherent whole. At this age even a genius like Mozart was capable only of brilliant imitation, not striking originality. Identity and originality are accomplishments reserved for adolescence. The child's task during latency is to assemble the alphabet and vocabulary from which her adolescent identity and creative accomplishments will later be composed.

In addition to the lying that occurs within play, defensive lying is seen in children this age, particularly those with bipolar disorder. The child's lies usually are not skillful, but the child's use of them can be upsetting to a parent. While such lies *are* manipulative, they are rarely cynical. Rather they are an attempt to manage a momentarily unmanageable world, a world that includes their parents' demands and expectations.

A bipolar child who is facing accumulating difficulties, academically or behaviorally, often lies in an attempt to cover the problems. The denial characteristic of bipolar disorder combines with the child's anxiety and increasing difficulties to make lying an almost inevitable defense. It helps to look at this kind of lying as a communication of distress. Your response should be to help your child speak more frankly about the difficulties. When a child is unable to articulate her difficulties, the parent's task is to articulate them for her, validating her discomfort without accepting the lie: "Homework is certainly hard for you right now—I know it makes you frustrated and worried—but you need to ask for help rather than saying you have no homework."

## SUMMER CAMP

Summer camp provides an excellent opportunity for developing peer relationships and a variety of athletic, musical, or artistic skills. But going to sleepaway camp requires facing some real challenges: separating from parents and home, falling asleep in a strange environment, managing aggression (one's own as well as others'), and tolerating the frustration of learning. Sending a child to sleepaway camp prematurely can be destructive and increase his anxiety, making his peer relationships even more difficult. If your child isn't ready for this kind of experience, day camp may be a better alternative.

If your child *does* seem to be willing and able to take on the challenge of summer camp, you must make sure several conditions are met.

· The camp must have a level of supervision that can handle your child's need for support.
· Counselors and staff should be fully aware of his special needs and able to accommodate them. Don't keep secrets from the camp.
· For children taking regular medication, arrange coordination between the treating psychiatrist and the camp. Usually this involves a letter stating the child's medications, their side effects, and any other potential dangers as well as a number where the doctor can be reached. In a camp that is appropriate for your child there will be a nurse to administer medication when needed.
· For children taking lithium or a major tranquilizer, the nurse and counselors should be made aware of the danger of excessive heat and dehydration.
· Homesickness occurs normally among campers, but a bipolar child is likely to become especially anxious, and this may require medication to help him fall asleep.
· As with school, it is important to pay close attention to the appropriateness of the camp's milieu for your child. This means taking your child's complaints seriously even when counselors and administrative staff are reassuring.

## BEAR IN MIND

· Remember self-regulation. As your child moves more and more out into the world, your task of watching over eating, sleeping, and exercise are all the more important. Does your child eat a proper breakfast? Does he need a snack before lunch? Is he spending too much time in sedentary activities (TV, computer games)? Does he sometimes still need a nap?

· When your child becomes overwhelmingly oppositional and has a meltdown, you need to change *your* agenda. Be ready to give up getting her on the school bus or back into the car. This takes the pressure off you and gives you flexibility and an ability to focus on what needs to be done. Helping your child out of this bind in a good enough way becomes the priority.

· You may see a big difference among the daytime, the afternoon, and the nighttime child. Sometimes children who have held it together all day in school need to let go when they get home. A bipolar child may also have lots of difficulty with homework and—as always—with getting to bed and sleeping.

· Dad cannot possibly overestimate his importance at this age, with girls as well as boys!

· As the bipolar child moves more and more into the world, the problem of dangerous and impulsive behavior continues, but it is harder to control and sometimes you will not learn of it until afterward. Watch out for it: traveling on public transportation, bicycle riding, playing in dangerous places or with dangerous things (especially fire). When problems with these things occur in your presence, it is an opportunity to intervene, not a disaster.

· Your child is now having more and more contact with other parents. Make sure you know them and that they know your child. Insist on appropriate limits and a continuing presence when your child visits another home. Also provide these things when other children visit your home.

· Birthdays and birthday parties now become frequent social events. Your child needs your presence here more than most children. Don't miss a chance to give your child a party. Also consider making the party a gathering for children *and* parents. This will decrease all the children's anxiety and foster your relationships with other parents.

· Boys will be boys. Even if you forbid them to have guns, they will invent them. But pay attention! Your child now has an increasing desire to watch TV, look at movies, and play video games. Exercise your judgment in what you allow. Bipolar children are particularly vulnerable to scary movies and violent video games. You need to know what is going on on the screen!—in your house or out of it. Children who have been traumatized have a particular (unhealthy) desire to play with scary games or watch scary movies. You need to protect them from their own emotional vulnerability.

# CHAPTER EIGHT

# Early Adolescence and the Middle School Years

## *Increasing Academic Demands, Cognitive Problems, and Hormonal Changes*

The middle school years can be especially difficult. To begin with, most middle schools take in students from several different lower schools, so the peer groups formed in lower school can disintegrate. This can be a disabling loss to a vulnerable child. Social anxiety increases for children across the board at this time. It can express itself in forming cliques, becoming more aggressive, and, at times, being cruel. In the increasingly competitive social atmosphere of middle school, any weakness carries a greater penalty.

Middle school is also a time of accelerated academic demands, and a child struggling with learning problems feels the pressure more intensely. Children with bipolar disorder often have learning problems, especially dyslexia (problems with the visual sequencing or the left-right orientation of letters or numbers) and dysgraphia (trouble with handwriting and written expression). In a child with a bipolar disposition, the frustration caused by these academic problems can be confused with oppositional behavior—that is, parents and teachers can see him as simply misbehaving. He can also be viewed as lazy, because these difficulties may not have shown up before. A child who has done well in the lower grades and demonstrated strong verbal or mathematical capacities may now begin to falter—and avoid academic work. Remediation can improve a child's performance, but it won't normalize it. Your child also needs your understanding and emotional support. However, timely and adequate remediation can make the difference between your child avoiding or compensating for a learning deficit.

## Dyslexia

Children with bipolar disorder commonly have problems reading. The cause of this difficulty is in dispute. Some optometrists maintain it is a problem integrating the left and right visual images, causing difficulty seeing things in a three-dimensional way and tracking objects in space, such as a line of letters on a page. Samuel Orton, an early and prominent authority on dyslexia, believed that the problem resided in a failure to suppress a visual image from the right hemisphere in favor of one from the left. Most proposed explanations for dyslexia, including other current ones, posit some discordance between the right and left hemispheres of the brain. Increasingly, we are also beginning to find evidence that (at least some) patients with bipolar disorder also exhibit deficits in coordination between the right and left hemispheres. Whatever the case may be with a particular child, dyslexia causes trouble with the decoding process in reading—the task of linking a series of letters to form words. As a result, the child guesses at words rather than fully decoding them. She reads more slowly, tires more easily when reading, and may also have particular difficulty when called upon to read aloud in class.

Vocabulary and comprehension are not directly affected by dyslexia, but the *work of reading* is increased. Dyslexia also impairs the child's ability to spell and to perform perfunctory mathematical tasks such as adding a column, multiplying larger numbers, or doing long division. Dyslexia manifests in psychological testing, limiting performance on nonverbal tasks such as coding, a subtest in the Wechsler intelligence test. Dyslexia also limits the speed and accuracy with which a child processes written or numerical information: there can be a significant difference in performance on tasks that are timed as compared to un-timed tasks—in school or on standardized tests.

Severe dyslexia may have been identified in the lower school years and the child may already be getting help before reaching middle school. Often, however, a bright child who has compensated for this difficulty in the lower grades begins to have trouble in fifth or sixth grade. The task in school changes at about that time from learning to read to reading to learn, and the amount of reading a child is assigned increases dramatically. One sign of dyslexia is a lack of interest in reading in a child with high intelligence and verbal capacity.

A problem with visual tracking can be diagnosed by a developmental optometrist—an optometrist who looks carefully not just at visual acuity but also at visual integration. (Often such an optometrist has a special program to help with visual coordination.) For children who are not helped by this approach, the Orton-Gillingham method, a multisensory approach to reading and writing, is more effective. Children are taught to read, write, and say a word aloud in order to reinforce their learning. Whichever method is best for your child, early intervention is crucial, because at younger ages the brain is more adaptable. It is important that you see to it that your child gets the help he needs and follows through with it.

When a child with bipolar disorder has dyslexia, additional difficulties can arise. As with other dyslexic children, a bipolar child tires more easily on longer reading assignments, but he also has a much lower tolerance for frustration and, very likely, a higher level of anxiety when reading—especially when reading material that is not essentially pleasurable. Also, because the flow of information is so slow, such a child may begin having interference from other thoughts—associations arising from what is in the passage—distracting him and introducing further inaccuracy in his reading and comprehension. (Remember, racing thoughts and loosened associations are common symptoms in bipolar disorder.) A stimulant such as Ritalin may remedy this inattention or help sustain motivation in some children, but in others a stimulant can cause increased anxiety, irritability, racing thoughts, or a flight of ideas.

## A DISTINGUISHED DYSLEXIC

Herman Melville almost certainly suffered from dyslexia. Although immensely talented verbally and intellectually, Melville had trouble reading the small-print editions of Shakespeare common at that time. While writing his masterpiece *Moby-Dick,* he obtained a large-print copy of Shakespeare's works and was able to reread them entirely. In 1849, Melville wrote to his publisher, "It is an edition in glorious great type. . . . I am mad to think how minute a cause has prevented me from reading Shakespeare. But until now any copy that was come-atable to me happened to be a vile small print unendurable to my eyes. . . . But chancing to fall in with this glorious edition I now exult over it, page after page." The experience of rediscovering Shakespeare was explosive for Melville, and he set to rewriting his masterpiece. The influence of Shakespeare's work can be seen throughout *Moby-Dick.*

It is unlikely that Melville's difficulty was weakened eyesight, because eyeglasses were readily available in his time. Melville clearly suffered from bipolar disorder: evidenced by a father who went insane, by Melville's own expansive letters to Nathaniel Hawthorne as a young man, and from the course of his life (which progressed from a prodigiously productive and adventurous youth to a contracted and depressed old age). Interestingly, the opening paragraph of *Moby-Dick* describes Ishmael as being possessed by moods "when it is a damp drizzly November in [his] soul" during which "it requires a strong moral principle to prevent [him] from deliberately stepping into the street and methodically knocking people's hats off." Ishmael suffers a seasonal bipolar swing with nearly irrepressible November irritability.

## DYSGRAPHIA

A second problem frequently encountered in children with bipolar disorder is dysgraphia, or an impaired ability to write letters, resulting in incorrigibly messy handwriting. As with dyslexia, dysgraphia increases the work needed to complete a perfunctory written task, so the child has to make a Herculean effort to complete the same assignment another child can dash off with ease. Dysgraphia not only affects a child's ability to do handwritten work, it can secondarily affect his ability to build paragraphs and arguments. In the same way that dyslexia secondarily interferes with concentration, dysgraphia can interfere with higher-level tasks in composition. This interference can be a particularly disabling problem, because expository writing is an important way of developing *thinking*.

## Christopher's Test Scores

In first grade, **CHRISTOPHER** was found to have dyslexia and dysgraphia. He received appropriate remedial help (the Orton-Gillingham approach) and then did well academically until the fifth grade, when his performance began to decline. A battery of psychological testing was done with the following results on the Wechsler Intelligence Scale for Children (WISC-III):

| Verbal Tests | Score | %ile | Performance | Score | %ile |
|---|---|---|---|---|---|
| Information | 16 | 98 | Picture Completion | 15 | 95 |
| Similarities | 16 | 98 | Coding | 7 | 16 |
| Arithmetic | 19 | 99 | Picture Arrangement | 17 | 99 |
| Vocabulary | 14 | 84 | Block Design | 17 | 99 |
| Comprehension | 16 | 98 | Object Assembly | 13 | 84 |
| Digit Span | 16 | 98 | Symbol Search | 11 | 63 |
| *Verbal IQ: 139 (99th percentile)* | | | *Performance IQ: 126 (96th percentile)* | | |

Christopher's scores are remarkable for what is called scatter, a wide discrepancy between one area of function and another. While eight out of twelve tests place him in the top 5 percent of his peers (and his verbal IQ places him in the top 1 percent), he performs in the bottom 16 percent on coding, a test that measures attention, speed, and accuracy on a perfunctory task of matching letters with numbers. Less dramatic but indicative of the same difficulty is Christopher's score on symbol search, placing him in the middle of his peers (63rd percentile), a low score for someone of his intelligence.

An examination of Christopher's reading found a large discrepancy between his performance on material that interested him and material that did not. With material he found uninteresting, he became inattentive and seemed to engage in empty decoding. He also had particular difficulty reading longer passages, due to fatigue.

When Christopher's abilities in writing were examined—despite his superior intelligence and verbal abilities, and despite schooling that paid careful attention to developing skills in writing—he was found to be performing at an average level. His spelling was particularly weak, and when writing longer, more complex sentences he struggled with syntax, grammar, and punctuation. He had great difficulty organizing a paragraph.

Christopher was described as inattentive and disorganized and diagnosed with ADD, despite the fact that his scores in most areas that required attention were in the superior range. A more careful examination of his testing shows something quite different. Christopher works so hard at perfunctory tasks (such as decoding in reading, spelling, and handwriting) that when he arrives at the task he is most capable in—abstract reasoning—he is so fatigued and uninterested that he does not perform at his best.

Over time Christopher's academic performance declined further and his interest in school predictably disappeared. He was particularly dismayed because his brother—who obviously was not as bright as he was—far outperformed him academically. Although

Christopher's parents had initially resisted the suggestion, they agreed to a trial of a stimulant. The prescribing doctor (a highly respected pharmacologist) failed to look into the family history. Had he done so he would have learned that although Christopher's parents were both high functioning and highly educated, each had near relatives who suffered from severe depression. This information might have set off a warning bell to take a closer look at Christopher and the nature of his academic problems.

The use of a stimulant made little difference in Chris's organization: he continued to hand in assignments late or not at all. He complained that he didn't like taking the medication. Another round of psychological testing (again the WISC-III) was done, this time on medication; the results were similar but with important areas of decline.

| Verbal Tests | Score | %ile | Performance | Score | %ile |
|---|---|---|---|---|---|
| Information | 16 | 99 | Picture Completion | 11 | 63 |
| Similarities | 16 | 99 | Coding | 2 | 0.4 |
| Arithmetic | 14 | 91 | Picture Arrangement | 11 | 63 |
| Vocabulary | 13 | 84 | Block Design | 13 | 84 |
| Comprehension | 16 | 98 | Object Assembly | 14 | 91 |
| Digit Span | 13 | 84 | Symbol Search | 7 | 16 |
| *Verbal IQ: 129 (97th percentile)* | | | *Performance IQ: 102 (55th percentile)* | | |

Despite the use of medication, on tests that require sustained attention—arithmetic, coding, digit span, symbol search—Chris's scores declined significantly. A noticeable drop also occurred in his score on picture arrangement, a test that correlates with social judgment. Even more significantly, Chris's performance IQ has dropped by 24 points; the discrepancy between his verbal and performance IQ has more than doubled (going from 13 to 27 points). A change of this magnitude is consistent with depression. Nonetheless, the interpreting psychologist, relying mainly on external observations made by Christopher's parents, persisted in describing him as suffering from ADD.

Projective tests (tests that look at unstated feelings) were also done at this time: they showed Chris to be bored with the tasks he was being forced to do and continually disappointed at the judgments being made of him. Chris's feelings of boredom and disappointment are also indicative of depression. The pharmacologist prescribing Christopher's medication was, however, unaffected by this second battery of tests.

When I was consulted, I advised Chris discontinue the stimulant and consider a school that made special accommodations to students with his difficulties. By this time, however, Chris had been to several different schools and was more concerned about a disruption in his friendships than any promise of academic success. He also didn't believe that anything would make much difference. I was particularly concerned at the level of Chris's discouragement and the damage that had been done to his self-esteem. I was equally concerned to notice in his projective testing a tendency to present a false self, an appearance designed to satisfy other people's expectations, but an appearance that was at odds with his deeper feelings.

*Christopher illustrates the discrepancy that can develop between a rich innate intelligence and an inability to succeed academically in a child suffering from dyslexia and dysgraphia. This discrepancy creates what I call cognitive dissonance, a continual collision among a person's sense of his own intelligence, the effort he makes academically, and the results he obtains. In a person like Christopher, the flow of information can be compared to water running through a wide pipe that must suddenly go through a narrow opening: only a trickle comes through and great pressure (work) is needed even to get that trickle. The cumulative impact of*

*such cognitive dissonance—especially when it is unacknowledged—on a
child's self-esteem is enormous.*

Quite apart from dyslexia or dysgraphia, bipolar children can experience a more subtle difficulty with expository writing that makes an observation and accounts for that observation logically on the basis of
particular information. Their quickness of mind combined with a
grandiosity that spurns proof makes the task of accounting for their
conclusions tedious. Some bipolar children's difficulties with logical argument also arise from the difficulties they have with the perception of
and tolerance of *time.* Logical thought requires the examination of the
relationship between events or forces that act causally over the course
of time, including over time in our own mind, as one thought leads to
another. Put another way, the impulsive learning style of some bipolar
children gives them particular difficulty with the task of *exposition*—
exposing the logical sequence of their own thoughts.

An adequate argument also requires an examination of contradictory points of view. The difficulty bipolar children have tolerating con-
tradiction affects their ability to make this intellectual move. Finally,
some bipolar children, because of their powerful imaginative processes,
tend to think visually rather than verbally, making it especially difficult
for them to insert logical verbal transitions between their thoughts. A
bipolar child may excel in imaginative writing but have persistent difficulty with expository writing.

Difficulties with expository writing typically do not become obvious
until children begin more advanced academic work and have their most
noticeable effects on more intelligent students who advance into an academic setting where this kind of work is crucial.

## Two Brilliantly Problematic Young Writers

JOHN, a former student of mine, is a good example of a person
with bipolar disorder who was brilliant but had great trouble

with expository writing. John was a charismatic leader and power-fully intelligent, but he also had dyslexia, difficulty with composi-tion, and persistent behavioral difficulties. He did quite well on quizzes for reading assignments he could do at home. But when he was called on to answer questions about a passage being read in class, John became evasive. He had difficulty reading things on the spot.

I once gave the class an early speech of Abraham Lincoln's, without telling them who the author was. They were to give me a written analysis of the speaker's character and account for their opinions with details from the speech. John wrote an intricate and astute description of young Lincoln's character. His perceptions were original and I could tell they arose from details in the speech, but he was completely unable to explain how he arrived at his con-clusions. I believe that John's charisma, his quick and perceptive mind, his history of misbehavior, his difficulties reading, and his difficulties with expository writing all had a common source—a bipolar mind.

**MARILYN**, a girl with pressured speech and a quirky and rebel-lious personality (who at one time required hospitalization for an eating disorder), was a brilliant creative writer. When given an ex-pository assignment, however, she artfully dodged the task with one verbally dazzling evasion or another. I had the chance to follow her path through a fine liberal arts college, where she continued to charm and dodge her teachers, avoiding true expository writing to the end.

## Mood Instability

Hormonal changes begin affecting a child's mood and behavior during the middle school years. Depression can either accompany or cause ac-ademic failure, social isolation, or school refusal. In my experience, twelve is the most common age for onset of both bipolar depression and mood instability. In girls, dramatic changes in mood often precede or accompany the beginning of menstruation. There is no obvious biological marker in boys, but mood changes tend to occur at about the same age.

## Recovery from Early Adolescent Depression

ALICIA had always been a shy child. She had been the victim of occasional bullying in her lower school years but by fifth grade had a solid group of friends, was doing well in school, and had begun to enjoy skiing and ice-skating. Sixth grade was unexpectedly difficult for her socially: her friends split off into different groups and paid less attention to her. Some friends had already begun to be interested in boys; others began to take on a tougher attitude, and she felt left behind. At lunchtime she couldn't find a table where she fit in. Abandoned by her former friends and upset by the increased aggression around her, Alicia turned in to herself. In response to these difficulties, her parents started her in individual therapy. During the summer between sixth and seventh grade she began to menstruate.

Problems got worse in seventh grade. She did not feel comfortable at parties. Her father and mother—both of whom had a family history of bipolar disorder—were in conflict over how to help her: her father took a stricter tone and was more distant; her mother was more protective and closely involved with her. Just after Halloween, which had not gone well, she became depressed and stayed in bed most of the day. She stopped going to school, missing more than a month of classes. She required medication in addition to her psychotherapy before returning following the Christmas break. Although she was able to resume academic function (with the help of some tutoring), she continued to be socially withdrawn. Her mood seemed to pick up on a winter skiing vacation but deteriorated when she returned. In February she took an assortment of pills in a suicide gesture. She was kept in the hospital overnight but did not require psychiatric hospitalization; further pharmacologic consultation was made, however. Her parents now were in even greater conflict and sought family therapy.

That spring her mood improved, and she began with a new skating coach who encouraged her to compete. She proved to be quite talented and the sport became a new focus in her life. Her competitions also required the support and mutual cooperation of her parents and became a uniting force in the family. The following summer, in addition to practicing skating she attended a camp that combined hiking and camping with peer group discussions led by counselors. The experience left her feeling much better about herself socially.

Nonetheless, her depression recurred the next three winters, and again she missed weeks of school. By this time, however, appropriate medication was in place (an antidepressant combined with a mood stabilizer), the family had resolved many of their conflicts, and Alicia's increasing athletic success began to bolster her self-esteem. Her athletic success also gave her entry into a peer group of equally talented children who respected and liked her. By the time she was sixteen, Alicia was an accomplished athlete and a top student; she made it through the winter of eleventh grade without a depression. In the twelfth grade she was accepted, early decision, into a top college on the basis of her athletic accomplishments, her academic excellence, and the depth of character she had developed as a result of her emotional and athletic struggles. She continues, however, to require ongoing psychotherapy and pharmacologic care.

*Alicia is a good example of a bipolar II child, with a family history of bipolar disorder in both parents, whose early development was largely normal except for some shyness and difficulty managing aggression with peers. The social stress of middle school intensified her difficulties with peers and she was appropriately placed in psychotherapy. (Having a distant father is associated with difficulty managing aggression with peers.) The onset of hormonal change—at about the age of twelve— precipitated her first depression; it also came on with seasonal change from fall to winter. The stress of Alicia's illness and particularly her overdose intensified existing family discord, requiring her parents to seek therapy as well.*

*Despite appropriate pharmacologic treatment, Alicia's depression recurred seasonally, causing extended absences from school. It took several years for the combination of individual therapy, family therapy, and medication to begin to stabilize her mood. Tutoring prevented her from losing ground academically during this difficult period. Her peer relationships were assisted by a camp experience that included group therapy. Alicia was also healthy enough to be able to take up a competitive sport. Her athletic development helped with self-esteem, her ability to assert herself aggressively, and her peer relationships. All these measures were necessary to help her get back on track developmentally, and at the end of the process she was a high-functioning, emotionally sophisticated adolescent.*

## ANTIDEPRESSANTS AND SUICIDE IN CHILDREN

Recent reports of an increased rate of suicide in children treated with antidepressants are worrisome, but they cannot be easily interpreted. These reports are based on a second look at studies not originally designed to look for suicide. That means the studies have not examined patients for other factors that increase the risk for suicide: a bipolar depression; a relative or peer who committed suicide; a history of physical, sexual, emotional, or substance abuse.

These reports also neglect the important fact that depression in a child is very commonly a sign of bipolar disorder, and the use of antidepressants in bipolar disorder requires special expertise. If your child is depressed and medication is advised, discuss concerns about suicide and antidepressants carefully with your child's psychiatrist. Don't hesitate to bring it up, and listen carefully to the response. If you are uneasy, get a second opinion.

Sometimes mood instability seems to be caused by seasonal change. For example, thirteen-year-old Jason appeared to be fine at the beginning of the school year, but he started having difficulties by early November. He was more irritable and anxious, didn't want to get up in the morning, and had a hard time staying awake during the day. He stopped paying attention in class, especially in the morning, and neglected his assignments. After winter break, he started refusing to go to school, although his parents struggled to make him attend. By February, his academic performance was at an all-time low. Things started to improve around April or May: Jason began having less difficulty getting up in the morning and was more alert in his classes; he did his assignments more regularly. By the end of the school year, his mood and performance were much improved. His parents and teachers thought he had just been lazy. His mother summed it up by saying, "He starts out okay, but after a while he slacks off. Then at the end of the year he exerts himself so he can squeak by and keep from going to summer school."

In reality, Jason suffers from a seasonal depression in the fall, with a shift forward in his sleep cycle. There is a significant overlap between bipolar disorder and seasonal affective disorder (SAD). Some clinicians see SAD as a form of bipolar disorder because seasonal changes in mood and dislocation of the sleep cycle can also be symptoms of bipolar disorder. Both SAD and bipolar disorder are characterized by an atypical depression (with increased sleep and sometimes increased eating). A defining characteristic of SAD is a drifting sleep cycle, either forward or backward. If the sleep cycle drifts forward, it becomes hard to fall asleep at night and harder still to get up in the morning. If the cycle drifts backward, there's fatigue early in the evening and early morning awakening.

A drifting sleep cycle is caused by a gradual change in the time when the hormone melatonin is released. This change in the release of melatonin is itself caused by a change in the person's exposure to daylight, especially at the beginning and end of the day. Detection of SAD can be complicated in adolescents because their sleep cycle normally shifts toward staying up later at night and getting up later in the morning. To make matters worse, classes in middle school and high school begin early, even earlier than most businesses—a deliberate convenience for working parents—making it hard for any teen to wake up at the proper time. In the bipolar adolescent, the normal adolescent drift can become more severe, especially in the winter when the hours of daylight lessen. Greater difficulties often appear when the clocks are turned back at the end of October. SAD is now better recognized and can be treated with light therapy and medication.

## LET THERE BE LIGHT!

Over the past twenty years, rigorous studies have shown that light of a particular intensity is an effective treatment for SAD, both depression and the disorientation of the sleep cycle. Sometimes a severe depression accompanying a sleep disturbance requires medication in addition to light. But light therapy is the best treatment for a dislocated sleep cycle. Exposure to special therapeutic light affects a neural pathway that runs from the retina to the pineal gland. Light striking the retina shuts off the release of melatonin from that gland and resets the body clock.

Achieving this effect requires a high-intensity light comparable to daylight. While the light in a well-lit room may be 500–1,000 lux (a measure of intensity), at least 3,000, and optimally 10,000, lux is needed to reset the pineal gland. Daylight ranges (even on a cloudy day) from 10,000 to 100,000 lux.

The time of day that light therapy is undertaken depends on whether the sleep cycle has drifted forward or backward, and how far. A child who has difficulty getting up in the morning needs fifteen to thirty minutes of light in the morning before school; a child who wakes up early and becomes sleepy early needs the same amount of light at about 5 P.M. or 6 P.M.

**P.S.** Your child may receive unintentional high-intensity light from a computer monitor. If he is using it too near bedtime, the effect of this exposure will shift his sleep cycle, making it harder for him to fall asleep and harder for him to awaken in the morning. In contrast to watching TV, most children (and adults) work at close range to their computer monitor. Because the intensity of light varies by the square of the distance from its source, at ten inches a monitor is thirteen times more intense than at three feet and twenty-three times more intense than at four feet.

## BEAR IN MIND

· Because the bipolar child can become intensely anxious, any academic tasks that aren't quickly mastered can make her back away from them. But failing to acquire basic skills will make future academic work even more difficult, which will provoke greater anxiety and greater avoidance. If you see your child beginning to avoid specific subjects, take action right away: try accompanying your child while she is doing her homework, or if basic skills are missing, get her a tutor to help make up the ground. Be in close contact with her teachers, so that you know when she is missing homework or faltering on tests. Be a guiding but not a harsh presence.

· The bipolar child's grandiosity and hurried pace (both of which are defenses protecting self-esteem) can make him dash through perfunctory tasks that don't come easily to him. Do your best to help him stay with the task until its details are mastered. Know what his homework assignments are and review his work with him. Set a minimum time for homework based on what you know the school's expectations are.

· Even when using a tutor, your interest, reassurance, and positive response to your child's effort are crucial in fostering success.

· A sudden increase in oppositional behavior, an abrupt decline in academic performance, increased daytime fatigue, sleeping during the day, or school refusal can be early signs of depression at this age. If you see them, consult a mental health professional.

· If you suspect depression, consult with a child psychiatrist. Remember, just as you must be careful of stimulants in ADD, you need to be careful of antidepressants in bipolar depression.

# CHAPTER NINE

# Adolescence

*Separation, Intimacy and Identity Formation,
Adolescent Rebellion, and Consumption Disorders*

In adolescence, three related developmental tasks stand out above all others: emotional separation from parents, achieving intimate relationships with peers, and the first phases of forming an independent identity. Biologically, two changes also stand out: the onset of sexual maturity signaled by the development of secondary sexual characteristics and enormous changes in size, strength, and mental capacity.

Cognitively, adolescents undergo a dramatic growth in their ability to think abstractly, to make independent moral judgments, and to understand complex causal relationships between different events and thus a new ability to imagine themselves more realistically in time. What does not mature at this age is judgment—that occurs with the maturation of the prefrontal cortex in the early twenties. This circumstance constitutes one of the most difficult problems facing parents of an adolescent: the blossoming of intellect, physical and sexual maturity, and an independent moral sense in the absence of mature judgment.

The adolescent with bipolar disorder—without considering developmental difficulties that may have preceded adolescence—experiences greater impulsivity, a grandiose sense of being perfect or an intense anxiety about lack of perfection, greater mood instability, and possibly hypersexuality. When there have been previous difficulties with separation, accepting limits, managing aggression, or acquiring basic skills, the necessary adolescent developmental tasks can be quite out of reach.

## SEPARATION, INTIMACY, AND IDENTITY

An adolescent is faced with three major developmental tasks: he must separate emotionally from his parents, learn to develop intimate relationships with his peers, and establish an independent identity. These tasks are interconnected. Healthy separation from parents requires intimacy with peers—just as in infancy the father acts as a pole to draw his child away from an exclusive relationship with his mother, in adolescence intimate relationships with peers act as a pole to draw the young adult out from an exclusive intimacy with parents. But intimacy with peers requires a developing sense of the self. Otherwise, allowing closeness with another person can threaten a loss of self. The successful achievement of these tasks depends on the mastery of earlier developmental tasks. The adolescent who can't maintain emotional equilibrium, handle conflict in ongoing relationships, or manage aggression won't be able to separate emotionally from his parents, tolerate intimacy, or begin the task of forming an independent identity.

### SEPARATING FROM THE PARENTS

In separating, an adolescent transfers emotional investment from her parents to her peers, but the transfer doesn't take place smoothly or all at once. Emotional investment is withdrawn from parents at a faster rate than it can be bestowed on friends. One result of this imbalance is an increased emotional investment in the self (heightened narcissism)—sometimes seen as a sense of omnipotence and at other times painful self-consciousness. An adolescent may insist on perfection (in herself and in others) while also being painfully aware of its absence. (Holden Caulfield, the central character in J. D. Salinger's *Catcher in the Rye,* poignantly illustrates this state of mind.) Positively, an adolescent's demand for perfection can encourage her to work intensely toward physical, academic, or athletic excellence. When an adolescent doesn't feel able to enter into this kind of competition, however, she can withdraw from developmental tasks and look for other destructive ways of finding emotional satisfaction.

## Separating from Mom

Typically, an adolescent begins to separate first from his mother, rejecting the care and affection that he recently sought. The child who used to have an inexhaustible need to be *seen* by his mother now demands *not* to be seen by her ("Stop staring at me!") and especially not to be seen *with* her ("Drop me off a block away from school!"). He also shows an increasingly fierce need to define his separate space—his room and his privacy become inviolable. At the same time, however, he acts in ways that beckon for Mom's involvement: he will have trouble getting himself up in the morning, he may insist on wearing outlandish outfits, adopt outrageous hairstyles, and/or cultivate a sloppiness that all but demands intervention. Because mothers and food are closely linked, unregulated eating—too much or too little—(short of an eating disorder) can also invite Mom's intervention. At this stage, Dad, if he is present, can be a crucial mediator. His limits are still respected, and he can, as in early childhood, draw an adolescent away from overinvolvement with his mother while also drawing the mother to himself and away from the adolescent.

## Separating from Dad

As adolescence progresses, however, Dad's position changes: his presence becomes an increasing barrier to an adolescent's moral independence and especially to her sexual and aggressive striving. Often, at a level beyond awareness, the adolescent rebels against her father's perceived opposition to her freedom. She questions her father's values and his position in the world. This skepticism can also be fluidly projected onto other adult authority: school administrators, police, or political leaders. The adolescent's rebellion most often is accompanied by *fear*— a fear of reprisal. This fear typically is masked, however, by defiance or a nonchalant disregard. An adolescent's fear and her defenses against it widen the generational divide.

Fortunately, just as a father can intervene in conflicts with the mother, some adults outside the home may be spared the adolescent's rejection and can serve as mentors or alternate sources of authority: teachers, coaches, aunts, uncles, or parents of friends often assume this role. It is important for Dad to recognize the value of such individuals and not become competitive with them, as long as their influence isn't harmful.

## Developing Intimate Relationships

Separating from parents results in an intense need for contact with peers. While a ten-year-old child in emotional distress goes to a parent for comfort, a fourteen-year-old more likely goes to his peers. Hanging out, talking on the telephone, text messages, instant messaging, and other online connections become crucial emotional lifelines. The adolescent is becoming increasingly aware intellectually, morally, and creatively and has an intense desire to share his thoughts and be appreciated for them. He wants and needs to enter into his peers' emotional and intellectual lives in a way that he never could previously. In doing so he embarks on one of his most important developmental tasks, which is the cultivation of intimate relationships in which he will bare his soul: aspirations, affections, and wrath.

### Forming an Independent Identity

The formation of an independent identity is an adolescent's most difficult and complex task. She must take an occupational, sexual, social, and moral stance in the present but also with an eye toward the future. Although establishing an identity begins in the early teenage years, the process isn't complete until the twenties and sometimes as late as the early thirties. If you ask a child what she wants to be when she grows up, she will probably recite a list of possibilities (president of the United States, astronaut, Olympic gymnast) that have no special relationship to each other or to her own abilities. If an adolescent wants to *be* something, however, she had better be able to imagine how she's going to get there. Otherwise she'll be called a wannabe, a term created by adolescents for adolescents. The adolescent must be able to imagine herself more realistically *in time*—or she feels foolish.

Similarly, a young child's idea of what is right and wrong tends to be the same as his parents'. (Even if the child does not do what her parents tell her, she assumes her parents are right and she is wrong.) But a teenager can envision the difference between what is truly right and what her parents say is right—and she may be pretty intolerant of any discrepancy between the two. (Once again I am reminded of Holden Caulfield's bitter rejection of everything that is "phony.") Forming an identity, then, entails developing a sense of what a person wants to do in the world and how to set about doing it; what stance she means to take in relation to her culture (a social reformer, a conservative, a revolutionary, an artist, a religious leader); what she believes is right and wrong; and what are her sexual needs and principles.

## Adolescent Rebellion

The idea that adolescent rebellion is normal has been discredited, but neither is it necessarily pathological. Indeed, it is each generation's job to question and improve upon the values of its predecessors. The adolescent's widening intellectual and social perspectives, emerging moral independence, growing physical capabilities, and drive to separate from his parents naturally lead to testing parental values and limits. Indeed, as an adolescent begins to form an authentic identity, he necessarily arrives at a sense of what he must *not* be well before he can know what he *must be*. However, the immaturity of an adolescent's judgment—his still limited sense of what he at least *needs* to be, his limited perspective on his culture, as well as his inability to distinguish between freedom and license—makes it necessary for parents to continue to set expectations and limits. The crucial distinction parents must make is whether their teen's rebellion is a part of development or an avoidance of it.


## NOT EVERY TROUBLED TEEN IS BIPOLAR!

Adolescence is such a volatile time that some of the symptoms or developmental difficulties found in the bipolar adolescent occur in adolescents who, although they are in turmoil, are not bipolar—and may not qualify for any psychiatric diagnosis. As with younger children, what needs to be assessed in determining the diagnosis is not a checklist but a pattern emerging over time, a pattern that may be composed of seemingly opposite cues: social withdrawal, flamboyance, intense competitiveness, grandiose withdrawal from competition, or a withdrawal that is depressed and paranoid. However, a single swallow does not make a summer: one or two of these characteristics doesn't add up to bipolar disorder.

Consider also that adolescents whose mental health is relatively sound are under so much pressure now—as compared to the society their parents and psychiatrists grew up in—that *normal* behavior requires redefinition. By pressure, I don't mean simply academic pressure. The insistent force of events around us—the prevalence of AIDS; the pressure of electronic media: the Internet (with its access to overwhelming amounts of information, e-mail, instant messaging, and chat rooms), video games of all kinds, the presence of cell phones just about everywhere (with calls, voice mail, and text messaging) all together eroding mental privacy; events such as Columbine and the attacks of September 11, 2001, have taken a toll on many children's sense of safety, trust, and optimism. The pressure of reality has increased unspeakably and demands a different standard of normalcy from today's adolescents. Finally, although I have gone to great length to describe developmental problems that can accompany and complicate bipolar disorder, those problems are not themselves symptoms of the disorder.

*Common Adolescent Behaviors—Not Necessarily Bipolar*

- rebellion
- irritability
- impulsivity
- seeing things in black and white
- grandiosity
- staying up late and sleeping far into the day
- intense anxiety about the self or the future
- excessive concern with appearance
- social withdrawal
- *talk* of suicide

*Special Problems of the Bipolar Adolescent*
(*in addition to the normal challenges of adolescence*)

- He can still have problems with self-regulation: eating, sleeping, and self soothing.

- Her intensity, as in earlier years, makes it harder for her to bear confrontation with peers as well as parents.

- A lack of developed academic and social skills hinders his formation of an independent identity.

- Her perception can be distorted by contempt and grandiosity.

- His desire for independence and perfection can lead him to refuse medication.

· Mounting social discomfort coupled with a shift in his sleep cycle can lead to chronic lateness or school refusal.

· Erratic eating habits can affect her mood. Some bipolar children or teens are sensitive to fluctuations in blood sugar and need to pay particular attention to what and when they eat to maintain mood stability.

· He may gain too much weight. Many of the medications prescribed for bipolar disorder—lithium, Depakote, most major tranquilizers, and SSRIs—promote weight gain in one way or another. Also, because of naturally increased levels of growth hormone during adolescence, weight gain occurs as an increase in the *number* of fat cells rather than an increase in the *size* of existing fat cells. The resulting hypercellular obesity is especially hard to correct.

## The Bipolar Adolescent

There are a number of ways that adolescents can falter at crucial developmental tasks, and when they do, the results can be disabling—school refusal, substance abuse, an eating disorder, delinquency, or promiscuity, to name the most common.

### Separating from the Parents

Any child with a persistent illness—including bipolar disorder—becomes more dependent on her parents (especially her mother) at every step along the way. During infancy and childhood, anxiety can make it hard for her to sleep alone. As she moves through school, her emotional, academic, and social difficulties increase a parent's presence in activities that other children learn to manage on their own (getting up in the morning, homework, eating, and traveling). An accentuated closeness between herself and her mother can also make it more difficult for her father to draw her out from intense dependency on Mom.

The resulting tension between the father and child makes it harder for Dad to fulfill his task of helping his child move confidently out into the world. These and other subtle influences can make separation during adolescence particularly difficult for a bipolar adolescent. This difficulty can show itself as an overattachment to parents (reluctance to undertake activities with peers and reliance on parents for companionship) or as a more violent effort at separation (refusing to accept limits, rejecting advice, or running away from home). Either way, the adolescent's difficulty in separating complicates other developmental tasks.

## Developing Intimate Relationships

Probably the most crucial skill in establishing and maintaining intimate relationships is the capacity to confront important conflicts without giving up your own boundaries, without violating the other person's boundaries, and without retreating from the situation. This capacity develops directly from the child's early task of learning to accept limits from his parents and then being able to limit himself—in order to stay connected. An adolescent who has not mastered this skill, at least partially, can't begin to let someone else inside emotionally because he lacks the ability to manage the inevitable collisions that occur. As a result, he either withdraws socially or experiences a series of intense failed relationships.

A related problem faces the adolescent who has not learned to manage aggression during the latency years (eight to twelve). Letting someone else draw near emotionally requires an ability to be comfortable with and limit aggression—to maintain one's own boundaries while respecting those of another person. The adolescent who has found himself excluded from the peer group is at a loss when it comes to negotiating boundaries, so that the mere act of approaching another person becomes problematic.

Another profound impediment to intimacy is a history of abuse—physical, sexual, or emotional. (As has already been mentioned, the bipolar child has an increased risk of having been abused in some or in several ways.) Abuse involves a violation of a child's inner sense of safety, a breach in the psychological membrane. It is as if there is a permanent hole in that membrane that prevents the person from establishing emotional equilibrium. Without such equilibrium, intimacy—the entry of another person into your emotional world—becomes terrifying.

## Forming an Independent Identity

Another crucial requirement for intimacy is developing a sense of the self. An adolescent who hasn't begun to develop an independent identity finds intimacy intimidating because she feels she has nothing to offer and may be envious of other adolescents' sense of direction. Intimacy also seems intolerable because closeness to another person risks the loss of self. Some adolescents (and adults) solve this difficulty by mirroring the person to whom they are attaching—their behaviors, interests, and desires are taken from a person they look upon as important to them.

Several things can contribute to an adolescent's problems establishing an identity:

· She failed during latency to acquire basic skills that help her construct an identity. As a result, she enters adolescence crucially unprepared.

· He has always done exactly what adults have demanded. A child who does his parents' bidding *at the expense of his own feelings* ultimately loses contact with an authentic emotional life. In adolescence, our feelings, *the things we want to do,* are necessary elements in the construction of an identity. This is one reason some model children implode when they reach adolescence: without access to their true feelings, they are at a loss about how to form an authentic self. But they can no longer accept having an identity imposed upon them—they feel lost or a painful sense of pretending.

· She may form a negative identity assembled in perfect opposition to what her parents want. A negative identity isn't an authentic self, however; it's only the opposite of parental values. Some teens develop a negative identity as a way of separating without having any real place to go. A negative identity can be a response to feelings of hopelessness about not being able to emulate a highly successful and distant parent. It can also be an expression of disgust with the values the parents espouse, a disgust that comes from a growing moral independence. In some individuals, however, the cultivation of a negative identity can issue in powerful originality and social or cultural challenge: Woody Guthrie in the 1930s, James Dean or Allen Ginsberg in the 1950s, Bob Dylan in the 1960s, Metallica in the 1980s, some rap musicians during this decade, and jazz musicians singers throughout the past century: Bessie Smith, Charley Parker, and Miles Davis are examples.

## SETTING LIMITS WITH THE REBELLIOUS ADOLESCENT

### HOLDING ON TO THE *No*

An adolescent, like a toddler, constantly tests your limits to prove what a tyrant you are. At this stage, as in the earlier one, the same principles apply:

· When it's important, don't give up the *no*.
· Stay even; don't get contaminated with rage.
· Don't leave the situation or allow the adolescent to leave.

However, some differences should be borne in mind when confronting a teen. You must exercise more caution about violating an adolescent's emotional or physical space. Because of the adolescent's need to separate from you, he needs to have a space that is practically inviolable.

(For example, it is not appropriate to go in and out of an adolescent's room without knocking.) In a conflict, he may need to withdraw into his own space—his room or a walk around the block. Unlike a toddler, it is usually okay to allow an adolescent to *temporarily* leave the situation. Because the adolescent (usually) has a more developed sense of time, the dispute can be resumed after a cooling-down period.

An exception to this occurs when the adolescent is in acute danger of hurting himself or is likely to run away. In this case, your goal is to contain the adolescent within the house—in his room if that is safe. If this kind of containment is not possible, hospitalization may be required. When hospitalization occurs, there will still be a later time when the conflict needs to be taken up again and resolved. In particularly difficult circumstances, the confrontation may need to take place during family therapy, at first in the hospital and later in outpatient treatment.

The exchange that takes place *in language* with an adolescent is far richer than that with a younger child. Your teen's advancing intellectual capacity and developing moral independence provide opportunities for genuine exchange. When handled well, moments of confrontation between a parent and an adolescent can be opportunities for moral and social growth on both sides. In addition to holding the situation, your most important task is to listen to your adolescent. As with the toddler, you have no way of making an adolescent listen to you, but you can make him feel *listened to.* When you do this with an adolescent, there is a possibility of real conversation. You can help him feel listened to by acknowledging any mistakes you have made and those parts of his position that are sound. Acknowledgment of these things decreases his anxiety and his need to fight you. When he is less impassioned, he can be more articulate. Just as with a toddler, delivering your adolescent *into language* is a crucial task.

Because of the adolescent's need to reject your authority, you may want to refer the dispute to another adult with whom the adolescent has a working relationship—his therapist, a coach, or a family friend. After the adolescent has had an opportunity to discuss the problem with another adult, there may be a greater chance for you and your child to have a meeting of the minds. Such a complex and protracted process is possible with an adolescent because he can entertain a dispute over a much longer period of time without losing track of the discussion and its emotional importance.

## WHEN YOUR TEEN REFUSES TO TAKE HER MEDS

You can make a young child take medication, but you have no such power with an adolescent. She will demand concrete reasons for taking the medication and may refuse it for a number of reasons.

Taking medication frustrates her normal developmental need to be perfect and independent. Adolescents are known for their sense of invulnerability, so she may deny that there is anything wrong with her, especially if she hasn't mourned her illness. Finally, if the medication causes weight gain or tremors, if it interferes with appearance, athletic performance, or ability to think clearly, her protest will be particularly fierce, and justifiably so. You should know about any medication your teen is taking, how it works, what it's for, and what are its side effects. It's vitally important that you get your teen in treatment with a psychiatrist who can work with her questions and resistance to medication. If her psychiatrist can't do that, you may need a new one. Fifteen-minute med checks by a psychopharmacologist are not adequate for an adolescent and are likely to inspire contempt. When there is a split between an adolescent's psychiatric and psychotherapeutic care—often an appropriate arrangement—there must be much closer coordination of treatment between the psychiatrist and the therapist.

Unfortunately, at times, experiencing symptoms of the illness is the only effective confrontation of an adolescent's denial. It is not a recommended approach, but it may be a necessary passage.

## STAYING SAFE

When language fails, physical danger can increase. Just as your teen is increasingly articulate in his protests, he can also become more forceful physically. An adolescent can be intimidating and potentially dangerous to you or to himself. If you strike him (or if he's been struck in the past), there is now a real possibility that he will strike back. He may also run away. These dangers underscore the importance, from the very beginning, of your not becoming contaminated with rage.

An adolescent's increased ability to defy limits also underscores the importance of setting limits from early on. When your child is fourteen or even sixteen, he is still largely under your sway. By eighteen, however, possibilities for containing him markedly decrease. Even in residential facilities, an eighteen-year-old legally can't be held unless he wants to stay. An eighteen-year-old who can't accept limits is also much farther off track developmentally, which raises the risk of dangerous impulsivity and lifelong developmental failure.

If you haven't been able to hold the line well enough, or you haven't been able to hold it in the right way—and this can happen for reasons that have nothing to do with you being an inadequate parent—you need to get help. Some crises require hospitalization to keep your child safe—if he is suicidal, is dangerously impulsive, or is abusing substances in a way that puts him in immediate danger. A hospitalization usually is brief—about two or three weeks. It allows time for limited biological stabilization, possibly some family work, and appropriate referral. It is a bridge to more effective long-term treatment.

Another acute measure that is sometimes effective is a therapeutic wilderness program. Under the supervision of trained professionals, limits set by a wild terrain help adolescents who have been unable to accept less stringent limits. The wilderness is more than a measure to prevent flight—it provides a setting in which to acquire self-reflection and self-confidence. Group therapy and cooperative activities are used to bring an adolescent to a point where he is open to less restrictive treatment. These programs usually last longer than a hospitalization—six or eight weeks—and can be used when there is a crisis but danger is not imminent. The programs vary in quality and appropriateness for any particular adolescent. If you are considering a wilderness program, you need to consult with an expert familiar with these programs who also makes himself or herself familiar with your child's needs and your family.

When the problem is more chronic but still beyond your control, there are different options depending on the child's age and ability to cooperate with someone else. The best case is when the child accepts some form of psychotherapy. When this is not an option, or an option that has already been tried unsuccessfully, you may need to go to family court and petition for court supervision. This usually results in your child being assigned a probation officer with whom he is required to meet. As grim as this sounds, sometimes the presence of social machinery can help a teen take stock of his situation and rein in.

Finally, if none of these measures are successful or appropriate, residential treatment is needed. Residential treatment can also be the outcome of a wilderness program, when it is clear that an adolescent cannot cooperate with less restrictive measures. Usually the cost of such a program is borne by the school district or the Department of Social Services. Again, as cruel as this may sound, it can be a life-changing experience for some adolescents.

## A Long, Hard Sail

After his parents' divorce, **DAMON**'s early years were spent in the custody of his mother, who suffered from bipolar disorder and substance abuse. She was unpredictable, inconsistent, and at times harsh in her treatment of him. His father also suffered from depression but was a highly accomplished professional who had remarried and had another child. When Damon was eight, his father gained custody and brought him into his home.

Damon had always had a close relationship with his stepmother, but as time passed she became increasingly involved in the care of her daughter and less tolerant of Damon, whose quietly oppositional behavior had begun to intensify. His father frequently traveled for work, and he could not always be an effective presence in setting limits with his son. His stepmother had difficulty confronting Damon, so that his father, when present, had to enforce discipline. Damon began displacing his rage at his own mother onto his father. His stepmother was spared and to some extent idealized in comparison to his father.

Damon was extremely bright, but by the time he entered high school he consistently neglected homework and became increasingly unwilling to engage academically. He was not, however, disrespectful. What is more, he had good relationships with peers, and his friends were among the brightest and most capable in his class. They became the emotional center of his life. Damon had also developed an interest in sailing, and during the summer he worked at a nearby sailing school, earning the respect of its owner.

By the time he was sixteen, however, Damon's refusal to cooperate at home and in school had begun to cause intense conflict in the household. He flatly refused his father's attempt to get him into psychotherapy. That winter Damon showed increasing signs of depression, and when he began having repeated accidents while driving, a difficult situation became imminently dangerous. After consultation, Damon's father arranged for Damon to be abducted into a wilderness program, hoping that technique would get through his son's intense oppositional behavior.

Damon was tougher than the program, however, and he refused to cooperate or talk. He was transferred to a secure residential school for an extended stay. Not surprisingly, Damon was furious, particularly at his father. It took almost a year for him to begin to cooperate, however grudgingly, with psychotherapeutic care. Tentatively he began to approach early issues of rage at his mother, but his father remained the main focus of his outrage. (His stepmother continued to be a positive figure for him.) Finally, after a few successful home visits, Damon returned, having promised to work in psychotherapy and attend a special high school.

Damon's oppositional behavior at home was temporarily improved. But he soon refused to cooperate with psychotherapy, and after a few months he also refused to attend the special school. His behavior in the household continued to be cooperative, however, and he bargained to attend the local high school with his friends. Nonetheless, before long he again refused to do assigned work and began attending erratically. Finally he announced a plan to get an equivalency diploma and stopped attending school altogether. During this time, although disappointed, his father did not withdraw from or become punitive with his son.

Damon never carried through with his promise to get an equivalency diploma. After much delaying, he obtained a job and worked responsibly for a while. When the evening hours of the job interfered with his ability to see friends, however, he quit. That summer he again worked in the sailing school and spent time with his friends. The following fall his friends went off to college, and he became more withdrawn. He again took a job, working a night shift for a time, but he soon quit. His sleep cycle was advanced: he stayed up late and slept during the day, a schedule that also allowed him to avoid other members of the household. Developmentally he seemed to be completely stuck.

Although he was no longer doing anything dangerous, Damon's withdrawal and inactivity caused tension in the household. His stepmother increasingly resented his sullen presence; his father, who continued to be supportive, was completely shut out by him. Damon still blamed his father for having sent him away and having him confined against his will.

That spring, his father learned of a well-reputed school in a foreign country that taught advanced seamanship and navigation. Graduates from the school were highly credentialed and sought after. When his father offered to send him to the school, Damon agreed, but without any clear expression of excitement or apprehension. Nonetheless, Damon's separation from home (this time voluntarily) caused him anxiety. He did not demonstrate his anxiety overtly, however; rather, he appeared to be unconcerned and out of contact with the necessary preparations for the trip. He permitted his father to accompany him on the plane but subtly ridiculed his father's attention to the details of travel, as if they were unimportant and his father's attention to them ridiculous.

The program in seamanship lasted six months. While Damon was away, his father continued to make contact by letter and occasionally by phone. He also made funds available for his son to use at his own discretion: the privilege was not abused. As it turned out, Damon was the youngest but the most proficient student in his class. Indeed, Damon was so motivated that he worked to obtain extra training in nautical engineering and navigation. By the time he returned home, his demeanor had changed. Although still very private, he was more cooperative and took pride in his accomplishments, sharing photographs with his family and his friends.

That winter during the darker months, he was again inactive and withdrawn. With the coming of spring, however, he obtained a job to help take a ship across the Atlantic. The trip was not easy. The skipper broke his leg in a storm and had to spend much of his time belowdecks. Damon was crucial in bringing the ship across safely. He had proved himself to be a highly responsible seaman under dangerous conditions at an unusually early age. At about this time he also began his first relationship with a girl. Within a year, his father had helped him purchase a boat to live and work on. Damon left the household and moved to a southern coastal state. His relationship with his father underwent a dramatic change—he expressed gratitude and remained in contact with him on the phone.

*Damon has some symptoms of bipolar disorder—a recurrently depressed mood in the winter with dislocation of his sleep cycle and* fierce rebellion appearing at the time of adolescence. His depressions, although recurrent, are not disabling. He also has a history of emotional neglect and abuse in his early childhood, in direct consequence of his mother's mood disorder and substance abuse. It is difficult to discriminate in his case between biological and developmental difficulties. Damon managed his early developmental tasks by toughing it out—forming an emotional membrane that was relatively impermeable, a shell—and becoming compliant at the expense of accumulated rage. His adaptation allowed him to function well enough at home and in school prior to adolescence. His father's consistent protective presence may have allowed him to develop sufficient trust to manage intimate relationships with male peers. With the onset of adolescence, however, Damon's residual rage from childhood, his moral independence, his need to challenge authority, and his consequent inability to continue with the process of formulating an identity resulted in increasingly oppositional behavior. This put him off track in developing skills with which to formulate an identity; it also threatened his ability to live in his father's household. Despite his defiance, he was not prepared to separate. His anger began to become dangerous when it was expressed in his driving, a circumstance in which rage can often express itself with unpredictable destructiveness.

The attempt to set limits with Damon's rebellion encountered enormous and sustained resistance and was only partially broached in a strict residential program. Damon's confinement was, however, a forceful limit set by his father in an attempt to protect his son and get him back on track developmentally. As severe as it was, his father's action was not contaminated by rage. Within the limits set by that residential program, Damon was able to approach, albeit briefly, his powerfully conflicted feelings about his mother. Although Damon's refusal to cooperate with conventional education persisted, his dangerous behavior resolved.

Damon's character had areas of strength: he had lasting, stable relationships with male peers, and he was able to work responsibly at the local sailing school in a task he valued. His failure to take on the *developmental task of acquiring academic skills was the result of accumulated rage, which also prevented him from identifying with either parent or most adult authority. (The owner of the sailing school was a crucial exception.) Developmentally, he suffered from what Erik Erikson, the originator of the psychoanalytic concept of identity, termed* identity diffusion. *His rebellion can be understood as a refusal to accept authority with which he could not identify.*

*Damon's stable relationships with his peers suggest, however, that he benefited from his father's abiding presence and the nonpunitive environment his father provided. With his father's help, Damon ultimately succeeded in accepting an apprenticeship and formulating a preliminary identity in which he was industrious, accomplished, and highly responsible.*

*Having begun to establish an identity, Damon was then able to attempt intimacy with a woman. His deep-seated conflicts with his mother are likely, however, to make this a difficult task without psychotherapeutic help. Emotional disappointment in such a relationship could precipitate a serious depression, stressing his bipolar tendency into a mood disorder.*

## Becoming Grace

GRACE was a thirteen-year-old adopted child whom I first saw at her parents' request because of their concerns about her depression. At the time she was sullen and furious about being brought to a psychiatrist. She did, however, enter the room and stayed while her parents explained their concerns. She would not speak or acknowledge that she had a problem.

Grace had been having increased difficulties in school since the age of ten or eleven, especially in subjects requiring reading. These difficulties, as it happened, coincided with the onset of menstruation, which took place just before she was eleven. At that age, her mother remembered Grace for the first time having greater problems with organization and assigned research reports. She also noted Grace experiencing mood changes and increasing frustration. During her early school years, between kindergarten and fourth grade, Grace had no prominent academic or behavioral problems.

Grace's ability to function decreased dramatically approximately a year prior to my seeing her (age twelve). She became depressed and had active thoughts of wanting to die with a specific plan of cutting her wrists. The prior winter, during January and February, she had a period of depression as well. There was an attempt to treat that episode with counseling, but it was stopped after five months without much perceived benefit. In October or November of that year (age thirteen), Grace began experimenting with amphetamines and marijuana, and once again the following February she had a period of depression. This time she began work with a therapist in a program for the treatment of substance abuse, a treatment that would ultimately succeed.

To begin with, however, her oppositional behavior continued, and in May she ran away from home and was arrested after attempting to burglarize a trailer. Just prior to her coming to see me she had wanted to get a tattoo and had been forbidden: in reaction, she cut her boyfriend's initials into her arm. At the time I saw her, Grace had a delayed sleep cycle with difficulty falling asleep and a tendency to get up late in the day. She denied any current suicidal thinking but described intense anxiety that was generalized rather than episodic. She denied panic attacks.

Psychological testing available at that time showed a significant discrepancy in intertest scores with verbal scores higher than her performance scores. Grace was also two years behind the norm for visual motor capacity. Achievement tests showed her to be between two and four years behind grade level, depending on the subject. These scores, together with her academic history, indicated a severe difficulty with visual tracking. In a girl of average intelligence, this was a formidable academic handicap.

In my presence Grace was sullen, denied any difficulties with mood, and tended to see her problems as coming from outside, caused by adults. Her recurrent seasonal depressions, coming on with menarche, led me to a diagnosis of bipolar disorder, complicated by oppositional behavior and substance abuse. Because of their insurance coverage, Grace's parents were required to follow up with a psychiatrist in their plan, who began her on lithium: her oppositional behavior improved initially but recurred after a few months. When her parents again consulted me the following January, I increased her dose of lithium, which lessened her irritability, but she remained chronically depressed. A trial of an antidepressant caused an abrupt increase in irritability and was discontinued. For the first two years that I saw her, Grace continued to be sullen, replied in one or two words to any questions, and was otherwise uncommunicative. On one occasion she came wearing a black Marilyn Manson T-shirt with the devil's symbol on it, taking grim satisfaction in her negativity. During this period of time she maintained her relationship with her boyfriend, who served as a counterfamily, an exemplar of the values her parents feared.

Sometime in the fall of 1996, I learned of lamotrigine, a new mood stabilizer reported to have antidepressant as well as stabilizing properties (the medication also did not promote weight gain; Grace had gradually put on weight with lithium). Using that medication, I was able to lower Grace's dose of lithium without the return of her irritability. Her mood also improved and her affect (range of facial expression) became wider. She became more communicative and was able to complain about the side effects she had been having with lithium.

That winter, however, she began to experience a more pronounced shift in her sleep cycle, causing her to have significant difficulty falling asleep and awakening for school. Even when she was able to get up, she did not feel awake and had a hard time functioning. Fortunately, her school district had just begun a program allowing some students to begin school in the late afternoon and attend evening classes. Grace was willing to go along with this program. By the springtime this difficulty improved, although it did not disappear. By this time she had lost weight and was feeling better about herself.

Grace had been abstinent from drugs now for some time, and under the influence of her therapist she had begun to take an interest in nutrition. She also began to inquire about how to decrease her smoking—she was at a pack and a half a day. Nonetheless, in my office she continued to be verbally withdrawn, a somewhat unwilling presence. We had been struggling all this time with the Committee on Special Education to get Grace classified to receive special educational resources. Further psychological testing documented problems with visual tracking and intermediate memory; Grace's IQ was also in the low average range. When I suggested that in the fall she attend a vocational program directed toward culinary skills, she agreed.

With the coming of fall and winter, Grace again had difficulties with her sleep cycle, but, with her parents' help, she began using a therapeutic light in the morning and her attendance improved. Grace completed the culinary course that year, achieving honors. She minimized the accomplishment, saying it was mainly because she had helped with cleanup, but it was clear that she was functioning at a higher level than at any time since I had first seen her. A year later she began to work part-time as a cook in a fast-food restaurant while still going to school.

Things went well until the spring of her senior year, when I got a call from her parents telling me that, in an argument with them about going to school, she had put her hand through a window. When I explored the incident, it did not appear to be related to a change in mood: rather, the prospect of leaving high school, after all its ups and downs, was troubling to Grace—as an adopted child she had great difficulty with separation. I spoke briefly with Grace about the ways terminations can arouse angry feelings, that high school is in most cases not a pleasant experience, and much less so for her given all the difficulties she had had.

The other question that Grace needed to address at this time was where she was going after high school. This entailed more than finding a job. That part was simple enough: she began full-time work at the fast-food restaurant where she had been a part-time chef and soon was promoted to manager. But Grace had aspirations to go to culinary school and had an idea of where she needed to go. Her plan would entail moving out of the area, however. Her boyfriend, whom she had been with now for four years, was in no way ready to make such a move. He had not kept pace with Grace's growth: he was still using marijuana and had nowhere near her ambition. He was in many ways the same troubled, immature boy she had gone out with originally. Grace also had difficulty leaving her family. Among other ties, she was playing a very nurturing role with her cousins. She had come a long way since the time she ran away.

Grace is now working as a chef in a somewhat better restaurant chain where she has room to develop. Her former boyfriend is still underemployed. Grace has given up the idea of going to culinary school, saying she could not afford it. Nor was she willing to accept money from her parents to pay for it. It seemed to me that separation and independence, not finances, are more the problem for this adopted child who had now become a woman. At her new position, Grace began seeing a man who matched her responsibility and motivation. Within that mature relationship, Grace conceived and delivered a daughter. She remained on a reduced dose of Lamictal during her pregnancy, increasing it following delivery, and thereby reversing a postpartum depression. Grace continued for eight years on a stable dose of medication. Her mood was normal; she was industrious, pretty, and softer in her appearance. During the whole time, her parents, now grandparents, had been unwavering in their support.

*Grace suffered from bipolar II disorder, with prominent oppositional behavior, dysthymia (mild chronic depression), and seasonal depres-*

sion all appearing around menarche and complicated by specific learning difficulties, substance abuse, and adoption. Like many adopted children she also had an episode of running away from home. Grace's parents continued to be caring and firm in the face of her opposition: they provided treatment and worked to get her a proper educational placement.

Grace was of average intelligence with areas of significant learning disability. As school became more demanding, she stopped making an effort. Seasonal depression and a drifting of her sleep cycle complicated Grace's problems at school, making attendance and punctuality additional problems.

Grace's attempted burglary was an isolated episode of stealing, and it occurred in the context of substance abuse—both stealing and substance abuse are consumption disorders. These difficulties suggest that her relationship with a boyfriend did not indicate a capacity for intimacy. That conclusion is also supported by her failure, at the time, in the task of accumulating skills with which to formulate an identity.

Grace's initial pharmacologic care was not ideal: lithium helped lessen impulsivity but did little to improve her mood. A limited response to lithium is typical in bipolar II disorder. Grace's increased irritability in response to an antidepressant is common enough but not always the case. The availability of lamotrigine as a mood stabilizer with antidepressant properties was crucial for her lamotrigine had the additional advantage of helping her lose weight, gained as a result of lithium. Grace's difficulties with a recurrent displacement of her sleep cycle in the winter required light therapy. She was also fortunate that her school district had an afternoon and evening program for students having trouble with an early morning schedule.

Although Grace was in rebellion against most adult authority, she was ultimately able to form a more trusting relationship with her substance abuse counselor. Through that relationship—at the same time that she was successfully losing weight—she began to take an interest in nutrition, an interest that would develop into culinary training and

*the beginnings of a substantial career. Before that could take place,
however, Grace needed an appropriate academic setting. That required
a sustained effort by her parents together with neuropsychological
testing before they could convince the Committee on Special Education
to properly classify her.*

*As Grace began succeeding in developmental tasks, her opposi-
tional behavior lessened and disappeared. Her ability to sustain her
relationship with her boyfriend shows her capacity for intimacy, as
does her connection with her younger cousins. Once her substance
abuse was under control, her capacity for intimacy was crucially fostered by her therapist's work with her. That relationship also helped
Grace get back on track with her adolescent developmental task of
accepting an apprenticeship. Both these accomplishments enabled
her to give up substance abuse entirely even when her boyfriend
did not.*

*As an adopted child, I suspect that Grace's problems with separa-
tion may have also played a role in maintaining her relationship with a
boy she had outgrown. Difficulty with separation also prevented Grace
from following through on her plans to go to culinary school. As she ad- ·
vanced professionally, Grace formed an appropriate relationship: her
achievement of identity and true intimacy coincided. Grace's developmental moves were made possible by parents who provided a firm,
nonpunitive holding environment, who also provided appropriate psychiatric and psychotherapeutic care and insisted on an appropriate academic setting.*

## Consumption Disorders

During middle school and high school, a number of related problems
begin to arise for some adolescents: drug abuse, alcohol abuse, eating
disorders, compulsive shopping, compulsive use of the Internet or
video games, compulsive promiscuity, and in some cases compulsive stealing. What links these problems—although they arise in very different

people—is their appearance in early adolescence *and* their common feature of an attempt to put something inside oneself in order to feel less empty. Additionally, adolescents who struggle with these disorders all have difficulties establishing or maintaining intimate relationships. These disorders are extremely common in adolescents suffering from bipolar disorder.

Studies confirm a strong overlap between bipolar disorder and consumption disorders but have little to say about why this overlap exists. Speculative answers include: these children are self-medicating; substances aggravate bipolar disorder, cause rapid cycling, and perpetuate the use of substances; and alcohol or drug abuse is inherited along with bipolar disorder. These suggestions fail to account for consumption disorders not related to mood-altering substances; they also have nothing to say about why these disorders arise at a particular time in a child's development.

The clinicians making these speculations also have little to offer about how parents can protect their child from these disorders. At best they suggest warnings, surveillance, behavioral limits, or enforcing compliance with medication. None of these measures grow out of an understanding of what affects the person rather than the illness.

Consumption disorders commonly arise at the time adolescents face the task of separating from parents and depending more crucially on their relationships with peers. The disorders also arise in adolescents who, having failed at the developmental task of carrying on intimate relationships and the task of beginning to formulate an identity, feel overwhelmingly anxious, socially isolated, and *empty*. Each of these disorders provides adolescents with a way of quickly changing their state of mind, giving them the illusion of control and fulfillment. In some cases the disorder also provides a pseudo society. Consumption disorders are common in adolescents with bipolar disorder not simply because of their moods or their genetic loading but also because bipolar disorder complicates the developmental tasks of intimacy and identity formation.

## Smoking

Many middle school children begin to experiment with smoking. Research shows that cigarettes are often a gateway drug, a precedent to more serious substance abuse. Cigarette use beginning at the age of eleven or twelve is a strong predictor of later substance abuse. The bipolar child is at particular risk for smoking for several reasons: cigarettes can be used as an illusory shortcut to being an adult, an escape from low self-esteem, or an escape from an unpleasant state of mind. Cigarettes also actually relieve anxiety and depression. Indeed, recent studies have demonstrated a significant overlap between people with recurrent depression and a history of persistent smoking despite efforts to stop. Because the middle school years are also a period when the onset of hormonal activity brings on a sharp rise in the rate of depression, it is no surprise to see smoking appear at the same time. Children with low self-esteem and difficulty with peer relationships can also be tempted to gain entry to a peer group by smoking. Finally, smoking can serve as an act of defiance that fits with a bipolar child's oppositional streak.

The most effective way to prevent smoking is not to smoke yourself—children often don't do what we tell them; they almost always do what we do. Graphic education about the effects of smoking—pictures of its effects on the body or of people suffering from diseases caused by smoking—can be effective when words fail. (Remember, adolescents are highly invested in physical perfection.) Information about the difficulty people have quitting once they start can speak to an adolescent's desire for independence. You might consider asking your doctor to arrange for your child to visit a hospital to see patients who have end-stage lung disease or cancer. Sometimes an adolescent's sense of invulnerability requires a frontal assault.

Despite its health risks and its potential as a gateway to substance abuse, smoking cigarettes is not properly seen as a consumption disorder—it is not invariably accompanied by the developmental failures seen with substance abuse, eating disorders, compulsive shopping, promiscuity, and stealing.

## SUBSTANCE ABUSE

Substance abuse is virulent and common in all neighborhoods. Drug abuse begins in the middle school years, when tobacco and marijuana are the most widely used substances. The fact that depression also increases markedly at the age of eleven or twelve may account for some substance use as a form of self-medication. A genetic predisposition other than a mood disorder may also increase a person's vulnerability to substance abuse, but sustained use isn't merely an attempt to self-medicate, or merely an inherited problem—deeper character problems are always present as well. Whatever the choice of drug, lying and law-breaking are also always involved. The use of illegal drugs is usually one or two steps away from organized crime, so that their use requires the user to deny that uncomfortable facet of reality.

Marijuana has different effects on different people: most, at least initially, experience a decrease in anxiety and a pleasurable intensification of sensory experience. Some of the reduced anxiety is due to a decreased awareness of negative emotional cues. Problems seem distant, everything is mellow. However, tetrahydrocannabinol (THC)—the active agent in marijuana—is highly fat soluble. With consistent use, it accumulates in fatty tissues (including the white matter of the brain) and is released in continuingly higher amounts. As the length and level of exposure increase, the effects of the drug can change. Some people with bipolar disorder begin to become more anxious and may even become psychotic. More often a person becomes dependent on the drug to manage the chronic anxiety that accompanies bipolar disorder. However, there frequently is also a loss of motivation, fatigue, and an inability to manage normal stress, effects that perpetuate use and decrease the person's level of function.

Marijuana is addicting and causes physiologic dependence. There can be a powerful and long-lasting withdrawal syndrome when marijuana use is stopped, although, because marijuana accumulates in fatty tissue, the withdrawal may not appear immediately. Psychological dependence also develops: the person who has used the drug to shield himself from negativity in his environment becomes less and less able to deal with that stress. In addition, many users neglect their day-to-day responsibilities—homework, job, personal relationships—and when they stop must contend with an even more stressful environment.

Less acknowledged is the role any drug plays in substituting for intimate relationships. (It is for good reason that marijuana has been called a rainy day woman.) When you stop the drug, you are not only faced more directly with the task of managing intimacy, but the friends—the pseudosociety—with whom you used the drug become uncomfortable with your abstinence. Stopping the drug requires the development of missing social skills and the establishment of a new social network.

Cocaine, like amphetamines used to treat ADD, increases levels of dopamine in the brain. The difference is that recreational use of cocaine or amphetamines—nasally, intravenously, or freebase—delivers the drug much more quickly and at higher concentrations to the brain. The sharp increase in activity—the high—is followed by a dramatic falling off. This creates an oscillation that is dangerous to anyone but particularly to a person with bipolar disorder. The rapid rise and the ensuing falloff also create craving for continued use. In addition, the high levels of neural excitation caused by cocaine (or ecstasy or crystal meth) cause cell death. PET scans (positron-emission tomography) of the brain show holes in metabolic activity in chronic users.

Cocaine always causes mood instability; in some bipolar patients the use of cocaine precipitates psychosis. The character problems that accompany other consumption disorders are also seen with cocaine; in addition, cocaine is associated with a higher level of violent and impulsive behavior. Cocaine can also cause a stroke or sudden death from cardiac problems—a loss of circulation or a fatal arrhythmia.

The dangers seen with cocaine, ecstasy, crystal meth, or high-dose amphetamines are not present when stimulants are given at the low doses and with the gradual delivery used in the treatment of ADD or ADHD. To the contrary, studies show that children with ADD/ADHD treated with stimulants have a lower rate of substance abuse than children who go untreated. Other studies show that the craving caused by the rapid delivery of amphetamines or cocaine does not occur when the drug is introduced gradually. It is also true that when given in low doses, an amphetamine or methylphenidate (Ritalin and others) does not cause cell death.

Opiates—heroin, codeine, oxycodone—work to mimic a different set of neurotransmitters: endorphins. In addition to the risks of withdrawal and addiction, an overdose of opiates causes respiratory suppression and can be lethal. Although opiates do not aggravate symptoms of bipolar disorder, their abuse is associated with more severe defects in personality—more profound avoidance of intimacy and more difficulties with normal levels of social functioning. Getting someone to give up opiates is more difficult than achieving abstinence from alcohol, cocaine, or marijuana.

## Alcohol

Alcohol differs in several ways from other substances that are abused: like cigarettes, it is legal for adults to use, it is widely advertised, and it is often readily available in the home. Also like cigarettes, children often see their parents or older siblings use it on a regular basis.

A genetic profile—inherited independently of bipolar disorder—can increase the risk for alcoholism. The traits seen with this profile include a relatively high level of anxiety (including social anxiety), restlessness when trying to sleep, and an ability to drink large amounts of alcohol without feeling uncomfortable. The dangerous consequence of this constellation is that the person experiences welcome relief from anxiety and social awkwardness by using alcohol, and this practice is reinforced because he finds himself able to tolerate it so well. The practice is also reinforced because after alcohol leaves the brain, anxiety and irritability not only return but are increased.

This ability to tolerate alcohol is the result of a particular bio-chemistry. The liver converts alcohol from ethanol to acetaldehyde to acetone. Of these three compounds, acetaldehyde causes us to feel physically and mentally uncomfortable. In familial alcoholism, because of a metabolic quirk, acetaldehyde doesn't accumulate, so the person doesn't feel uncomfortable when drinking, even to excess. On the contrary, the alcohol decreases her anxiety and helps her feel more at ease socially. Nonetheless, when she drinks large amounts of alcohol—even when she is not uncomfortable—her judgment is impaired, especially about when to stop drinking, her reflexes are slowed, and she can have blackouts.

The problems increase when alcohol leaves her brain. Alcohol has reached higher levels in the brain and stayed there longer. Although she tolerates the *metabolism* of alcohol quite well, her brain is no less susceptible to the inherent toxicity of the drug. That damage is not apparent while she is intoxicated, but when the alcohol is cleared it leaves her brain in an irritable state. The brain's increased irritability then drives up her anxiety levels. The increased anxiety encourages continued use of alcohol, which in turn leads to an even greater irritability of the brain and a greater desire for alcohol to relieve it. A vicious cycle is established.

With or without this genetic profile, alcohol causes a person with bipolar disorder to be more anxious, depressed, and irritable. Mood instability increases along with depression and impulsive behavior, and the risk for violence and self-destructive behavior rises dramatically. Alcohol potently increases the risk for suicide in anyone, but more so in bipolar patients.

## A Model Child Grows Up

CHARLOTTE was an attractive and brilliant young woman of twenty-five when she first consulted me for management of medication. She had grown up in a prosperous household and had appeared to be a model child. There was, however, a history of al-coholism on her mother's side of the family—her mother was a functional alcoholic as well as a heavy smoker. There was also, I later learned, an unacknowledged history of mood disorders in both families.

As a child, Charlotte was extremely shy but on occasion had an explosive temper, which kept her from being the target of aggres-sive peers. Nonetheless, her social difficulties in elementary school led her parents to enroll her in a private high school. Prior to this time, Charlotte had never abused substances, nor did any of her friends. She was a nonsmoker. Experiencing overwhelming so-cial anxiety in the face of going to a new school, however, Charlotte went to the family liquor cabinet and sampled the vodka. She expe-rienced immediate relief from her anxiety—the first she had known—and found that she was able to drink large amounts of al-cohol without any noticeable disturbance in her functioning. In-deed, the relief from anxiety she experienced allowed her to improve her social function. She went on to have an apparently brilliant high school career: a top student, she was also a leading athlete and highly popular. She never, however, felt truly recog-nized by or close to her peers. (Popularity and intimacy are very different accomplishments.) During the whole of her high school years she drank heavily in as well as outside of school, completely undetected by her parents or teachers. By her junior year she be-gan to experience severe changes in her mood, with a significant depression in winter and a manic high in the spring. Charlotte's mood changes also went unnoticed.

Charlotte was accepted at a top-level college, where she began to use cocaine to manage her depression, while still drinking enormous quantities of alcohol to manage anxiety. Remarkably, her academic performance continued to be excellent, although she often missed classes and ceased to compete athletically. She was now having fre-quent blackouts and her social life was organized around the use of drugs and alcohol. She was also physiologically dependent on alcohol and began to experience withdrawal if she did not drink constantly.

One evening while intoxicated, Charlotte was brutally raped. She was brought to an emergency room, cursorily treated, but never offered psychiatric help. Her rape, like her substance abuse, continued to go unrecognized by her college. Charlotte graduated cum laude without either her substance abuse or her rape being acknowledged.

Following college, she returned to her parents' home, completed a master's degree in a skilled profession, and began to work in her own business. Her substance abuse escalated, however, until one day—during the winter—she made a nearly fatal attempt at suicide. When measured in the emergency room, her blood-alcohol level was lethal. After a brief hospitalization, during which she underwent withdrawal from alcohol, she began a dual diagnosis program, having been diagnosed with bipolar disorder and multiple substance abuse. She remained silent about her sexual abuse. Over the course of the next six months, she remained abstinent but relapsed in response to psychosocial stress.

After a second hospitalization, she was again stabilized and began serious participation in Alcoholics Anonymous. She cut off association with friends who used substances, which included virtually all of her former friends. With the help of AA she was able to tolerate the consequent social isolation. In psychotherapy she began working on the problem of formulating an identity. That developmental task had been impossible because of her compliant personality and her severe social anxiety. Her substance abuse had followed and aggravated those problems but had not caused them.

Her substance abuse effectively brought the development of her personality to a halt, and with sobriety she had to begin from the emotional position of an early adolescent. This meant that she also had to begin authentic separation from her parents and sort out her own desires and intellectual capacities. As she did this, she began to question the appropriateness of her occupation and made tentative preparations to enter graduate school. Having relinquished denial and grandiose defenses, she began contending with anxiety about her academic capabilities, sorting out exaggerated from realistic concerns.

At first Charlotte's mood continued to be unstable, requiring continuous pharmacologic adjustment including the use of benzodiazepines, which she never abused. With continued abstinence from drugs and alcohol, participation in AA, and regular psychotherapeutic work, her mood began to stabilize. She began the process of mourning the time she had lost and the developmental damage she had suffered. Once she became sober—in addition to being abstinent—she also began the task of forming and managing intimate relationships with family and sober friends. This task could not be fully achieved, however, because of her untreated sexual trauma. Approaching that injury needed to take place during a later phase of treatment.

*Charlotte has bipolar I disorder complicated by severe social anxiety and familial alcoholism, and later by severe sexual trauma. She also has a narcissistic personality disorder, of the compliant type (see the discussion of this personality disorder below). Her mood disorder began with severe anxiety and occasional episodes of violent temper; she was also tremendously impatient. Her compliant personality, formed in response to parental expectations, made it difficult for her to manage conflict—difficult for her to say no—which meant that her relationships with peers were shallow and unfulfilling. Her social anxiety exacerbated this problem. Her parents looked upon her as a model child—obedient, intelligent, and attractive—and did not see her distress. The presence of alcohol abuse in the family had entrenched a coping style of secret keeping, avoidance of conflict, and denial.*

*Charlotte's entry into substance abuse took place entirely without peer pressure, but it did occur as a response to social anxiety. Her use of alcohol was dangerously augmented by its capacity to relieve her anxiety and her capacity to drink large amounts of alcohol without apparent intoxication. Her alcohol abuse then undermined her mood stability. It is impossible to know now how her bipolar disorder would have developed without substance abuse, whether it would have become as severe as it is. Without abstinence, however, her mood could not be stabilized. Yet even when she stopped drinking, stabilizing her mood was still difficult because of the years of severe substance abuse. It will take several years of pharmacologic treatment together with the reestablishment of stable personal and professional relationships before her mood will be stable.*

*Charlotte needed the support, structure, and knowledge of AA members and the AA program to secure her abstinence, establish sobriety, and leave her free to return to work on adolescent developmental tasks. She was healthy enough to acknowledge these needs and tolerate the dependency they entailed. She did not use denial, a grandiose sense of omnipotence, or contempt to evade her need for this help.*

*Charlotte's personality is more stable and she has a greater capacity for connection than Maureen (discussed below). Her personality is termed narcissistic because her self-esteem is largely based on her ability to satisfy other people's expectations: that is, how she appears to other people. Psychotherapeutically, an important task is for her to distinguish between her authentic needs and the demands others place on her.*

## EATING DISORDERS

Eating disorders have a number of contributing causes. Like other consumption disorders they are fostered by problems with adolescent developmental tasks—especially those of intimacy and identity formation—but because they involve eating they are often also rooted in developmental failures at the earliest stage of development. The preponderance of eating disorders in girls is thought to be culturally as well as individually determined. However, in a child with bipolar disorder who has unstable blood sugar—usually accompanied by a family history of adult onset diabetes, obesity, or early cardiovascular disease—the stage is *metabolically* set for an eating disorder.

For a person with bipolar disorder, the physical sensation of low blood sugar can become confused with preexisting feelings of psychological emptiness and anxiety. An increase in blood sugar causes an increase in serotonin levels in the brain and consequently a temporary relief of anxiety, so eating can become a way of addressing both anxiety and psychological emptiness. Eating as a way of relieving psychological emptiness and anxiety occurs in boys as well as girls. Culturally, however, there is a far greater pressure on women to be thin, so that weight gain in an adolescent girl is accompanied by more distress. The adolescent's intense concern with physical perfection also exacerbates the problem, in some cases leading to fasting, purging, or compulsive exercise. In addition, the seasonal swings some bipolar children experience can cause depression and carbohydrate craving in the winter.

Whether a person moves toward anorexia (unrelieved fasting) or bulimia (recurrent bingeing on food most often followed by purging) is probably multiply determined—both family dynamics and genetic predisposition are thought to play a role. Anorexia in some cases is thought to be associated with obsessive-compulsive tendencies and stubbornness, bulimia with impulsivity, and both are associated with depression. Because eating disorders also involve early developmental problems, family dysfunction is almost always involved. The particular nature of those difficulties varies from one family to another. Questions have also been raised about a connection between eating disorders and sexual abuse. Because sexual abuse necessarily entails an injury to a person's capacity for intimacy, it is not surprising to find several consumption disorders associated with it.

Because eating disorders include biological factors, along with problems with intimacy and with family function, a combination of pharmacologic, individual, group, and sometimes family therapy is required in their treatment. In addition to psychic suffering, these disorders can cause substantial medical problems that not only can affect the person's life expectancy but can be life-threatening. A pediatrician or a specialist in adolescent medicine is usually a required member of the treatment team.

## Excessive Spending, Promiscuity, and Stealing

Excessive spending as a way of compensating for feelings of emptiness is a common type of consumption disorder, reaching epidemic proportions in an affluent society such as ours, to the point that it has become fashionable. Nonetheless, the practice fits Melanie Klein's psychological description of compulsive pleasure seeking as a manic defense against loss. When compulsive spending is seen in a person with bipolar disorder, however, mania and hypomania may give the behavior an additional biologic as well as psychological force. When this is the case, mood stabilization needs to accompany psychotherapeutic work.

Sexual promiscuity used to be, and probably still is, more common in men. However, in some adolescent circles young women use fellatio as a way of asserting control over boys and achieving status among peers. Like compulsive shopping, promiscuity has a certain level of social acceptance and glamour. Nonetheless, promiscuity is an attempt to substitute physical excitement for emotional intimacy. Moreover, there is usually a dimension of anger and contempt beneath the appearance of affection. Also, as with compulsive shopping, this behavior can take on additional biologic force in bipolar disorder, since hypersexuality can be part of both mania and hypomania.

Stealing, although it is obviously related to the other consumption disorders, has an aggressive, angry dimension to it, like some forms of promiscuity. There is a sense of triumph in the act as well as a satisfaction of neediness. Since the neediness and the anger are emotional, not economic, it is not surprising to find stealing among children raised in affluence. There is a difference between stealing that occurs in the latency years and stealing in adolescence. The adolescent's capacity for planning, appreciation of social consequences, and capacity for moral choice make stealing at this age a more serious problem. In assessing an adolescent with this behavior it is crucial to look for a sense of remorse. When remorse is absent, the degree of character pathology is far more serious. Stealing always requires psychiatric evaluation and is primarily treated psychotherapeutically, but it does not occur in isolation. Its treatment needs to be part of a larger set of psychotherapeutic goals.

## Gambling, Video Games, and the Internet

Gambling, gaming, and excessive use of the Internet are attempts to create or live in a world that competes with reality, where the normal consequences of behavior are magically suspended. Virtual experiences allow the person a potential power wholly unrelated to his real accomplishments. Obviously, like shopping, these activities are enjoyed in moderation by healthy children and adults. When they are motivated by a deep sense of inadequacy and become a substitute for social contact or real development in the world, they become a consumption disorder and are driven by the same developmental failures that drive the other consumption disorders.

Increasingly, psychiatrists are encountering children who spend excessive amounts of time playing video games or playing on the Internet. The problem, whether encountered in latency or adolescence, is associated with problems entering the peer group. The behavior has a more ominous quality in an adolescent than in a younger child, in part because it represents developmental failure occurring at a later age. Adolescents are also more capable of acting out the fantasies they pursue online or in a video game, making them potentially more dangerous to themselves and others. Because a child with bipolar disorder is at significant risk for the developmental failures that drive these behaviors, he may choose them as a way to compensate for feelings of loneliness and inadequacy. Some obsessive gambling is understood to have a biological dimension related to obsessive-compulsive disorder; another set of gamblers suffers from deficits in the activity of dopamine. I have seen gambling in bipolar patients as part of hypomanic pleasure seeking. Like most of the other consumption disorders, there are twelve-step programs that offer effective help to people able to accept it.

## HANDLING CONSUMPTION DISORDERS

If a consumption disorder has already reared its head, take it seriously. Helping your teen with it is much, much more than a problem of setting limits, although limit setting is required.

If the problem is caught in early adolescence, it may be helpful for you and your teen to go into family therapy. Later in adolescence, because your teen has (or needs to have) separated from you, family therapy is less effective. Family therapy must then be conducted separately from the adolescent. In both cases, however, individual and group therapy are needed for the adolescent. Failures in the peer group need to be addressed in a group; problems with intimacy are better treated individually.

The twelve-step programs are essential for many people with these disorders: they provide immediate emotional support, a transitional identity, and a clear structure within which first abstinence and then sobriety can be accomplished. It is no accident that the twelve-step programs that address the various consumption disorders all call themselves anonymous: their members enter with a crucial lack of identity, and the group's first healing act is to allow them to enter anonymously, that is, without an identity beyond membership in the group.

Adults who view substance abuse as an effect of peer pressure have it backward. Adolescents don't turn toward obsessive consumption from external pressure but from an *internal* emptiness, an emptiness that has been building long before their teenage years. Such adolescents find other empty peers with whom they consume.

Members of twelve-step programs often understand the pitfalls of these disorders and of recovery from them better than most people, including many physicians and therapists. It is important for a psychiatrist or therapist not trained in substance abuse to consult when a patient develops substance abuse. What is more, the psychiatric and psychotherapeutic treatment cannot be effective while substance abuse continues.

People with bipolar disorder may encounter a difficulty in some twelve-step groups because of the groups' opposition to the use of *any* medication. The bipolar adolescent with a consumption disorder most often requires medication, sometimes medications (like tranquilizers) with a potential for abuse. It is my experience that bipolar patients who are being effectively managed pharmacologically *and* are engaged in psychotherapeutic treatment seldom abuse their prescribed medications. A lack of pharmacologic treatment poses a greater risk than its presence. There are, however, twelve-step groups that recognize the need for medication and cooperate with psychiatrists to coordinate its use with their program. When there is a difficulty, it may be important for the psychiatrist to speak with his patient's sponsor. The help these programs offer should be prized.

Finding an appropriate twelve-step program is like finding any other kind of medical care. Professionals and organizations that specialize in the treatment of substance abuse are known throughout the medical community. The psychiatrist you are working with may not know what program to refer you to, but he or she will (or should) have a colleague who does. His or her job is to refer you to that colleague who will help you find an appropriate program or meeting.

The greatest obstacle to entering a twelve-step program is denial. Consumption disorders deny basic problems in the self or the family, and they are sustained by continued denial. The first of the twelve steps requires surrendering denial and accepting some measure of helplessness. This kind of surrender is particularly difficult for the bipolar adolescent because a sense of omnipotence and denial are such fundamental features of both adolescence and bipolar disorder.

Denial in bipolar disorder is worth expanding on here, for it is one of the illness's core symptoms and is almost always the first problem that must be confronted in psychotherapy. Denial of the illness, at whatever age it is encountered, is fundamentally an attempt to evade loss. As such it resembles psychologically a toddler's attempt to avoid an unrelenting *no*. Defenses of manic distraction, rage, and contempt all are brought into play. The goal of a therapist—or parent—in working with denial must be to help the adolescent acknowledge a loss of perfection and independence and begin mourning the illness. For this reason, reassurance cannot initially be helpful. Validation of the person's fear, anger, and sadness must come first.

In mourning, before sorrow and resignation can be reached, rage must be experienced, expressed, and validated. It is important to bear in mind that beneath an adolescent's nonchalance or contempt, beneath assertions of invulnerability, is rage at the unfairness of this illness.

A parallel mourning must also take place in the parent and may take place recurrently at each developmental stage. It is crucial for you to identify the source of your rage, lest it be directed at a caregiver, an educator, your child, or yourself. Moving through mourning gives you and your child a capacity to cope with the disorder and its effects. On the other side of mourning there is a tragic strength that accrues, if only the process can be borne.

## BEAR IN MIND

· As in the past, pick your battles carefully. Don't become provoked by your adolescent's dress, hair style, or even hair color. (Body piercing is an exception because it is not just a matter of appearance; it includes self-mutilation.) If there is a school dress code your child is breaking, let the school handle it, at least to begin with. Confine yourself to issues of development—schoolwork, peer relationships—and safety.

· If you have a partner, be willing to hand over a situation he or she can handle more effectively. As in the past, resolve disputes between parents privately and present a united position.

· Pay attention to your teen's anxieties. Some children with bipolar disorder still need your presence once in a while in going to sleep. Some clearly need your presence when doing homework.

· Keep an eye on any sleep disturbance. Don't let it go on for more than a few days without bringing it to her psychiatrist's attention.

· Develop a relationship with your child's guidance counselor. Let him or her know about challenges or special needs.

· Your child's school may need to know what medicines your child is taking, if they are administered at school. It is not appropriate for a teen to administer his own meds.

· On the other hand, your teen may be increasingly concerned about privacy in this regard. Speak with her psychiatrist to see if that privacy can be safely maintained by rescheduling doses.

· Know what is happening on the screen—video games, the Internet. Parental controls are appropriate, even if they are only partially successful. Violent video games, like scary movies, are not appropriate for some teens.

· Limit time on the screen—TV, computer (except for homework), video games. Limiting does not, however, mean eliminate!

· Unless it is absolutely necessary, don't violate your teen's privacy! Stay out of his e-mail; don't touch a diary or read an opened letter; knock before you enter his room; ask permission before going in when he isn't there. The need to clean the room is real, but there are times when even that can be secondary. An important exception is when you suspect drugs. Danger supersedes boundaries.

· The decision of whether to have a TV in the bedroom is important. Some teens use it as a blanket, for calm and comfort. Some teens can't regulate themselves in its presence.

· Preserve your teen's contacts with peers: phone calls, e-mail, instant messaging are crucial. Many teens IM constantly while doing homework. If they are getting the work done, don't interfere.

· Be ready for your teen to question her diagnosis or treatment. Questioning at this age is appropriate. Putting questions into words is a step in the right direction. Your teen's questions may be part of a struggle to accept her illness at a new level.

· If your teen—especially a girl with an eating disorder—has problems about her appearance, be matter-of-fact but limit your comments. These issues are rarely open to rational discussion.

· Curfews are appropriate, and they needn't conform to what other parents allow.

· Know the parents of your teen's friends; know how permissive they are; know how much supervision they provide when your teen is with them.

· When it's appropriate, let your teen separate. Another family may provide an important refuge or alternate experience.

· Handling money is an important issue. You should know how much your child is spending and where he gets the money. Learning to manage an allowance is obviously positive, if your teen is up to it. If your financial circumstances don't impose limits, you need to.

# CHAPTER TEN

# Late Adolescence

## *College and Other Moratoriums*

There is no specific age at which adolescence ends. For some, completing the developmental tasks of adolescence is one measure. However, there are people who settle on a career, marry, and have children who have achieved neither intimacy nor an authentic identity and who don't function like adults. On the other hand, some of the most talented people in history—Martin Luther, William Shakespeare, Bernard Shaw, Mahatma Gandhi—went into a holding pattern during their twenties and completed adolescent tasks only in their thirties, after which their productivity blossomed. Erik Erikson (who, in the 1950s, formulated the psychosocial concept of identity) described this pattern of development as a delayed identity crisis prior to which the person creates for himself a *moratorium* during which he avoids making a commitment to any particular identity and also avoids commitment in intimate relationships. The activity he pursues during the moratorium—in a job or in school—has the requirement of *not* leading to a specific goal. The purpose of the moratorium is to give him time to formulate an authentic identity, especially when there are significant conflicts that make the task more difficult.

Biologically, the frontal cortex reaches its full development in the early twenties, which means the apparatus of judgment is finally in place. Socially, an individual is expected by then to be well on the way to developing an identity: that is, professional, sexual, and moral choices have autonomy and integrity together with a sustained depth and level of commitment. As our society has become more prosperous, however, the available choices for careers and social roles have become more complex and educational demands more extensive (for those who can meet them). Consequently, adolescence has been prolonged, and there is often a need for a period of time during which a person who has reached physical and intellectual maturity can delay the final stages of personal definition. College is an institution socially authorized for this purpose. For other adolescents, less socially privileged or unwilling to undertake such an apprenticeship, the military can serve a similar purpose. It is also possible for a young person to work at a job that doesn't define him (and to which he is not committed) but which provides a time-out until he is ready to define himself. Currently it is not uncommon for a person to reach his thirtieth birthday without having completed adolescent business.

## AN IMPORTANTLY DEFERRED IDENTITY

Shakespeare married before the age of twenty and had three children before he took off for London to escape a premature set of commitments. There he spent a number of years as an actor—someone who plays at being someone he is not. During that moratorium he struggled with questions of how he fit into the sophisticated London scene, whether he would be a writer, and for whom he would write—the public, in the theater, or the nobility, as a poet with a patron. At the age of thirty he bought a share in an acting company, making a commitment to be not only an actor and writer but also an owner. The decision resulted in his spectacular literary accomplishments as well as his becoming wealthy and securing a title and coat of arms. At the same time, in both his comedies and tragedies, he challenged his audience's pieties and the emotional ground on which they stood, taking a moral as well as a professional stand.

## LEAVING OR STAYING

Under normal circumstances, going away to college is a freeing and expanding experience that assists development by creating a geographical separation that complements an emotional one, and expanding a person's social and cultural horizons at just the time they need to be. For a young adult with bipolar disorder, however, the decision of whether to go away to college or stay close to home can be complicated.

### GOING AWAY TO COLLEGE

For many young people, college represents the first definitive, prolonged separation from home. It is common for a college freshman to return home on break and unexpectedly realize that she is no longer *at home*. Home has become not only the college campus but also the society and tasks taking place there. Being able to form sustaining intimate relationships, exercise intellectual and moral independence, and at some point to find a professional direction have assumed crucial importance. In some ways these are the same tasks that took shape in earlier years—separation, intimacy, and identity—but now their developmental and personal urgency is increased.

Separation from home can be particularly strenuous for a person suffering from bipolar disorder. If she has suffered from separation anxiety or has had an intensified dependence on parents, she can find the first year of college particularly difficult. If she has also had difficulties establishing adequate relationships with peers, the separation is all the more difficult. She must take responsibility for the crucial tasks of self-regulation (sleeping, eating, and exercising), but the environment of college makes all of these things more difficult because of all-night cramming for exams, late-night philosophic discussions, responsibility for one's own diet, and a more or less complete lack of restraints on substance abuse.

As the choices leading to the formation of an identity become more urgent, the conflicts inherent in those choices assert themselves more forcefully: the risk of surpassing a parent or of acceding to his or her expectations is felt more painfully; the pressure to become an integrated part of society—and the risk of surrendering one's own values—becomes greater. Intense conflict with parents, school administrators, and society at large is common.

## LIVING ON ONE'S OWN: THE BIPOLAR ADOLESCENT'S CHALLENGES

For the average young person, living away from home can be a challenging experience. But the young person with bipolar disorder faces extra hurdles as he struggles to maintain his independence and his mental, emotional, and physical equilibrium. Certain requirements, such as taking medication, attending therapy, continuing developmental tasks that others completed long ago—managing aggression, handling conflicts with authority, managing time, organizing and presenting thoughts, and establishing personal and sexual intimacy—can complicate an already difficult phase of life.

### TAKING MEDICATION

The bipolar adolescent, who up to this time has had parental supervision of his medication, must now obtain it and take it regularly on his own. Psychologically this requires a new level of acceptance of the illness and the need for medication. Old feelings of shame and negative comparison to peers can assume new intensity. Resistance to taking medication can come in the form of deliberate discontinuation or forgetting to take (or obtain) medication. Episodes of substance abuse can disrupt the therapeutic effects of the medication or interact dangerously with it—in both ways alcohol is a big offender. These difficulties need to be addressed psychotherapeutically: the behavior needs to be understood, and the loss that the illness causes must be mourned again, this time at a deeper level.

## Continuing Therapy

Going away to college commonly disrupts the relationship with a psychotherapist and psychiatrist. The trust inherent in these relationships develops over time and cannot be easily transferred. It is important for a psychiatrist to help the student find someone in the new locale and to help coordinate the transition. Even when there is a person of equivalent expertise, the student must tell her painful story yet once more and reestablish a relationship of trust and understanding. In some areas there may not be an equivalent person, and psychotherapy and pharmacology must be managed with phone consultations—as long as there is also a person at the college who is in regular contact with the student and with her caregivers. The student needs to be *seen:* there are important things—weight loss or gain, fatigue, eye contact—that can't be assessed over the phone. A student can skip medication and psychotherapy can become less regular at a time when she needs more, not less, support.

# Working on Old Developmental Tasks

To make matters more difficult, the college student with bipolar disorder often needs to master earlier developmental tasks while taking on newer ones.

## Separation and Self-Regulation

Separation from home and self-regulation cannot be taken for granted. A student who has had panic attacks, has become enmeshed with his family, or has difficulty forming new relationships quickly feels isolated, adrift, and anxious at college. Sleeping can also be a problem: due to separation anxiety, anxiety generated by academic problems, a lack of structure making it hard for the student to keep to a regular schedule, and sometimes an uncooperative or hostile roommate. Eating regularly and maintaining stable blood sugar are more difficult without a kitchen and a stocked refrigerator, to say nothing of a mom who does the shopping, selects and cooks the food, and keeps after her child to eat.

## Managing Aggression

Some young adults with bipolar disorder must again deal with managing aggression in college, particularly if they have moved through their earlier years outside the peer group and the mastery of aggression has eluded them. At the start of college, a person who draws attention to himself as anxious and withdrawn generates anxiety in other students who are struggling with their own (less obvious) anxiety. On occasion these students may try to bolster their own self-esteem by playing pranks on the loner. If the bipolar student is passive, he may be repeatedly attacked; or he may have an explosive, violent response that further alienates peers. When the bipolar student finally manages to begin a closer relationship, difficulties handling conflict and aggression can cause an abrupt and angry end to the relationship when a powerful conflict occurs.

## Establishing Personal and Sexual Intimacy

The new degree of separation that college entails also makes personal and sexual intimacy more pressing needs, which, if they cannot be met, increase the risk for depression, consumption disorders, and consequent academic difficulties. For a person who is able to take advantage of them, college offers an abundance of opportunities for personal contact. The person unable to make these contacts, however, feels all the more isolated and draws negative attention to herself, an attention she is painfully aware of.

If a person is unable to manage personal intimacy, sexual intimacy feels unreachable, especially when her peers are having sexual relationships all around her. The heightened sensitivity of many bipolar adolescents makes this circumstance all the more painful. When the bipolar student does begin a sexual relationship, there is a risk that intimacy may prove unbearable. The end of the relationship may then occasion a severe depression. In fact, the first major depression for a person with bipolar disorder often occurs around the loss of an early relationship.

## COLLEGE WRITING

Given the impulsive thought processes of a bipolar mind, mastery of the basic skills of writing and organized thinking are more difficult. The very task of expository writing requires subordination of one idea to another and a developed sense of the sequence in which thoughts should be presented. In order to be an author, one must exercise authority over one's own thoughts. But the bipolar adolescent may well have a long history of being unable to tolerate any kind of subordination, including that of his own thoughts. An unruliness similar to that which affected his behavior as a child may now interfere with his ability to write. Difficulties contending with and assuming authority can also get in the way of the task of documenting an argument: college-level work demands that a student consult scholarly authorities, incorporate their ideas, and begin to write with authority himself. Finally, some bipolar adolescents are intimidated by the thought of their writing being judged—the authority of the professor can be a paralyzing presence.

## MANAGING TIME

The management of time, another subtle authority, is also a crucial requirement in college. As we have seen, however, a bipolar child can come to adolescence with a defective sense of time. Getting to bed on time, getting up for class, managing large amounts of reading, planning the work that must be done on longer projects, and managing social demands all require an awareness of and a submission to the limits of time. Impulsiveness and a tendency to get lost in the present moment are characteristic of some bipolar adolescents. In order to have time, a person must *take* time from one thing in order to do another, one must subordinate—a challenge for the bipolar student.

## Staying Home

For a bipolar adolescent who is not up to these challenges, staying home (or at least closer to home) may be a better choice. At this age, however, staying home can intensify a young adult's struggle for independence and autonomy. There is a risk of sliding back into an inappropriate dependency or of intense conflicts regarding autonomy. The young woman will suffer a burden of shame for not being able to separate in an age-appropriate way. The presence of a college-age child in the household also places a demand on parents to manage an appropriate distance, not only from college responsibilities but also from personal relationships, especially sexual ones. A related difficulty for parents is avoiding the pitfall of treating the adolescent like a child whose time is at their disposal. Expectations that the adolescent contribute to the household need to be carefully assessed and clarified.

### A Deferred Separation

At the age of fifteen, **THOMAS** was referred to me by a colleague following a hospitalization for severe depression and anxiety. Although he was quite intelligent, Thomas had a particularly difficult time during elementary school: he suffered from severe separation anxiety, intense social anxiety, and a complex learning disorder. He was attacked by peers and excluded from the group. He had hoped high school would provide deliverance from these problems; instead, they intensified. Increased academic demands, social anxiety, anger, and shame brought on panic attacks and school refusal; conflicts with his parents over these matters also became more severe. During the winter of his sophomore year he was hospitalized for depression. A diagnosis of bipolar disorder was made, and he was discharged on a complex array of medications that compromised his thinking and caused excessive weight gain.

I made adjustments in Thomas's medication, and I reviewed his developmental, family history, and psychological testing, and explained to Thomas's parents the complex biologic, cognitive, and social difficulties he faced. I proposed a pharmacologic strategy and supported my colleague's recommendation for individual psychotherapy, family therapy, and group therapy. Junior year was an excruciating struggle for Thomas and his family, but during the spring of that year Thomas discovered his talent as a runner. With the help of a coach who took a special interest in him, by his senior year Thomas had been chosen as captain of the cross-country team and was one of the leading runners in his state. His academic work improved as well. His peer relationships were still extremely tenuous, however; Thomas attended an adolescent group ambivalently and intermittently.

Thomas began at a college about one hundred miles from home, but he still suffered severe separation anxiety and felt isolated socially. His relationship with his therapist was disrupted, and an attempt to begin with another doctor did not work out. Although he began his first term competently, by November he felt overwhelmed in several of his courses. By taking incompletes and finishing them during the winter break, he managed to get fairly good grades by term's end. He entered the second term anxiously and somewhat depressed. By that time his anxiety and social awkwardness had made him a target for other students' attacks. Social humiliation was more than he could bear: he was unable to continue the term and returned home. I assumed both his pharmacologic and his psychotherapeutic care.

Intensive psychotherapy and complex psychopharmacology enabled Thomas to make a slow recovery. By the summer he was able to find work as a counselor in a day camp, and that fall he enrolled in a local college while living at home. This arrangement allowed him to continue face-to-face psychotherapeutic work with me. Even with that support he suffered bouts of severe anxiety over academic work and struggled with depression during the winter. Nonetheless, he did well academically. His social relationships remained tenuous.

On the basis of his superior academic performance, he was able to gain admission to an excellent college—this one five hundred miles from home. There he joined a fraternity and was much less socially isolated. It seemed as if he had successfully made the separation from home. However, he now began having trouble completing written assignments. His difficulties had nothing to do with his academic capabilities. Rather, they were caused by an accentuated fear of his professors' judgment together with a magnification of their demands, which left him immobilized with anxiety and shame. He struggled through the first term, accumulating several incompletes. By the end of the first month of the second term he again had to return home, more discouraged and savagely angry at himself.

Again he entered intensive psychotherapy, but this time he made slower progress. His anger, humiliation, and guilt were paralyzing. He was barely able to work that summer and unable to make up his incomplete courses. That fall he enrolled in a community college and again lived at home. Once more he suffered severe anxiety about meeting academic requirements, and once again his grades were excellent. He also participated successfully in the school newspaper. His social anxiety persisted, however, and despite his participation in the paper, he ended the term with no lasting relationships.

His psychotherapy was still at an impasse. Thomas's severe conflicts with his father came up again and again, but interpretation of them was not helpful. One day, however, it occurred to me to examine Thomas for dissociative symptoms. His lack of eye contact, cognitive difficulties, profound shame, paralyzing fear of authority, tendency to space out, and persistent difficulties with peer relationships looked at as a constellation of symptoms suggested emotional trauma. The results of my examination showed moderately severe dissociation. Approaching Thomas's many difficulties as the results of overwhelming fear occurring repeatedly during his childhood proved more helpful than anything in the analytic approach I had tried before. Thomas experienced an alleviation of guilt, an improvement in eye contact, and above all relief at being able to understand his difficulties as an intrusion on his personality rather than part of it.

His writing was freed up that fall and he felt able to declare a major. He passed the winter without a depression, although not without intense anxiety. He was still very far from knowing what would become of him after college, and farther still from achieving intimacy, but he and I had a new way of understanding and working with his difficulties. He remained under pharmacologic and psychotherapeutic care.

*Thomas suffers from bipolar II disorder, complicated by seasonal depression, severe separation anxiety, intense social anxiety, panic attacks, a learning disorder, and a narcissistic personality disorder with an extremely punitive conscience. It took me a long time to discover that he also suffered moderately severe dissociative symptoms, as a result of long-standing emotional trauma.*

*When first seen, my task was to manage his anxiety and sleep disturbance with medications that did not cause weight gain. A major tranquilizer was discontinued in favor of a mood stabilizer and benzodiazepines, both for sleep and for his recurrent panic attacks. At that time he required a moderately high dose of benzodiazepines to manage his anxiety. He required the use of an antidepressant (an SSRI) as well. At the same time he was in individual psychotherapy and group therapy together with periodic parental counseling. Even with these supports, Thomas finished tenth grade and made it through eleventh grade with great difficulty: intermittent school refusal, recurrent panic attacks when going to school, difficulty completing assignments, and frequent family discord.*

*Thomas's athletic success, beginning in eleventh and culminating in twelfth grade, helped him regain control of his body, lost in the hospital, and built his self-esteem, although it did not improve his relationships with peers. At a time when he was in great conflict with his father, his coach proved to be a crucial mentor who escaped the anger directed at his father and at times at his psychotherapist.*

*During his first years of college, unresolved problems from latency— management of aggression, emotional separation from parents, establishment of intimate relationships—were disabling. Because of his powerfully ambivalent attitude toward authority and his lack of basic trust, Thomas also had difficulty establishing a new psychotherapeutic relationship. Fortunately, maintenance of his established relationship with me, by phone, was possible. When he returned home, the development of our relationship allowed him to recover from an initial defeat. His return home and attendance at a local college also allowed him to prepare for a more successful separation the following year.*

*As earlier problems were resolved, however, late adolescent conflicts with authority began to emerge. Thomas's powerful desire to satisfy other people's expectations made his distrust of authority excruciating. At times he completely abandoned his responsibilities; at other times the guilt and shame he felt were paralyzing; at still other times his internal conflict was so great that his thinking became disorganized. At the same time he had to contend with recurrent seasonal depression in the winter. The combination of his developmental struggle and his seasonal vulnerability brought on a particularly severe episode of depression and anxiety. It became necessary to use a monoamine oxidase inhibitor (MAOI)—a potent antidepressant that also had a powerful effect in calming anxiety. This medication required him to observe a special diet.*

*Thomas's persistent difficulties with earlier developmental tasks made his treatment especially difficult. His most important break-through psychotherapeutically came, however, when I recognized that the hypersensitivity common in bipolar patients had made his develop-mental experiences not just difficult but traumatic. Emotional trauma consists of an overwhelming of normal physiologic and psychological defenses, resulting in lasting symptoms of numbness, hyperarousal, and shame. These symptoms can be triggered by situations that faintly resemble an original trauma, which makes them hard to account for and often confusing. Seeing Thomas as both bipolar and traumatized helped explain symptoms that were complicated by—but not ac-counted for—changes in his mood. Thomas's story is particularly in-structive because none of his developmental experiences, even though they were hurtful, are normally considered traumatic—but the hyper-sensitivity characteristic of some bipolar patients made them over-whelming.*

## Sexual, Physical, and Emotional Abuse, Social Deprivation, and Academic Failure Overcome by a Brilliant and Resilient Woman

JEANETTE left home, a small town in the West, at eighteen to es-cape a childhood and adolescence filled with emotional and sexual abuse. Both her parents suffered from bipolar disorder, but that was the least of her problems. Her mother was erratic, immature, and unpredictably emotionally abusive; her stepfather abused her sexu-ally from the age of twelve. High school was a series of academic fail-ures: she managed to graduate by virtue of her wits rather than her work. Before she left home, Jeanette had already had one pregnancy and had placed her child with a distant relative. Originally quite beau-tiful, like many women who suffer sexual abuse, she began putting on weight.

She went east and joined the army, where she acquired a mea-sure of self-esteem and some recognition for her tenacity and intel-ligence. While in the army she married but was divorced within two years. She was, nonetheless, able to secure an entry-level position in a large corporation, where she worked for an executive who rec-ognized her abilities and took an interest in her. She received several promotions and at the same time used her health insurance to begin psychiatric treatment.

I diagnosed her with bipolar disorder, ADD, and post-traumatic stress disorder (PTSD) with moderate dissociative symptoms. Bio-logically she was able to tolerate a stimulant along with a mood sta-bilizer, but, despite recurrent winter depressions, she was never able to tolerate an antidepressant. During periods of depression and stress, including the stress of success, she had frequent dissociative episodes during which she blanked out and didn't remember the passage of time.

I insisted on psychotherapeutic as well as pharmacologic care. Psychotherapy focused on the articulation and emotional recounting of her early abuse together with validation of the suffering she con-tinued to undergo; the treatment also provided a place where she could safely express her rage and shame. I also acknowledged and encouraged her growing skills and professional competence. She occasionally disappeared from treatment without notice. Although she had some limited relationships with women, she remained somewhat isolated and had no sustained relationships with men. Despite these difficulties, she had a boisterous sense of humor, abundant energy, generosity, and a striking capacity for empathy. In quiet ways she gave of herself to friends and to social projects. The strength of her will showed in her ability to quit smoking amid the emotional struggles of treatment. Her attempts to lose weight were, in contrast, not successful.

Initially she could not follow suggestions that she continue her education and was convinced she would fail. As her professional success increased—including success at a course to become a notary—she was able to overcome her fears and begin work in an online college. (The privacy of that academic route gave her relief from accumulated shame.) As it happened, her tuition was partially paid by her employer, and she found to her surprise that she was given significant credit for her life experience. Most surprising was her discovery that she was an extremely competent student. Within a year she had earned her associate degree magna cum laude. She later told me, however, that she would never have been able to attend a regular college—the fear of embarrassment and face-to-face contact would have been unbearable. By now she had proved her competence to herself, saved enough money to buy a condominium, and secured a place she could define as hers. She continued with her college education, obtaining her bachelor's degree, also magna cum laude.

Intimacy is still a problem for her. Shame keeps her from forming relationships with people of her own caliber, and an intimate sexual relationship with a man is a distant goal. She has, however, reconnected with her brother, confronted her abusive stepfather, and established a growing relationship with her daughter. Her mood is stable but she requires continued pharmacologic and psychotherapeutic care.

*Jeanette suffers from bipolar II disorder with seasonal depression, ADD, and the effects of severe sexual, emotional, and physical abuse. She is, however, one of those remarkable people who have come through a horrible childhood ordeal not unhurt but, nonetheless, resilient. Her positive bipolar qualities include her gregarious personality, quick wit, and high energy level. She also has an aggressiveness and ability to set limits with people that are unusual in victims of profound abuse. She suffers from marked dissociative symptoms and searing memories of her abuse. Her anxiety is not apparent to most people, but she experiences intrusive thoughts and the intense shame seen in many people suffering from PTSD. Like Grace, her bipolar disorder is made worse by antidepressants, even when combined with a mood stabilizer; she is, however, able to tolerate a stimulant. Her oscillation includes seasonal swings but not premenstrual symptoms.*

*She is an example of a child who suffers more from her parents' mood disorders (and substance abuse) than from her own. The abuse she suffered severely damaged her self-esteem and her capacity for sexual intimacy, but she retained to an unusual extent a capacity for self-regulation. Her ability to have stable relationships personally and professionally separates her from those victims of abuse and bipolar disorder who develop a borderline personality (see discussion pages 232–235). In spite of her family history, Jeanette has also managed to avoid substance abuse: her self-regulation and her more stable personal relationships help explain her ability to do this. By contrast, like many women who are victims of sexual abuse, Jeanette has suffered weight gain, possibly as a protection against sexual approach, possibly also as a result of the change trauma causes in the cortisol response to stress, which disrupts the effects of insulin on the metabolism of carbohydrates.*

*Developmentally, Jeanette used the army and relatively menial employment as a shelter until she could develop her strengths in preparation for the construction of an authentic identity. A mentoring relationship with an executive and a psychotherapeutic relationship helped compensate for a profound lack of parenting until mood stability, success in her occupation, and increasing self-esteem allowed her to begin the process of discovering and developing her talents. Despite tremendous gains in self-esteem, personal function, and a developing sense of identity, her severe abuse has left her with enormous shame and continues to interfere with her capacity for intimacy.*

## BEAR IN MIND

· Finding the proper distance can be particularly difficult both for you and your college-age child. The amount of space needed differs not only with different persons but also from one time to another. Mothers, who are acutely aware of their child's internal vulnerabilities, have a more difficult time finding the proper distance. This circumstance—once again—makes Dad's role even more important.

· Each developmental stage carries with it a potential disappointment about the difference between a bipolar child and his peers. As he matures, the disappointment is increasingly felt and acknowledged by the adolescent as well as by his parents. For the adolescent, this acknowledgment comes in stages, accompanied by various levels of denial and sensitivity. It is particularly important at this time for you to avoid comparing him to his peers, openly or in your expectations.

· At this stage, bearing the passage of time can be an ordeal for an adolescent struggling with bipolar disorder, particularly one who is behind on developmental tasks. She is troubled not so much by an inability to wait (impulsivity) but by an inability to feel comfortable in time itself. She has trouble bearing a lack of direction or a lack of accomplishment—compared to where she *should* be.

· Deans and college guidance counselors can be key figures to work with in late adolescence. They can help get the student extra time on examinations and papers or, if needed, help him drop a course or arrange a leave of absence. When therapy is being conducted on the phone, a guidance counselor can be a valuable observer. Frequently a bipolar college student has difficulty approaching people in authority and may (inaccurately) assume they will be punitive. He needs help with this.

· Be aware that your adolescent may temporarily need to withdraw entirely from school in a therapeutic retreat. This may be occasioned by a severe change in mood, accumulated overdue academic work, or social difficulties. Usually a college is more than willing to take a student back when she has recovered. The retreat may need to go on for an extended period of time, even years, while the adolescent gathers self-esteem and a sense of accomplishment that allows her to accept the task of apprenticeship and the circumstance of being judged.

# CHAPTER ELEVEN

# Diagnoses That May Accompany Bipolar Disorder

Because bipolar disorder can be accompanied by other conditions—ADD and ADHD, panic attacks, obsessive-compulsive disorder, various learning disorders, substance abuse, an eating disorder, or a personality disorder—it must sometimes be recognized in the context of these conditions. Addressing bipolar disorder when it occurs together with these conditions is particularly important because treatment of bipolar disorder usually must precede treatment of the accompanying problem.

## ATTENTION DEFICIT DISORDER AND ATTENTION-DEFICIT/ HYPERACTIVITY DISORDER

ADD and ADHD are defined as sets of symptoms rather than as specific neurological conditions. The official list of those symptoms is defined in *DSM-IV,* published by the American Psychiatric Association.

## *DSM-IV* CRITERIA FOR ADD/ADHD

Six (or more) of the following symptoms of *inattention:*

· often fails to give close attention to details or makes careless mistakes in schoolwork, work, or other activities
· often has difficulty sustaining attention in tasks or play activities
· often does not seem to listen when spoken to directly
· often does not follow through on instructions and fails to finish schoolwork or chores (not due to oppositional behavior)
· often avoids, dislikes, or is reluctant to engage in tasks that require sustained mental effort (such as schoolwork or homework)
· often loses things necessary for tasks or activities
· is often easily distracted by extraneous stimuli
· is often forgetful in daily activities

Six (or more) of the following symptoms of *hyperactivity-impulsivity:*

### HYPERACTIVITY

· often fidgets with hands or feet or squirms in seat
· often leaves seat in classroom or in other situations in which remaining seated is expected
· often runs about or climbs excessively in situations in which it is inappropriate
· often has difficulty playing quietly
· acts as if "driven by a motor"

### IMPULSIVITY

· often blurts out answers before questions have been completed
· often has difficulty awaiting turn
· often interrupts or intrudes on others

ADHD is defined as meeting criteria for *both* inattention and hyperactivity. ADD/ADHD—Inattentive Type is defined as only meeting criteria for inattention. ADHD—Hyperactive-Impulsive Type is defined as meeting only the criteria for impulsivity.

These symptoms are required to have been present at least since age seven, to be present in at least two situations (e.g., home and school), and to cause significant impairment in social or academic functioning.

Parents of a child with ADHD might say, "Right from the start he was kicking in the womb; he can't pay attention or sit still in school; he distracts the class; he chews his pencils; he can't sit through a meal; he is going from one end of the day to the next, and has a motor mouth!" The parents of a child with ADD might say, "She has her head in the clouds; she loses everything; her room and school bag are a mess; she never listens!" As the criteria suggest, the boundary between ADD and ADHD is not always a sharp one, but it is important not to overlook a child who is quietly adrift. For example, girls are often overlooked as suffering from this condition—because they tend to be less disruptive, their difficulties with attention are often missed.

Many of the symptoms of ADD/ADHD are typical to some degree of all children; what is different is the degree in affected children. Certain symptoms stand out: difficulty sustaining play, difficulty carrying through on things (when there is no question of oppositional behavior), or losing important items that the child (as distinct from the adult) values. What is also significant is the degree to which these difficulties impair a child's ability to carry on normal developmental tasks. The child with ADD/ADHD will continue to suffer from these difficulties beyond an age when they typically resolve in other children.

Children with ADD or ADHD experience difficulties that are not strictly part of the syndrome: school failure, decreased self-esteem, a deterioration of relationships with adults in authority, and eventually a habit of doing things to get people off their back rather than getting the task done or getting help to do it. I see this last trait most commonly in adolescents who have lived with the disorder for years, and especially those in whom it was not diagnosed early enough. They have a particularly worrisome problem because the defense of getting around things has become an entrenched part of their character.

There has been much public attention focused on the dramatic increase in the diagnosis of ADD/ADHD, particularly its treatment with stimulants. It is important to emphasize, however, that for the majority of children with the syndrome of ADD/ADHD, stimulants can have a dramatically positive effect not just on their school performance but also on their development as a whole. Studies show that, far from increasing the risk of substance abuse, there is a lower rate of substance abuse in children with ADD/ADHD who are treated with stimulants than in children who have the syndrome and are not treated. Properly used, stimulants are a flexible and quickly effective remedy for a condition that is potentially disabling both in its immediate impact and in its long-term effects on a child's development. Stimulants may be overprescribed, but this circumstance does not discount their ability to help children with ADD/ADHD cope, achieving success at school and at home. The potential danger of stimulants used to treat a child with bipolar disorder is not a reason to reconsider their use generally, or even in those bipolar patients who can tolerate them.

## ADD AND ADHD ON THE RISE

It seems like everybody is being diagnosed with ADD or ADHD. Although this diagnosis and its treatment have been beneficial for many children, the dramatic increase in labeling children ADD/ADHD has caused concern among medical professionals and laypeople. Why are there so many more kids with ADD or ADHD today than there were, say, ten years ago?

· New treatments for a disorder help increase professional awareness of that disorder and consequently their diagnosis of it. (This
has also been the case with bipolar disorder and obsessive-
compulsive disorder.)

· For reasons that are not fully understood, there has been an increase in several psychiatric illnesses in the past two decades—
depression, bipolar disorder, and obsessive-compulsive disorder
—not completely explained by the increased awareness and ability
to treat them.

· Parents want their children to have every possible advantage
and so seek treatment for a child who seems to have more than
usual trouble paying attention, being organized, or sustaining
motivation.

· The use of medications for ADD and ADHD can also benefit
teachers, allowing them to focus on teaching rather than taking
care of behavioral or motivational problems. In fact, it's often a
teacher who brings up the question of medicating a child.

· Our society has become increasingly willing to accept the benefits of psychiatric medication as the efficacy and variety of medications available have increased. More and more people have
been helped or know someone who has been helped by a psychiatric medication.

## CONFUSING BIPOLAR DISORDER WITH ADD OR ADHD

The danger of confusing bipolar disorder with ADD/ADHD has
increased with the rise in frequency with which ADD/ADHD is
being diagnosed and treated. *There are no pharmacologic treatments
for ADD/ADHD that don't pose some risk for a bipolar child,* so the
distinction between the disorders is important. The confusion of the
two conditions is common for several reasons: bipolar disorder and

ADD/ADHD have overlapping symptoms, ADD/ADHD is also present in some children with bipolar disorder, bipolar disorder itself varies in its appearance and the age when a child becomes symptomatic, and, finally, many of the physicians treating ADD/ADHD are pediatricians and neurologists who don't regularly encounter bipolar disorder.

*Symptoms Present in Both ADD/ADHD and Bipolar Disorder*

- hyperactivity
- distractability
- impulsivity
- difficulty following rules or behavioral limits
- talkativeness
- difficulty following through on certain tasks
- a lack of contact with what is being said

## CHILDREN AND ADULTS WITH BIPOLAR DISORDER HAVE A SEPARATE TYPE OF ADD/ADHD

Resemblances between ADD/ADHD and bipolar disorder can be further complicated by the fact that many people with bipolar disorder suffer from their own version of ADD, but also have tremendous ability to concentrate in some circumstances. Children with the more common version of ADD/ADHD cannot concentrate intensely, have difficulty *staying on track,* and tend to be distracted by the *external* environment: activity in the room, what's happening outside a window, a strange noise. Children with bipolar disorder, in contrast, have difficulty *changing tracks,* and they tend to be distracted by their *internal* environment: they can often focus intensely on something that interests them but have difficulty when they are asked to stop one thing and move on to another. In these cases of bipolar disorder, it is not just a matter of the children's symptoms resembling ADD/ADHD; they have a particular form of the problem—and their symptoms can benefit from the same medications.

However, those same medications, if not used cautiously, can aggravate bipolar disorder.

## Bipolar Disorder Is an Evolving Diagnosis, Especially in Children

The diagnosis of bipolar disorder in children is evolving: children who are now recognized as suffering from the condition would not have received the diagnosis as little as five years ago. Also, like a number of other medical conditions, bipolar disorder has different symptoms at different ages, and even children of the same age can have different symptoms. What is more, a child without obvious symptoms of bipolar disorder may be vulnerable to the condition if stressed with medications used to treat ADD/ADHD.

## ADD/ADHD Is Often Diagnosed by Physicians Not Familiar with Bipolar Disorder

Because its appearance can be so variable, physicians not used to treating bipolar disorder, especially childhood bipolar disorder, can have difficulty recognizing it. Many physicians diagnosing and treating ADD/ADHD are family practitioners, pediatricians, or neurologists who don't regularly encounter bipolar disorder. Additionally, many clinicians diagnosing ADD/ADHD make the diagnosis on the basis of a list of symptoms or a continuous performance test without examining developmental and family history (except for assessing the presence of ADD/ADHD). This method of diagnosis can overlook accompanying symptoms and details of developmental and family history that suggest the presence of bipolar disorder.

## Distinguishing Bipolar Disorder from ADD or ADHD

There are, however, a number of features that clearly distinguish bipolar disorder from uncomplicated ADD/ADHD:

- emotional intensity
- elevated or depressed mood
- oscillations of mood and activity level
- intense anxiety
- severe oppositional behavior
- deliberate destructiveness
- a sleep disturbance, before or after initiation of a stimulant and especially as an infant
- a history of nightmares or night terrors
- a family history of bipolar disorder or depression

All this being said, there are children who have a form of ADD/ADHD who benefit from conventional treatments, and become symptomatic with bipolar disorder only later—during adolescence or following pregnancy. I have also seen young adults (for example, Grace, pages 148–154) who during childhood did not appear to have ADD/ADHD but after becoming symptomatic with bipolar disorder in early adolescence developed the type of ADD/ADHD particular to bipolar disorder—with difficulties carrying through on tasks and increased impulsiveness, which make it more difficult to perform academically. These symptoms can be present in the absence of depression or a hypomanic episode.

## Oppositional Defiant Disorder

The difficulty children with bipolar disorder have tolerating *no,* and the difficulty parents often have holding the situation with them, can lead to oppositional defiant disorder, which is seen in the child's behavior in school, with other adults, and even with peers. To qualify for this diagnosis, these behavioral difficulties must be persistent and must interfere with the child's ability to carry on developmental tasks.

Although not all children with oppositional defiant disorder have bipolar disorder, these children all have in common an inability to manage the word *no*. In a bipolar child, this can be attributed to the child's intense rage or the difficulty he has tolerating intrusion into the flow of his mental life. Oppositional defiant disorder can also be the result of the chronic collisions with parents and authority that befall a child with ADHD. When those conflicts are not handled well, or when they become the predominant interaction between the child and adults, a child who is unable to satisfy authority may resolve to defy it. The child's defiant behavior may be fueled by a sense of isolation from adults and by accumulated anger and disappointment. Oppositional behavior can also be the result of family dysfunction or of parents who incite rather than quell their child's rage. Finally, oppositional behavior can be the result of physical or sexual abuse, especially in boys. It is not necessary to assume a manic state or a bipolar disposition to account for widespread conflict with authority. It is important with such a child, however, to rule out a mood disorder as a contributing factor.

## *DSM-IV* CRITERIA FOR OPPOSITIONAL DEFIANT DISORDER

A pattern of negativistic, hostile, and defiant behavior lasting at least six months, during which four (or more) of the following are present:

- often loses temper
- often argues with adults
- often actively defies or refuses to comply with adults' requests or rules
- often deliberately annoys people
- often blames others for his or her mistakes or misbehavior
- often touchy or easily annoyed by others
- often angry and resentful
- often spiteful or vindictive

The two cases you will now read about are both children with oppositional defiant disorder. Maureen developed more severe difficulties because she was more vulnerable biologically, her parents had more trouble setting limits, and she successfully resisted treatment. Eric had a better outcome, even though there was serious early neglect and a more fragmented family, because he received more comprehensive treatment earlier and was less vulnerable biologically.

## A Severely Oppositional Girl

MAUREEN was an adopted girl of ten whose development was reported to have been normal until she was about two. At that age several problems became apparent: severe oppositional behavior (trouble with the word *no*), a high level of anxiety, and extreme tactile sensitivity. Competent psychotherapeutic care was begun at age four, and for a time Maureen progressed well in treatment. In addition to help with her behavior, her therapist identified learning difficulties subtly affecting Maureen's ability to comprehend language.

Conflict arose, however, between Maureen's parents regarding discipline: her father had little patience for Maureen's tantrums and he became enraged himself and punitive; Maureen's mother was more consistent, but she was less frequently at home and her interventions were often superseded by her spouse. Maureen's father became increasingly impatient with his daughter and reacted to Maureen very differently on different occasions. Maureen became more unpredictable herself, not knowing what to expect. Her parents began having more severe arguments, increasing her insecurity.

By the time she was eight, Maureen's oppositional behavior had become so severe that it was often difficult to get her to go to school, and when she did attend, she refused to participate in activities or attempt assigned tasks. She was falling behind socially and academically. A pharmacologic consultation was made. Maureen initially responded well to an antidepressant (her tantrums became less frequent and less intense), but these benefits deteriorated after six months: Maureen became worse, with major tantrums and explosive episodes of anger. Her anxiety also continued to be very high. A second consultation resulted in the use of a mood stabilizer, which was partially helpful, but Maureen had difficulties with the side effects of sedation. Her mood never stabilized, and her oppositional behavior continued, frequently disrupting family activities.

Maureen continued to have problems in school: her presence became more and more disruptive to the class; at home she adamantly refused to do homework. Other children began to withdraw from Maureen: her tantrums and her disruption of class activities made them uncomfortable and angry. Her teachers also reached a limit to their tolerance and in their ability to help Maureen.

An attempt to improve Maureen's peer relationships by sending her away to camp was unsuccessful. Maureen could not manage her anxiety or the limits camp imposed, and, as an adopted child, she perceived separation as abandonment. At the same time, an impending divorce between her parents angered and frightened her. As an adopted child, the disruption of her family was particularly threatening. Finally, like many parents, Maureen's had mixed feelings about pharmacologic intervention. The side effects Maureen had suffered and their uncertainty about her diagnosis made it difficult for them to accept recommendations. Their hesitation fortified Maureen's resistance.

In junior high school, Maureen was transferred to a school specializing in children with severe emotional problems. With the help of the school's skilled faculty, their consistent but flexible expectations, and their sincere interest, Maureen began to improve: she was able to accept some limits and perform academic tasks. Maureen's increasing academic success then bolstered her self-confidence, enhancing her ability to tolerate limits. Her mother was even able to get her to attend a summer program to further improve her academic skills. Under the guidance of the school, together with parental counseling, her parents also began cooperating more effectively. Problems with anxiety, oppositional behavior outside of school, and peer relationships persisted, however. Maureen's compliance with medication was erratic.

At about this time Maureen became intensely involved in collecting Yu-Gi-Oh! cards, but her collecting had a desperate quality and she put relentless pressure on her parents to buy her rarer (and expensive) cards. She had tantrums in which she demanded an expensive card: she felt entitled to have it and believed she had been mistreated when she was refused. Questions began to arise about whether Maureen was stealing money to buy additional cards.

Maureen continued in individual therapy, but her relationship with her therapist was tenuous: she was frequently unconnected, distant, and bored, and she pretended to sleep; at other times she was warm and related and allowed herself to be fed and to explore different foods. Occasionally she talked about a matter of pressing emotional importance, but she could not connect what happened in one session with what went on in another. In treatment, Maureen functioned at a much lower level than her age: she could not enjoy or tolerate playing games; she sometimes listened when spoken to and sometimes talked about her own feelings, but she was not able to carry on a meaningful conversation. Being spoken to and speaking herself remained largely separate. Eventually her attendance became more erratic; her parents' efforts to enforce her attendance were only partially successful.

Toward the end of her thirteenth year, Maureen's behavior and school performance declined. By this time, unquestioned episodes of stealing had occurred. Her growing interest in sexuality led her to experiment with classmates and to make dangerous contacts on the Internet. Maureen was also confused about her sexual orientation, adding to her anxiety. Her doubts were more frightening because of her tenuous peer relationships. She was unable to discuss sexual matters with anyone and consequently experienced stronger impulses to act on them. By the middle of her fourteenth year, she firmly refused to comply with psychotherapeutic and pharmacologic treatment. Episodes of sexually promiscuous behavior began occurring with classmates and, it was feared, with strangers. Her mood became more unstable, and she began having persistent thoughts of suicide.

Maureen was hospitalized, at which time she was found to have symptoms of mania and a psychotic depression. Efforts to intensify her treatment and pharmacologic management came too late, and she required residential placement. After two years of both psychotherapeutic care (including strict limits and extensive group work) and consistent pharmacologic treatment, Maureen improved enough to return home. Having acquired mood stability, an understanding of her condition, some acceptance of her need for medicine, a measure of academic success, and an experience of satisfying peer relationships, Maureen was able to begin work on appropriate developmental tasks. She continued to need individual and group psychotherapy and careful pharmacologic care, but her oppositional behavior had resolved.

*Maureen was a child with bipolar II disorder, complicated by prominent anxiety, oppositional behavior, learning difficulties, adoption, and severe family discord. Because of her anxiety, she had difficulty feeling comfortable in her own skin; she moved on to oppositional defiant disorder. Her subtle difficulty comprehending language may have contributed to her difficulty accepting limits. Over time she also developed a borderline personality disorder (see pages 232–235). As she reached early adolescence, Maureen showed signs of three consumption disorders—compulsive consuming (Yu-Gi-Oh! cards), stealing, and promiscuity.*

*Because she was an adopted child, family history was unavailable. Her anxiety and oppositional behavior lasting into latency together with* a negative response to an antidepressant strongly indicated bipolar dis-order. Nonetheless, the diagnosis was not accepted by her parents un-til accumulated developmental failures and adolescence brought on undeniable symptoms.

Although early psychotherapeutic intervention provided some improvement, persistent anxiety, irritability, and oppositional behavior severely impaired her ability to function in school. Attempts at pharma-cologic intervention at first made matters worse and later were only partially successful. Parental ambivalence and intensified resistance by Maureen ended effective pharmacologic care for a time.

An appropriate school setting improved Maureen's academic perfor-mance and increased her self-confidence, but her peer relationships continued to be tenuous, making normal development impossible. Mau-reen was unable to benefit from camp because of her extreme anxiety and difficulties with separation. Maureen's intense interest in Yu-Gi-Oh! cards resembles other latency-age children's desire to collect, but in Maureen they served an additional purpose of magically increasing her personal power and defending against feelings of helplessness. Playing Yu-Gi-Oh! also gave her some connection to her peers. Her vociferous demands that her parents buy her more expensive cards was ominous, however, heralding the beginning of compulsive consumption.

As she grew older, Maureen began exhibiting more serious symp-toms than mere oppositional behavior; she began to show symptoms of a borderline personality. In treatment, there were abrupt and extreme changes in her mood and in the quality of her contact with her therapist, an inability to tolerate competition, boredom, a problem with attach-ment, difficulty connecting one event with another (e.g., one psy-chotherapy session with another, or a behavior with its consequence), and an inability to carry on meaningful conversation. Other symptoms—intense episodes of rage and intense unstable relationships with adults and peers—were also apparent.

Maureen's personality disorder developed from her inability to feel comfortable in her own skin—her intense anxiety and irritability—which fostered a defense of frequent splitting (see page 234), resulting in *changing perceptions of herself and of other people, fluctuating emotional states, and a need at times to cut off feeling more or less entirely. Effective treatment for this personality disorder requires, among other things, firm limits set in an emotionally neutral way. From very early on, Maureen's parents could not provide such limits, in part because Maureen was such a difficult child, but also because of their conflicts with each other. Because of her tendency to split, when her parents divorced, Maureen had more difficulty than most children moving between two households with different rules.*

*Family therapy helped to improve parental cooperation, but the improvement was too late and too little. As Maureen entered adolescence, she experienced not only increased difficulties with mood instability but also severe problems with identity, including sexual identity—also characteristic of a borderline adolescent. These problems were intensified by the circumstance of her adoption. Grandiose demands for presents, stealing, and sexual acting out began to be problems because Maureen—unable to solve earlier developmental problems of emotional stability, tolerating limits, and managing aggression—could not establish intimate relationships. Mounting depression, defended against by increasingly dangerous and impulsive behavior, finally resulted in hospitalization.*

*Maureen's inability to cooperate with outpatient psychotherapeutic or pharmacologic care meant that residential placement was necessary. Within a residential setting she received consistent limits (which she could not evade), appropriate pharmacologic care, and both individual and group therapy. These resources enabled Maureen to begin again at developmental tasks that had not been accomplished: feeling comfortable in her own skin, tolerating limits as a result of her connection to people (rather than to avoid punishment), managing aggression, academic skills, and healthy peer relationships. Appropriate pharmacologic care was crucial in Maureen succeeding at these tasks, but it could not be offered until she could accept appropriate limits. Once those two things took place, the more difficult and essential psychotherapeutic work could begin.*

## Terrors of the Terrible

ERIC was eight when he was brought to me by his grandmother, with whom he lived, together with his older brother, Jed, and his grandfather. Eric had been extremely disruptive in his third-grade class and recently in a fit of anger had stabbed another child with a pencil. Eric's rages were so severe that his teacher raised the question of whether he might be psychotic. He had also repeatedly been in fights with neighborhood children and had been shut out by his peers. At home he was in constant conflict with his grandfather, whom I was told was quite irritable himself.

Eric's mother, a recently recovered alcoholic, lived in another state; his father was remarried and also lived in a distant state. Although Eric regularly visited his mother for holidays and during the summer, she did not visit him at her parents' house; Eric's contact with his father was less frequent. The people Eric was closest with were his brother and his grandmother, although (as I learned in his treatment) he had an intense desire once again to live with his mother.

It was 1990 and wider concepts of bipolar disorder had not yet emerged, much less the array of medications we now have to treat it. Managed care had also not yet made its appearance and intensive psychotherapy was not regarded as extravagant, even in the middle-class community where Eric lived. I diagnosed Eric as having oppositional defiant disorder and recommended individual psychotherapy twice weekly with family sessions every two weeks.

Eric began treatment unwillingly. He would not speak or interact with me, but he did begin playing by himself with blocks. He built structures composed of wall upon wall, sometimes with a central compartment. He was uninterested in the towering structures I encouraged him to make (the ones I thought boys were supposed to build). So I just watched. One day after about two weeks, while Eric was building a solidly walled compartment, I asked, "What's inside?" He fleetingly turned his head toward me and said, "My mother." Nothing more was said, but after that Eric tolerated more interactive play. In chess I showed him how to build walls of pawns; then we drew walls.

I discovered that Eric was intensely interested in and talented at drawing. At first we copied knights in armor. Then we drew battles with many knights, walls, and castles—with more walls. We also fought each other with plastic swords. Soon Eric began creating his own drawings of battles with fantastic creatures. Occasionally I attempted to interpret one of Eric's drawings or refer to something about his life. Whereupon, without commenting, he would pick up a sword and begin to fight savagely. As his oppositional behavior (and the feelings that drove it) were expressed in his play, Eric's behavior improved in school.

Eric continued to draw, week after week. His drawings became more original and elaborate. He would work for several weeks on a single one: there were monsters, peculiar creatures engaged in struggles within a fantastic landscape against fantastic adversaries. His use of color was brilliant. I have never had a child who drew so intricately and with such sustained attention. Eric's intense concentration and his fantastic drawings are excellent examples of the wonderful—and at times terrifying—imaginative life of the bipolar child.

Meanwhile I worked with Eric's grandmother and brother to gather Eric's developmental history and to help with behavioral measures in the household. I learned that during his infancy and earliest childhood, Eric had been repeatedly left alone with his brother while his mother went out at night. At times the party moved into the apartment where they lived. It was such behavior, together with unremitting alcohol abuse, that finally led Eric's grandmother to take custody of the boys. I also learned about a secret that had been kept from Eric, a secret never revealed during the course of our treatment: Eric and his brother had different fathers. The secret gave an additional meaning to Eric's walled-in structures. There were also school meetings to determine what difficulties occurred in the classroom: I established

communication with Eric's teacher; she felt less isolated, and Eric's behavior in school soon ceased to be a problem.

Eric still had difficulties in relationships with peers: his unpredictable anger and aggression continued to isolate him. Fortunately, during the second year of Eric's treatment, a colleague and I formed a boys' activity group to help boys learn to manage aggression in the peer group. The group worked through the boys' interactions with each other rather than by any specific instructions or any interpretation of their behavior. The activity group worked more powerfully to correct Eric's relationships with peers than anything I could achieve within individual or family treatment. Eric's problems in the neighborhood began to subside.

There remained the problem of Eric's relationship with his parents. I had phone contacts with his mother, and eventually she came for a family session. His father could not be engaged. We discussed what it would mean for Eric to live with his mother. I was concerned about Eric's mother's ability to consistently care for him, but after a

few trial visits his mother and grandmother agreed that Eric would rejoin his mother, which ended our treatment.

One of the last drawings Eric made was of a volcano erupting with bright red and orange lava. Just as he finished the drawing, he added a giant boot descending on the mouth of the volcano. In the picture Eric represented himself twice: as the volcano and also as a small figure raising a sword bravely and defiantly in the face of these terrible forces. I cannot think of a more poignant portrayal of the oppositional child's image of himself in the face of authority.

In writing this book, I recontacted Eric (now twenty-four) and his grandmother. By this time Eric had suffered several seasonal depressions, confirming my impression of him as a bipolar child. His talent as an artist had also persisted.

*Eric started out with oppositional defiant disorder. He also had what I now recognize as a family history of bipolar disorder and substance abuse in his mother and his maternal grandfather. Just as important, he had a history of inadequate care as an infant and a problematic home life during his preschool and early latency years. Eric had a genetic risk factor and*

*several symptoms suggestive of bipolar disorder: he was highly imagina-*
*tive, prone to fierce irritability, and oppositional. Because my contact with*
*his mother was minimal, I never obtained a clear developmental history*
*of his infancy and toddler years and had no way to know how he might*
*have developed under better circumstances. His oppositional and defiant*
*behavior resulted from an inadequate holding environment, one in which*
*he could learn to articulate his rage and manage conflict. In his drawing*
*and his play, Eric was able to express his feelings in exquisite—although*
*nonverbal—detail. At the age I saw him (eight to nine), Eric's tempera-*
*ment was not volatile enough to need medication in order to work in psy-*
*chotherapy. Conversely, medication without complex psychotherapeutic*
*treatment would not have been effective in helping him.*

*Eric's problems with aggression and his isolation from the peer*
*group fit the pattern I have observed of an absent father and, in his*
*case, a lack of adequate mothering—resulting in a tendency toward ex-*
*plosive paranoid aggression directed outward. He worked wonderfully*
*in individual and family therapy, but his problems with peers resolved*
*only with activity group therapy. He needed a group to get the feel of*
*setting limits with peers and with himself.*

## IF YOUR CHILD HAS OPPOSITIONAL DEFIANT DISORDER

· Psychotherapeutic help is needed, because your child is off track
developmentally and your efforts to help him are not succeeding.
· First you need to determine what has kept your child from
managing limits:
  · a mood disorder?
· ADD/ADHD?
  · parents' problems with holding the situation?
  · discord between the parents?

· more serious family dysfunction?

· trauma outside the family?

· Begin by addressing the underlying causes, whatever they are.

· When there has been damage to the relationship between child and parent, individual (play or talk) therapy may be needed to help the child work through difficulties that have become too hot to handle with the parent.

· When there has been serious damage to a family's ability to function, family therapy is needed.

· Appropriate limit setting is always crucial.

## CONDUCT DISORDER

Children and adolescents with conduct disorder have progressed from opposing limits in anger to serious violation of rules, violation of the rights or property of others, and in some cases threatening or causing physical harm to others.

### DSM-IV CRITERIA FOR CONDUCT DISORDER

A repetitive and persistent pattern of behavior in which the basic rights of others or major societal norms or rules are violated, as manifested by the presence of three (or more) of the following criteria in the past twelve months, with at least one in the past six months:

#### AGGRESSION TO PEOPLE AND ANIMALS
· often bullies, threatens, or intimidates others
· often initiates physical fights

· has used a weapon that can cause serious harm to others (e.g., a bat, brick, broken bottle, knife, gun)
· has been physically cruel to people or animals
· has stolen while confronting a victim
· has forced someone into sexual activity

### DESTRUCTION OF PROPERTY
· has deliberately engaged in fire setting with the intention of causing serious damage
· has deliberately destroyed others' property

### DECEITFULNESS OR THEFT
· has broken into someone else's house, building, or car
· often lies to obtain goods or favors or to avoid obligations
· has stolen items of nontrivial value without confronting a victim

### SERIOUS VIOLATIONS OF RULES
· often stays out at night despite parental prohibitions, beginning before age thirteen years
· has run away from home overnight at least twice
· is often truant from school, beginning before age thirteen years

As discussed earlier, an ability to manage conflict appropriately leads to impulse control as well as a capacity for empathy (an ability to imagine other people's emotional life as distinct from one's own) and guilt not related to a fear of punishment but to a desire to maintain contact with other people. Children with conduct disorder have some failure in impulse control, in empathy, and in their capacity for guilt. These children most often *plan* their violations—unlike the child with oppositional defiant disorder who commits them impulsively, usually in anger, and just at the time a limit is set. Planning suggests that the behavior is not merely the result of an abnormal mood state; it suggests a lack of respect for authority and, at least, an episodic loss of empathy and guilt.

There is an important distinction between children suffering with conduct disorder who have a capacity for guilt and empathy and those who cannot experience these emotions. The degree to which empathy and guilt are present determines how treatable the conduct disorder is. The presence of depression in a child with conduct disorder actually predicts a better outcome, because the abnormal mood may contribute to the lapses in judgment or to lapses in guilt and empathy.

At the far end of the spectrum of children with conduct disorder is the psychopath, who is without a capacity for guilt and empathy (or normal emotions) and rarely suffers depression. This diagnosis is uncommon in adolescents, but it does occur. There is little that can be done in the way of treatment for psychopathy other than containment—close supervision or confinement. There is no certainty about what causes a person to become psychopathic: developmental and genetic factors are both thought to play a role, but a mood disorder is *not* the cause.

In many cases of conduct disorder, appropriate treatment can restore a child's capacity for empathy and guilt. As with oppositional defiant disorder, it is necessary when treating conduct disorder first to determine what has given rise to the child's developmental failure. The oppositional disposition of bipolar children and the consequent difficulty they have negotiating conflict puts them at risk for conduct disorder. Also, as with oppositional defiant disorder, family dysfunction can be a contributing cause. The anger that results from emotional, physical, or sexual abuse can also bring about a conduct disorder. Finally, a parent's serious disregard for rules or other people's rights can help foster conduct disorder in a child. The difficulty of any child with conduct disorder handling conflict usually results in serious obstacles to intimacy. These difficulties account, in part, for the substance abuse often seen as part of or accompanying this disorder. In a bipolar child, it is not necessary to assume a manic or irritable state to account for conduct disorder.

Treatment of conduct disorder depends on its causes but always includes enforcing limits. Usually this task has failed at home, so limits need to be set, at least in part, from outside the household. When a child cannot be contained within the household—does not observe curfews, runs away, or engages in dangerous or illegal behavior—a wilderness program or residential facility is needed. These programs are not, however, ultimate solutions; they are bridges to establishing effective outpatient treatment.

## Ethan in Trouble

ETHAN was in the middle of eighth grade when he came to see me, after he'd been put on probation for deliberately breaking windows in an unattended building. He had also been stealing since the age of ten and had been getting into trouble outside the home over the past six months. Ethan expressed remorse for his behavior and said that he "felt like a loser."

His academic work had declined since the fifth grade, he was having a hard time concentrating, and he was having increasing difficulties with his handwriting. He said he didn't think he needed treatment, but he also said that he wished he weren't alive. For the past year he had been having night terrors and had recently had a terrifying and violent dream about a woman stabbing a man. Ethan also lately had been having difficulty falling asleep. He described episodes during which he felt "spaced out and numb," and others when he had a "fast feeling." He scored an 18 on the Hamilton Depression Scale, indicating severe depression. He had no history of substance abuse.

Ethan's mother drank heavily from the time of his birth until he was three years of age. Until then, he was cared for principally by his older sister. His father was also drinking at the time, and Ethan was exposed to almost constant arguments between his parents. In addition, Ethan was physically abused by his older brother until about the age of twelve, when his brother left the household. The family history was significant for alcohol abuse, physical and sexual abuse, and depression on both sides.

At the time of his evaluation, both his parents were abstinent: his mother, an effective substance abuse counselor, was appropriately concerned and cooperative; his father denied his son's distress, noticing only the disturbance in his behavior and in his performance in school.

Because of his problems with attention, questions were raised about whether or not Ethan suffered from ADD. I placed Ethan on imipramine, a medication used at the time for both depression and ADD. His depression responded well to a low dose of medication, but I requested psychological testing nonetheless. The testing gave no indication of ADD—a Connors Scale (a set of questions about a child's behavior answered by parents and teachers) was negative. Rather, Ethan's difficulties with concentration were the result of his tendency to become emotionally overwhelmed. The pattern described in the testing—"a tendency to his being disrupted by anxiety more with meaningful information . . . than rote or essentially meaningless data"—was opposite to what is seen with ADHD. This pattern of distraction, together with his episodes of spacing out and becoming numb, was more consistent with post-traumatic stress disorder.

I treated Ethan psychotherapeutically, and he became more open and willing to come. He benefited from a validation of his trauma and from emotional support. His resistance to treatment lessened but did not entirely disappear because it was supported by his father's denial that there was a problem in the family. From Ethan's father's point of view, talking about what went on in the family was a betrayal. Ethan's mother was healthier than his father and appropriately cooperative. With her help, I was able to carry on family therapy to a limited degree. Ethan's behavior and academic performance improved, and he discontinued therapy when he was back on track academically and no longer depressed. Further psychotherapeutic treatment would have been beneficial, but his family had limited resources and depended on managed care, which would not approve further treatment. It was recommended that he attend an Alanon group for adolescents.

*Conduct disorder was the least of Ethan's problems and resolved quickly when his depression and his history of abuse were addressed. When he had gotten back on track developmentally, however, Ethan continued to be at risk because of his father's minimization of his distress and of the abuse that had gone on in the family. As is the case in many families in which abuse occurs, Ethan's family experienced intense shame and strove to keep the abuse a secret. Ethan was part of this secret keeping. Indeed, at the time of his evaluation, Ethan kept the secret of his abuse from himself. His secret keeping was, however, only the most recent in a history that extended far back into the families of both his parents.*

*Establishing a diagnosis of bipolar disorder in Ethan would be problematic even today. His report of times when he felt racy might raise suspicion. His depression could have been attributed to the trauma he suffered as well as to any genetic vulnerability. Alcohol abuse, physical abuse, and sexual abuse were so widespread in both his parents' families that it would be difficult to see past them. In Ethan's case, a diagnosis of bipolar disorder would need to be made over a longer course of time. Ethan—like Charlotte, Thomas, Jeanette, and Maureen—had symptoms of dissociation. Charlotte, Jeanette, and others each had suffered obvious trauma. But Thomas and Maureen had not.*

## PANIC DISORDER

Bipolar disorder is almost always accompanied by high levels of anxiety, sometimes masked by intense activity or irritability. At times, however, it is accompanied by additional anxiety disorders. Not all bipolar patients have panic attacks, but when they are present their treatment is crucial to the stabilization of the bipolar disorder.

## Symptoms

A panic attack has a sudden onset and typically lasts for about ten minutes. During an attack, a person experiences overwhelming anxiety, sometimes with thoughts that he is going crazy or must flee from the present situation. The most common physical symptoms accompanying a panic attack are shortness of breath, rapid heart rate, increased blood pressure, chest or abdominal discomfort, a cold sweat, and gastrointestinal discomfort. Following a panic attack, a person's level of anxiety does not return to normal but remains high. The likelihood of another attack then increases—that is, the threshold for triggering an attack is lowered. This heightened state of anxiety can lead to a sleep disturbance and in some cases to depression.

## Causes of Panic Disorder

A panic attack is a sudden overactivity of the sympathetic nervous system—the fight-or-flight response. A propensity for panic attacks can be inherited, and frequently the family history of a person with panic attacks includes other family members who have suffered from them. In susceptible persons, a panic attack can be triggered by a chemical change—such as an increase in lactic acid, carbon dioxide, or caffeine— or a minor environmental stress. In some persons, a visiospatial challenge, such as traveling over a bridge, entering a shopping mall, or finding oneself at a great height, can trigger an attack. When a panic attack has a chemical or sensory trigger, it is not necessarily a sign of psychological difficulties, but if it is allowed to persist without treatment, psychological difficulties can result. A fear of leaving one's house— agoraphobia—is one common consequence of untreated panic disorder.

In other people (children or adults), a panic attack can have a psychological trigger. I have frequently seen the onset of panic attacks in a person who becomes angry but fears to express that anger. Persons who have suffered trauma also experience frequent panic attacks—sometimes from normal stress and sometimes in a situation that recalls the original trauma.

In young children, there is a high correlation among panic attacks, separation anxiety, and school refusal. Children tend to complain of a stomachache rather than anxiety, perhaps because anxiety is something they do not understand or cannot articulate. They probably also experience discomfort around their diaphragm, which they identify as their stomach. Panic attacks can also accompany school refusal in an adolescent, especially when there is massive social anxiety or intense inexpressible anger (as was the case with Thomas, pages 181–186).

## Panic Attacks and Bipolar Disorder

A panic attack increases the level of arousal throughout the central nervous system and in a person with bipolar disorder exacerbates that condition. Sleep disturbance that may accompany panic attacks also undermines mood stability. The intensification of bipolar disorder that follows then brings on more panic attacks and a vicious cycle ensues— the panic attacks aggravate the bipolar disorder, and the bipolar disorder perpetuates the panic attacks. Mood stability cannot be maintained in a bipolar patient until the panic attacks are stopped.

In a vulnerable person, the probability of panic attacks varies with daily as well as monthly hormonal cycles. On a daily basis, hormonal changes, especially in the evening and in the early morning hours, increase the likelihood of an attack. These same cyclical changes affect bipolar disorder. It is common, for example, for children with bipolar disorder to become hyperactive in the evening as their cortisol level drops. Bipolar children with panic attacks can also have the onset of an attack at that time. Panic attacks can also come on in the early morning hours when the hormone ACTH is released. It is common for a person suffering with panic disorder to awaken at 4 or 5 A.M. with either a panic attack or acute anxiety.

In women with bipolar disorder, premenstrual hormonal changes can cause an increased vulnerability to panic attacks as well as to an increase in irritability or depression. In some cases, the onset of panic attacks can be the first symptom of the onset of bipolar disorder, particularly when they are accompanied by mood changes or depressive thoughts.

## Strange Thoughts Accompanying a Panic Attack

LAURA was a beautiful, dark-haired, olive-skinned girl of fourteen who was experiencing panic attacks accompanied by intrusive and angry thoughts of killing someone. The thoughts, which were distressing to her, had come on abruptly toward the end of her menstrual cycle and while watching a movie that depicted angry women. They were followed by a panic attack the next day. Her developmental history was entirely normal except for an incident in fifth grade when, after two friends died of cancer, she had irrational fears of getting cancer herself. I initially treated her briefly with a minor tranquilizer, and she fully recovered. Working with a psychologist, she learned cognitive behavioral techniques for managing her anxiety.

Four years later she suddenly became depressed with intrusive thoughts of suicide but no desire to act on them. She could think of no cause for her depression, although it came on toward the end of her menstrual cycle and slightly improved at the beginning of her next cycle. She responded to a combination of two mood stabilizers with mild antidepressant effects (Neurontin and Lamictal). In late August, however, as the daylight began to change, she had the acute onset of anxiety with no apparent cause other than the seasonal change. At that time, slight adjustments in the schedule of her medication were effective, but depression recurred in the fall just after the clocks were changed. Treatment with a light box in the morning aggravated her symptoms, but use of it in the late afternoon was effective without any alteration of medication. Symptoms of anxiety and depression recurred yearly with the change of seasons.

Laura's family history included two paternal aunts with mood instability, one with an eating disorder and the other with panic attacks, mood swings, and prominent premenstrual mood changes.

*Laura has bipolar II, which appeared at first with the sudden onset of panic attacks. The accompanying uncharacteristic and troubling murderous thoughts suggested an incipient bipolar disorder, so I treated her with a benzodiazepine without an antidepressant. Even when she later presented with depressive symptoms, mood stabilizers were used rather than an antidepressant. Light therapy eased her seasonal depression.*

*Laura's developmental history was entirely normal. Her diagnosis rested on the peculiarly violent thoughts accompanying her panic attacks, a correlation of symptoms with menstrual changes, prominent seasonal changes, and a family history of mood disorders. Her symptoms were almost entirely depressive—although accompanied by intrusive violent thoughts that were wholly out of character. Her depressive symptoms oscillated with hormonal and seasonal swings. Some psychiatrists would diagnose Laura with premenstrual dysphoric disorder, seasonal affective disorder, and a recurrent major depression. The coincidence of these three, together with thoughts that border on psychosis, argues for an illness in the bipolar spectrum. The distinction is important because it affects the choice of pharmacologic intervention.*

## Treatment for Panic Attacks

In patients without bipolar disorder, the preferred treatment for panic attacks is an antidepressant (usually a selective serotonin reuptake inhibitor, SSRI) accompanied by cognitive-behavioral treatment. In bipolar patients, however, an antidepressant can aggravate the panic attacks and destabilize mood. The drug of choice for them is a benzodiazepine. (Occasionally children have a paradoxical response to a benzodiazepine, becoming agitated or disinhibited; in such cases another choice must be made, but an SSRI is rarely effective.) A benzodiazepine can shut down panic attacks within hours and can be used for a longer period of time to provide sustained protection against recurring attacks. For some children after a period of a week or two, with the use of cognitive-behavioral techniques, the drug can be tapered and panic attacks do not return. Other children need to continue the benzodiazepine over a sustained period of time. If panic attacks are part of or have triggered an arousal of the bipolar condition, that arousal must be calmed separately with a mood stabilizer or a major tranquilizer. In most cases, however, the medications that treat the bipolar disorder are not by themselves effective for panic attacks.

When panic attacks have a psychological basis, medication must be accompanied by psychotherapeutic care. When a young child has panic attacks associated with separation anxiety, it is important to determine if the panic attacks and their accompanying anxiety have caused a change in boundaries within the home. Is the child able to sleep in his own bed? If not, parental counseling may often be needed to help the situation. The possibility of abuse must also be explored, especially if there has been a change in the child's behavior or control of urine or bowel movements. Panic attacks occurring in an adolescent in the context of school refusal indicate significant developmental problems: chronic difficulties with peer relationships and problems within the family are commonly present.

## OBSESSIVE-COMPULSIVE DISORDER

Obsessive-compulsive disorder (OCD) is an anxiety disorder characterized by intrusive *thoughts* (obsessions) that a person knows to be irrational but cannot evade and repetitive *behaviors* (compulsions) that serve no rational purpose but that the person feels compelled to do.

### SYMPTOMS OF OCD

The symptoms of obsessive-compulsive disorder include recurrent, inappropriate, intrusive thoughts, usually involving fear of injury to the self or someone else, accompanied by marked anxiety. A person with OCD knows that these thoughts are inappropriate and are all in her mind, so she tries to stop them—but cannot. OCD is also character-ized by repetitive behaviors or mental acts the person feels compelled to perform, such as hand washing, counting, praying, silently repeating words, or repeatedly checking to see if something has been done. The disorder can also include rituals (a need to perform certain tasks in a fixed way). These behaviors are performed to avoid anxiety or incurring .an irrational injury. Concerns about contamination, a preoccupation with symmetry, and exaggerated grooming behaviors are common, as are religious scruples and superstitions. People suffering from OCD have great difficulty making decisions and can find themselves frozen in situations where other people are able to act quickly.

## BIPOLAR DISORDER AND OBSESSIVE-COMPULSIVE DISORDER APPEAR TO BE OPPOSITES

In several ways, obsessive-compulsive disorder is the opposite of bipolar disorder. People who suffer depression and anxiety fall along a spec-trum. At one end of the spectrum are people who, when they are depressed or anxious, become impulsive and do things that hurt them-selves or other people—these are people with bipolar disorder. At the other end of the spectrum are people who, when they become de-pressed or anxious, worry about hurting themselves or someone else and have difficulty making the decision to act—these are people with obsessive-compulsive disorder. People with a bipolar disposition tend to be creative and disorganized and have intense, obviously expressed feelings; people with obsessive-compulsive disorder tend to be meticu-lous and well organized but not creative and are constricted in express-ing their feelings. Pharmacologically the two disorders also tend to be opposite. Patients with bipolar disorder usually respond quickly to low doses of an antidepressant; patients with obsessive-compulsive disorder require higher doses of medication and take longer to respond.

Despite these thorough differences, symptoms of both disorders can appear in the same person. This is probably because both disorders are inherited and can be inherited simultaneously from different family members. When they appear together, however, bipolar disorder must be regarded as the more dangerous condition because it can lead to impulsive and dangerous acts. What is more, the SSRIs used to treat OCD can aggravate bipolar disorder when used alone or in the high doses commonly used to treat OCD.

The diagnosis of bipolar disorder in the presence of prominent symptoms of OCD can be difficult to make, but impulsivity, intensely oppositional behavior, irritability, a prominent sleep disturbance, or a family history indicative of bipolar disorder should arouse concern that both conditions may be present. Concern should also be aroused if treatment of OCD with an SSRI worsens anxiety or brings on impulsive behavior.

## Bipolar Disorder Appearing as OCD

ALEX was eight when he abruptly had the onset of irrational thoughts and compulsions. When I later evaluated him, he told me, "About a year ago some thing came to my brain, and things I don't like I would have to say twice." Alex was also preoccupied with hand washing and fears of contamination (at times spending twenty minutes washing his hands). He often had difficulty crossing the threshold into his room and was preoccupied with neatness and symmetry. He had episodes in which he felt compelled repeatedly to count silently by threes. Unlike many patients with OCD, however, Alex also reported difficulty falling asleep; he could be explosively irritable, and at times he heard his name called when no one was there.

Alex was an adopted child and a family history was not available, so his developmental history was especially important. Adopted shortly after birth, he had been well cared for up to that time. As an infant he was always restless and did not sleep through the night for almost two years. Developmental milestones were on time, but as a toddler he had difficulty sustaining play and "fidgeted with whatever he could touch." He was highly active and was difficult to calm when he was aroused. Alex had problems getting along with other children; he was strong willed and controlling in his play at nursery school. Positively, Alex was strikingly imaginative and had a good sense of humor, communicating his mirth easily to other people, but he could become uncontrollably silly. He liked to draw, although he had some difficulty controlling a line; he was "fabulous at color." In school, Alex had difficulties with the decoding process in reading and had to repeat third grade. No symptoms of OCD had been seen in him prior to their sudden onset at the age of eight.

Alex's symptoms of impulsivity, his few incidents of auditory hallucinations, restless disposition, high level of activity as a toddler, imagination and sense of color, and emotionally infectious disposition all aroused my suspicions. The abrupt onset of his obsessions and compulsions without any prior history was also striking. His problems with visual processing, although not diagnostic, fit in with the picture of bipolar disorder. I chose to treat him first with a mood stabilizer and later with a low dose of an SSRI. Alex responded well to lamotrigine, with a decrease in irritability but a more gradual and less complete improvement in his symptoms of OCD. After six months on lamotrigine I added a small dose of an SSRI; his symptoms of OCD diminished further over the next four weeks.

Alex's treatment required much more than appropriate medication, however. His adoptive mother and father were both anxious people but they had very different styles. His father was superficially calm, soft-spoken, and restrained up to a point, when he would become explosively angry. Alex's mother was quite anxious, detail oriented, and intrusive. Although Alex's mother tried to control and mask her anger, Alex (like many bipolar children) was attuned and sensitive to her emotional states. His mother's unseen anger made him tense, causing him to be even more provocative with her.

Despite Alex's positive response to medication, he had particular difficulty tolerating his mother's intrusions. Like many bipolar children, he struggled to maintain an inner calm. His difficulty soothing himself had been obvious as an infant and may have been aggravated by early separation from his biological mother. As his conflicts with his mother intensified, Alex became more violent, sometimes deliberately destroying his toys; at times he ran out of the house. (Adopted children frequently exhibit the defense of running away. Having been left once, they attempt to reverse the situation when they feel threatened.) Unfortunately, Alex's father had a job that kept him away much of the time, and he was often not available to help Alex's mother set limits. When his father was home, the parents' very different styles of discipline could provoke conflict between them and confusion in Alex.

Alex's parents, recognizing difficulties in school with limits and with other children, were concerned enough to place him in psychotherapy from the age of six. With his therapist's help, Alex was able to stay on track developmentally—managing in school and marginally with peers—but tension in the household was high. His symptoms of OCD appeared at a time of particularly intense conflict at home. It was through his therapist's intervention that he was referred to me, and we have worked closely together to coordinate his care.

Alex's difficulties in school intensified conflict at home. His parents placed him in a very competitive school with high academic standards that prided itself on producing graduates who went on to the best colleges. In order to help him succeed, Alex's parents hired a tutor for him four days a week. As well intentioned as this was, it increased pressure on Alex and limited his contact with friends; arguments about homework occurred frequently.

Alex's mother did not allow herself to become alienated. She continued to be concerned and active in supporting Alex's peer relationships. She encouraged playdates, attendance at parties, and summer camp. She stayed in close contact with Alex's teachers and maintained good communication among home, school, and Alex's psychotherapist. She also strongly supported Alex's talents as a painter when they appeared. She had difficulty, however, accepting suggestions that Alex be placed in a less competitive school.

As Alex moved closer to adolescence, further conflicts arose about privacy in his room and his communication with friends over the Internet while doing homework. The conflicts between Alex and his mother also became more violent. There was a marked difference in his behavior with his mother and his behavior in other circumstances. There could also be a difference in his behavior toward his mother on one occasion as compared with another. Indeed, the change could be so marked that it seemed as if Alex were a completely different child.

*Alex is now almost twelve, and there has not yet been a marked change in his mood stability. He does not qualify for the diagnosis of bipolar disorder. Nonetheless, his response to medication (positively to a mood stabilizer and quickly to a low-dose SSRI) and his developmental history confirm the presence of a bipolar disposition. Without appropriate pharmacologic treatment, his risk for developing severe symptoms of this disorder would be quite high. As he undergoes the hormonal changes of adolescence, he will also be at increased risk.*

*With the help of psychotherapy he has stayed on track developmentally and has some solid peer relationships. His capacity to develop an intimate relationship with his therapist bodes well for his capacity to manage intimacy with peers, despite his early difficulties with peers and his difficulty managing conflict at home. There is no indication of any consumption disorders. However, given Alex's history of difficulty soothing himself and the profound changes in his behavior with his mother from one circumstance to another—powerful use of a defense of splitting—his therapist and I are concerned about him being at risk to develop a borderline personality disorder. (See pages 232–238 for the association between bipolar disorder and borderline personality disorder.)*

*We are also concerned about adolescent rebellion as he matures and explores moral independence. His parents' continued support of his psychotherapeutic treatment gives us reason to be optimistic.*

## Bipolar Disorder Underlying Tourette's Disorder

SUE was nine when she was brought to me with several difficulties: prominent vocal and motor tics, obsessive-compulsive symptoms, a sleep disturbance that had persisted despite moderately high doses of a major tranquilizer, periods of depression, and problems with peers who teased and tormented her. Sue's difficulties had come on quite abruptly in the midst of heightened tension between her parents, who were divorced. She lived with her mother but had been visiting with her father when she became symptomatic.

Sue's older brother had suffered significant problems previously. In early winter he had developed severe symptoms of obsessive-compulsive disorder and depression also in the context of a parental dispute. When I treated him with SSRIs, he became worse, at length requiring hospitalization. He improved, however, when placed on Lamictal, although the improvement took several months.

When Sue first became ill, prior to my seeing her, she too required hospitalization. Because of her brother's experience, antidepressants were avoided and she was begun on Lamictal right away. Possibly because her dose was increased too quickly, Sue developed a severe ulcer in her mouth and had to be taken off the drug. An attempt was then made to treat her tics, her anxiety, and her sleep disturbance with an atypical major tranquilizer and clonidine. When I first saw her, however, she still had moderately severe vocal and motor tics, some depression in the morning, and an inability to sleep through the night. She was also suffering continual attacks from peers. Attempts to help her with individual therapy had been unsuccessful.

I knew from the family history and my experience with her brother that behind Sue's symptoms of Tourette's disorder was an underlying bipolar disposition. She had already had fairly vigorous trials of medication, and I was reluctant to push harder pharmacologically. Instead I recommended treatment with acupuncture (for her anxiety, tics, and depression) and group therapy to help her manage peer relationships. I did not, however, discontinue the medications she was on. Sue's tics abated, she began sleeping through the night, and her mood improved. Relationships with peers remained a problem for a while, but after two months with a group for girls her age, she was beginning to hold her own.

*Sue and her brother both resembled Alex in that their symptoms came on abruptly with no preceding problems in early childhood. Sue's brother had a harder time because there was no developmental history suggesting bipolar disorder, the family history was obscured by denial, and his depression and obsessive-compulsive symptoms were quite severe. Consequently, he underwent several attempts to treat him with vigorous doses of antidepressants (SSRIs) and his suffering increased. I was experienced enough to know that lamotrigine had to be started very gradually; he tolerated the medication and slowly responded.*

*Sue's introduction to lamotrigine in the hospital was more hurried, which may have been the reason she developed early signs of Steven's Johnson syndrome, a severe autoimmune reaction (see pages 292–293). Sue illustrates the usefulness of an alternative biological treatment for psychiatric symptoms (acupuncture) when pharmacologic treatment reaches a limit. She is also an example of a girl with a distant father who develops problems managing aggression with peers but is helped by treatment with group therapy.*

## SOCIAL ANXIETY DISORDER

Shyness rises to the level of social anxiety disorder when a child's fear of being embarrassed in a social or performance situation affects his ability to carry on developmental tasks, such as playing with other children or participating in group activities, or, in school, asking or answering questions, performing on tests, or speaking in front of a group.

Children suffering from this disorder are exquisitely sensitive to criticism or to rejection; they may also be subject to bullying. Such children cling to familiar adults, cry, freeze, or have tantrums when faced with the task of entering a social situation. They may also refuse to go to school or to separate from parents in other circumstances, such as being left with a babysitter or going to camp. They have difficulty being assertive and asking for routine kinds of assistance (directions, help in a store or in a restaurant). Their self-esteem, social relationships, performance in school, and sometimes ability in sports suffer.

## *DSM-IV* CRITERIA FOR SOCIAL ANXIETY DISORDER

· A marked and persistent fear of one or more social or performance situations in which the person is exposed to unfamiliar people or to possible scrutiny by others. (In children there must be evidence of the capacity for age-appropriate relationships with familiar people and the anxiety must occur in peer settings, not just in interactions with adults.)

· Exposure to the feared social situation almost invariably provokes anxiety, which may take the form of a panic attack. (In children, the anxiety may be expressed by crying, tantrums, freezing, or shrinking from social situations with unfamiliar people.)

· The feared situations are avoided or else are endured with intense anxiety or distress.

· The avoidance, anxious anticipation, or distress experienced in the feared situations interferes significantly with the person's normal routine, occupational (academic) functioning, or social activities or relationships.

· The duration is at least six months.

· The fear is not due to the direct physiological effects of a substance of abuse or a prescribed medication or a general medical condition and is not better accounted for by another mental disorder (e.g., panic disorder, separation anxiety, body dysmorphic disorder, a pervasive developmental disorder, or schizoid personality disorder).

## SOCIAL ANXIETY DISORDER AND BIPOLAR DISORDER

Although many children with a bipolar disposition are impulsive, silly, exuberant, irritable, and aggressive within the family, these same children can often be intensely shy among peers and in unfamiliar situations. Their shyness grows out of the high anxiety that almost always accompanies bipolar disorder and is compounded by the intensity of their needs—needs so intensely felt that they can make the child feel embarrassed and unable to join in. When recurrent depression also occurs, a child's anxiety, self-esteem, perception of social situations, and initiative can be seriously challenged.

A child's shyness can also be intensified by interactions within the family. For example, a bipolar child's impulsivity and difficulty accepting limits can arouse irritability and impatience in her father. If the father is too harsh in setting limits, or if he withdraws, the child will have more difficulty separating from her mother. In the face of this, a mother can become overprotective or ally too closely with her child, fostering anxiety, difficulty separating, and a tendency to be passive.

Shyness can hinder a child's ability to make friends, limiting both her mastery of aggression during elementary school years and her formation of deeper personal relationships later in adolescence. When the anxiety is so severe that it inhibits one-on-one relationships and participation in sports or group activities, both individual and group therapy are essential to prevent serious problems in adolescence and later life.

If difficulties with social contact have not been mastered to some degree by adolescence, the child is at risk for adolescent school refusal, which is a more serious problem than school refusal at an early age. The risk of consumption disorders is significant. In my experience with adults, the coincidence of bipolar disorder, social anxiety disorder, and alcohol abuse is strikingly frequent. In an older adolescent attending college, performance on examinations and assignments can be markedly affected by this disorder.

Treatment of social anxiety disorder needs to be both pharmacologic and psychotherapeutic. When bipolar disorder is present, the same pharmacologic precautions that apply to panic disorder and depression apply: care must be taken when using antidepressants for anxiety, so benzodiazepines—clonazepam, lorazepam, alprazolam—play an important role. As with other anxiety disorders, bipolar disorder must be treated before the social anxiety can be approached effectively.

Psychotherapy for this disorder, when possible, should include both individual and group therapy. The value of group therapy with social anxiety disorder cannot be overemphasized. The form of individual and group therapy will vary with the child's age and capacity to work verbally. (Chapter 12 clarifies the choices to be made and how each form of therapy works.) A psychiatrist managing medication, if he or she does not take on the psychotherapy himself or herself, should help with finding an appropriate therapist.

## BORDERLINE PERSONALITY DISORDER

A personality disorder is a characteristic set of emotional defenses that have become fixed in a person and tend to distort the way she conducts relationships, how she perceives herself and other people, and how she perceives her circumstances. In contrast to a mood or an episode of anxiety, which are both transient and perceived as separate from the self, a personality disorder is both constant and accepted *as the self,* even when it is disturbing.

A person with a borderline personality disorder makes a pervasive use of the defense of splitting—dividing *perceptions* of people and situations absolutely into the good and the bad, or the loved and the hated. The borderline also splits one set of *emotions* from another, so that she shifts from one emotional state (affection) into another (rage) suddenly and irrationally. When the borderline finds herself on one side of a split, she cannot appreciate or reach to the other side: she cannot see that the person she now despises is someone she admired moments ago. Splitting is a primitive way of escaping from the anxiety caused by powerfully conflicting feelings. The borderline's use of this defense is a remnant of infancy that has become a fixed way of life.

The continual attempt to escape from intolerable thoughts and feelings causes a painful sense of emptiness and chronic boredom. This painful emptiness makes it impossible for the borderline to feel comfortable alone, resulting in a need to make intense impulsive attachments to other people. But her inability to tolerate disappointment and her shifting perceptions of herself and of other people make these relationships unstable and unfulfilling. The borderline's emotional instability and intense interpersonal conflicts foster impulsive behaviors—substance abuse, an eating disorder, self-mutilation, and attempts at suicide are common in people suffering with this disorder.

The borderline can also shift rapidly from one sense of self to another—from grandiosity to shame—and she is unable to modify one sense of herself with the other. Even if she can recall the other state, it seems distant and no longer valid. These changes can be so abrupt and extreme that she can feel as if she were a different person from one moment to another. A borderline is subject to episodes of intense fervor, longing, emptiness, and rage. Lost amid these drastically changing states of mind, she at times is unable to distinguish between what's real and what she simply imagined. In effect, she moves back and forth across the border between reality and unreality.

## CAUSES OF BORDERLINE PERSONALITY

In bipolar disorder, a borderline personality can stem from a child's failure to master the earliest developmental task of achieving emotional equilibrium and basic trust, causing intense emotional uncertainty during interpersonal conflict. In an attempt to master this uncertainty, one set of perceptions and feelings (the good) are split off from the other (the bad) as a way of reducing anxiety. Because feelings are isolated, they cannot modify one another and so continue to be undiluted and intense. A pervasive use of this defense (splitting) results in emotional instability, a fragmented and shifting sense of the self and of other people, and an inability to tolerate intimacy. In some ways, the person with borderline personality resembles a toddler trapped in the *no* stage. Both are subject to episodes of intense rage during which the sense of self and of other people changes abruptly from one extreme to another. Whereas this is normal in a toddler, in an adolescent or an adult it is a disabling developmental failure.

Another circumstance that can result in a borderline personality is emotional, physical, or sexual trauma. Overwhelming fear, pain, or sexual assault permanently destroys a person's ability to maintain emotional equilibrium and consequently the ability to achieve basic trust. Afterward, the capacity to manage interpersonal conflict or even normal stress is damaged and the defense of dividing conflicting states of mind (splitting) becomes entrenched.

People who suffer trauma—especially in childhood—may manage their terror by isolating the entire traumatic experience from the rest of their mental life, using a more profound type of splitting known as dissociation. The dissociated thoughts and feelings are not escaped, however. They continually disrupt normal personal function, causing sudden overwhelming sensations (terror, rage, pain), a fragmented reexperiencing of the trauma, or abrupt losses of sensation or awareness (numbness, blackouts, memory loss, disorientation). In extreme cases, the use of dissociation is so profound that the personality is fragmented into multiple selves. The rapidly shifting mental states seen in borderline personality disorder are also fragmentations of the self.

Dissociation can also be brought about by an infant's early distress and difficulty settling in, especially if it is severe and if the infant has a capacity for dissociation. (The ability to dissociate varies from one person to another; a capacity to dissociate correlates with an ability to be hypnotized.) Some aspects of a bipolar child's distractibility can be understood as forms of dissociation—intense absorption in one pursuit with a loss of contact with surroundings, disruption of thought by intrusive emotion or by blanking out, transient confusion between internal and external reality. In adolescents and adults, more pervasive losses of contact known as depersonalization (a feeling of disconnection from one's body) and derealization (a sense that things and the world around one is not real) can occur. Depersonalization and derealization are seen commonly in persons with borderline personality.

One response some borderlines make to their feelings of dissociation and inescapable internal distress is scratching or cutting the skin with the purpose not to kill oneself but to relieve a sense of disconnection from the self and to escape intolerable internal stress. While cutting, the person usually does not feel pain; instead, the cutting restores a more normal ability to feel and an escape from a painful numbness. The cutting probably provides an actual physiologic release. Cutters often say that they experience relief just as they bleed. There are also psychological meanings that accompany cutting: punishment of the self, or an attack on the skin, which is the organ most closely connected to early body memories of infancy.

## DSM-IV DIAGNOSTIC CRITERIA FOR BORDERLINE PERSONALITY DISORDER

A pervasive pattern of instability of interpersonal relationships, self-image, and affects (expressions of feeling), and marked impulsivity beginning by early adulthood and present in a variety of contexts, as indicated by five (or more) of the following:

· frantic efforts to avoid real or imagined abandonment
· a pattern of unstable and intense interpersonal relationships characterized by alternating between extremes of idealization and devaluation
· identity disturbance: markedly and persistently unstable self-image or sense of self
· impulsivity in at least two areas that are potentially self-damaging (e.g., spending, sex, substance abuse, reckless driving, binge eating)
· recurrent suicidal behavior, gestures, or threats, or self-mutilating behavior
· affective instability due to a marked reactivity of mood (e.g., intense episodic dysphoria, irritability, or anxiety lasting a few hours and only rarely more than a few days
· chronic feelings of emptiness
· inappropriate, intense anger or difficulty controlling anger (e.g., frequent displays of temper, constant anger, recurrent physical fights)
· transient stress-related paranoid thoughts or severe dissociative symptoms

## WHY BIPOLAR DISORDER OVERLAPS WITH BORDERLINE PERSONALITY DISORDER

The intense reactivity of the bipolar child, her sensory hypersensitivity, and her daily ups and downs all impede the task of establishing emotional equilibrium and basic trust. This lack of equilibrium complicates the child's ability to accept limits. When a parent says *no*, a bipolar child who has not succeeded in feeling comfortable in her own skin has enormous difficulty managing rage: her perceptions of the parent and of herself are intense and shifting between opposite values of good and bad. Both the intensity and the instability of her thoughts and feelings accentuate the child's anxiety, which she manages by segregating opposing perceptions of herself, her parent, and her surroundings. This segregation or splitting can become the child's central emotional defense in managing personal conflict. The persistent use of splitting leads to the borderline organization of the child's personality.

An adolescent who begins experiencing symptoms of bipolar disorder can also undergo a dramatic change in behavior resembling borderline personality, because her emotional turmoil intensifies at a time when behavioral limits are being renegotiated with parents and when she is experiencing a drive for closer relationships with peers. The adolescent can manage her intense, rapidly changing emotions by an unrelenting division of opposite feelings and perceptions, fragmenting her sense of self and of other people. Substance abuse or another consumption disorder may also appear. When this pattern of feeling and behavior shows for the first time in adolescence, and especially if it coincides with changes in mood, the condition may be transitory.

The causal connection between trauma and a borderline personality also helps explain the overlap between borderline personality and bipolar disorder. Families in which bipolar disorder affects both a parent and child have a higher risk for emotional, physical, and sexual abuse, especially when there is ongoing substance abuse. Children in these families contend not only with the rage and emotional volatility of bipolar disorder—in themselves, in a sibling, or in a parent—but also the risk of a parent or sibling who is abusive.

Maureen, whose story was discussed in the section on oppositional defiant disorder (pages 201–206), is a good example of a child whose early bipolar disorder together with chronic family discord resulted in a borderline personality. By the time she reached adolescence, Maureen suffered from heightened reactivity of mood, intense rage, unstable interpersonal relationships, problems with identity, impulsive self-destructive behavior, chronic emptiness, and thoughts of suicide. Alex, discussed in the section on obsessive-compulsive disorder (pages 224–228), was at risk for developing a borderline personality disorder but had not yet manifested it. He had intense emotional reactivity, severe episodes of rage, and dramatic changes in his behavior and his sense of self, but these symptoms were confined to some of his interactions with his mother and had not spread into other areas of his interpersonal relationships. His symptoms of bipolar disorder were less severe than Maureen's. Alex also had the capacity to form a relationship with his therapist.

## NARCISSISTIC PERSONALITY DISORDER

The name of this disorder comes from the myth of Narcissus, whom the gods punished by making him fall in love with his own reflection. It is an oversimplification, however, to understand narcissistic personality as simply a love of oneself. A person with a narcissistic personality is intensely occupied with maintaining a positive image of himself, but this preoccupation is the result of a deeper lack of self-esteem. The narcissist constantly strives to maintain an unrealistically idealized image of himself as a way of warding off an opposite sense of worthlessness. When he is unsuccessful in supporting the positive image, the narcissist falls abruptly into an intensely negative sense of himself. Like the borderline, his sense of himself and of other people is black and white, but his perceptions do not shift as easily as the borderline's.

There are two almost opposite styles of narcissism—the exploitative narcissist and the subservient narcissist. When a parent says *no* to a child whose sense of emotional stability and basic trust is relatively well established, the child can feel safe to resist the parent's demand by imagining himself as more powerful than the parent, able to control him or her, and beyond needing his or her approval or help. These three defenses—grandiosity, imagined control, and contempt—can become relatively fixed when a parent gives up the limit and does not effectively challenge the child's resistance. We commonly call this spoiling a child.

In the exploitative form of narcissism, grandiosity, imagined control, imagined triumph, and contempt for anyone who threatens the person's exalted sense of the self are used to protect a sense of being special and to avoid feelings of helplessness or loss. Originally these defenses are developed when a child is threatened with the loss of a parent's approval. The child can make use of these defenses, however, only from a position of relative security. Unlike the borderline, he must be able to maintain a sense of self-assurance—although illusory—for a relatively long period of time. His parents must also fail to challenge his defenses, either by giving in to his demands or by being so out of touch with the child that they fail to challenge him because of their absence. Some parents are both materially indulgent and emotionally or actually absent. As these defenses are used repeatedly, a more consistent split develops between the child's idea of himself as special and powerful and his opposite sense of being helpless and worthless. (The borderline, because of a lack of basic trust and extreme emotional reactivity, cannot maintain this split as consistently.)

In order to avoid any loss of self-esteem, the exploitative narcissist tries to exercise control over the people he needs. He regards anyone who fulfills his needs as valuable and worthwhile; anyone who fails to satisfy him is expendable or contemptible. As a result, the narcissist forms shallow and exploitative relationships with people but feels no guilt about his treatment of them. This kind of narcissist has limited empathy for other people and may not even desire close relationships. Transient narcissistic behavior is normal in a child and in an adolescent who is separating emotionally from his parents but has not yet made a comparable emotional investment in his peers. When that behavior and way of thinking become fixed, however, a narcissistic personality disorder has set in.

Developmentally, a narcissistic personality arises from a failure at the second developmental task, an acceptance of limits—*no*—and an acknowledgment of dependence on others. A child with a bipolar disposition who has great difficulty subduing the demands of his internal life (but who feels safe enough to challenge his parent) can mount a manic defense against the parent's demand: denying dependence, the child asserts his superiority, retreating from guilt and a sense of loss into grandiosity and a pursuit of pleasure. In doing so, the child discards attachment to the parent and substitutes contempt and a sense of triumph. (His example for this may be a parent's own behavior.) When parents cannot successfully challenge this façade, or if they fail to challenge it because they are emotionally absent (cold or self-involved), these defenses can become relatively fixed. The child then experiences little attachment to other people, has problems tolerating frustration, and tends to seek satisfaction in possessions and control. Aggression has become a defense against attachment. Such a child has developed an exploitative narcissistic personality.

## DSM-IV CRITERIA FOR NARCISSISTIC PERSONALITY DISORDER

A pervasive pattern of grandiosity (in fantasy or behavior), need for admiration, and lack of empathy, beginning by early adulthood and present in a variety of contexts, as indicated by five (or more) of the following:

· has a grandiose sense of self-importance (e.g., exaggerates achievements and talents, expects to be recognized as superior without commensurate achievements)
· is preoccupied with fantasies of unlimited success, power, brilliance, beauty, or ideal love
· believes that he or she is "special" and unique and can only be understood by, or should associate with, other special or high-status people (or institutions)

- requires excessive admiration
- has a sense of entitlement, i.e., unreasonable expectations of especially favorable treatment or automatic compliance with his or her expectations
- is interpersonally exploitative, i.e., takes advantage of others to achieve his or her own ends
- lacks empathy: is unwilling to recognize or identify with the feelings and needs of others
- is often envious of others or believes that others are envious of him or her
- shows arrogant, haughty behaviors or attitudes

An apparently opposite style of narcissism can arise when a child cannot or does not contest a parent's demands. She has come to understand that defying her parent's demand will result in an unsustainable loss—she will lose her parent's love and approval or the parent will (she believes) be irreparably damaged. Consequently, she goes along with the demands but at the expense of her own feelings. In time, she loses contact with those feelings, contact with her own authentic desires. Eventually she even begins to experience her desires as bad or dangerous. Her self-esteem comes to depend on securing the approval of others by complying with their expectations, and she cannot afford to have independent desires.

But self-esteem based on what a person *does* for others, rather than who a person *is,* is fragile, lasting only as long as the person's last act. The subservient narcissist must keep proving her worth through continued striving to be a good girl, a model student, or an understanding friend. The unacknowledged personal desires do not disappear, however. They come to be segregated into a bad or inadequate self that can emerge whenever the good self fails or is unwilling to please. A fear of becoming that bad self becomes an unobserved but desperately motivating force for the subservient narcissist.

Both of these narcissistic styles put a child at particular risk during adolescence. The exploitative narcissist formulates a grandiose identity that he can't sustain; the subservient narcissist, out of contact with her authentic desires, can formulate only an identity that has been assigned to her. Both have constructed a false self and will have trouble achieving true intimacy.

## WHY BIPOLAR DISORDER CAN LEAD TO NARCISSISM

Narcissism is one of many ways of defending against loss, and it can arise for a number of reasons. At an early stage of development— before a child can distinguish his feeling from another person's—a narcissistic sense of self is entirely normal. At that stage, a child's sense of himself is appropriately a mix of fantasy and the parent's regard. Narcissism becomes problematic when it persists as an entrenched way of managing reality. As has been noted, many bipolar children are especially perceptive of another person's emotional state, and especially that of their parent. When their parent, especially their mother, is so self-involved that she cannot become attuned to the child—afflicted by her own narcissism, depressed, or in some other distress—some bipolar children can be adept at protecting their mother by fulfilling, even anticipating, her expectations. It is their way of gaining whatever affection they can. The child smiles to get the mother to smile, obeys to obtain affectionate attention. This behavior can, of course, develop in a child without bipolar disorder, but the capacity of some bipolar children to sense other people's feelings may dispose them in this direction, especially if they have a parent who is poorly attuned to them.

A bipolar child can also be at risk for an exploitative narcissistic style, but for different reasons. When a bipolar child settles in adequately (is comfortable in his own skin), he perceives that it is safe to rebel against his parent's demands. In this circumstance, the intensity of the child's internal demands makes it difficult for him to surrender to a limit or a loss. Since he has received a good enough sense of security, he is disposed to use a defense of omnipotence—"I can do whatever I want to!" Or he may take a stance of grandiose contempt: "I don't have to listen to you!" "You can't tell *me* what to do!" "I don't care what you say!" A child without bipolar disorder can also take such a position, but the bipolar child's intense inner life and heightened grandiosity give him particular force in using such tactics. If, then, his parent does not adequately challenge him, this kind of thinking is reinforced, leading to an exploitative style.

## HOW DO I KNOW IF MY CHILD HAS A PERSONALITY DISORDER? WHAT SHOULD I DO?

· Usually a personality disorder does not become fixed before adolescence, although it may appear as an ominous pattern of behavior before then.

· A personality disorder persists as a way of behaving and seeing the world regardless of a child's mood.

· If you are worried your child may have such a problem, consult with a child psychologist or psychiatrist or a therapist skilled in diagnosing and treating personality disorders.

· A personality disorder cannot be treated only with medication; psychotherapy is an essential part of treatment.

· In a person with bipolar disorder, however, mood stability is a prerequisite for effective psychotherapeutic work.

· Personality disorders take a long time to develop and a long time to treat effectively. Accept that treatment will be long term and at times intensive.

· A personality disorder is not necessarily a permanent condition. With appropriate psychotherapy, a person's characteristic defenses can change.

## DISSOCIATION AND BIPOLAR DISORDER

Dissociative symptoms—a segregation of one part of an experience from another, or a failure to formulate an experience that is overwhelming—are frequently seen in a person with bipolar disorder. It practical terms, a child tunes out language because the nonverbal parts of her experience are overwhelming or completely absorbing. Because she does not formulate an experience (translate it from an emotional and sensory event into thoughts and memories), she may have no memory of what has gone on—be entirely spaced out. The acute sensory reactivity of a bipolar child predisposes her to sensory and emotional overload, resulting in a need to use psychic defenses that are more commonly seen in traumatized patients. The emotional and intellectual characteristics of a bipolar child—hyperfocusing, an intolerance of intrusion, an imperviousness to verbal demands, and a tendency to go blank or become disorganized under stress—are all qualities seen in people who have suffered an assault that overwhelms their emotional and sensory defenses.

The tantrums seen in some bipolar children are sudden and unpredictable. During the course of these episodes, the child is not only unreachable verbally but also resists any approach by her parent. Following the tantrum, such children do not have the ability to connect with their recent state of mind, nor can the parent connect the stress that provoked the incident with the child's catastrophic response. Such tantrums have the quality of a flashback—a reexperiencing of a traumatic event—except that the children have no history of trauma.

I evaluated one such child who upon testing had a verbal IQ of 160 (highly superior) and a performance IQ of 109 (slightly above average). This discrepancy was traceable to severe problems with visual integration, but her visual apparatus was normal. One interpretation of this information is that the child's abstract reasoning is cut off from her ability to process nonverbal experience. Significantly, her perinatal history was characterized by extreme sensory reactivity (intolerance of normal visual and tactile stimuli), prolonged gastrointestinal distress, and an inability to be soothed. Her entry into the world was an overwhelming assault on her central nervous system (from the outside and from within), a trauma brought about by ordinary events.

We have evidence on the basis of brain imaging and hormonal studies that one result of emotional trauma is an injury to the hypothalamic-cortisol axis—the body and brain's hormonal response to stress. It is also common for bipolar children to become activated, anxious, disorganized, and sometimes psychotic in the evening when their cortisol level drops. I have seen such evening vulnerability far more severely in a young woman suffering from bipolar disorder and severe sexual trauma.

Borderline personality and narcissistic personality are highly prevalent in the bipolar patients I treat. Dr. Elizabeth Howell in *The Dissociative Mind* argues that both these personality disorders have at their core powerful defenses of dissociation. It may be that the tendency of bipolar children to use dissociation from very early on predisposes some of them to develop these personality disorders.

Recognition of a mental tendency in bipolar children to divide verbal from nonverbal experience carries with it important implications for parenting, education, and treatment. Work with bipolar children by parents, teachers, and therapists needs to be keyed toward an integration of nonverbal with verbal thought processes. For example, a parent needs to devise a physical complement to verbal commands, but a physical approach that takes into account the child's sensitivity to intrusion. When a child does not respond to words, verbal repetition or an increase in the volume will not work. Eye contact, movement, and touch need to be used to lead the way into verbal contact and compliance.

In school, a teacher's task is not simply to get a child to pay attention to what is said and written or even to minimize distraction, but to find ways to link movement, images, and sound to verbal concepts. The linking of movement, images, and sound to verbal concepts is central to the Orton-Gillingham method of working with dyslexic and dysgraphic children. The entire academic program of the Austin Harvard

School—the first school developed for children with bipolar disorder and ADD—uses a combination of visual, auditory, and kinesthetic materials to deliver the curriculum. The success of these approaches may have to do with more than multiple reinforcement of material: each entails an approach to verbal thought processes through simultaneous nonverbal stimuli as way of integrating the two.

Similarly, in psychotherapy, the task is not simply to join words to feelings but to use nonverbal *activity* as an entry into verbal thought processes. Psychotherapy conducted in this way is not aimed at releasing repressed thoughts; it is aimed at formulating unformulated material, experience that is dissociated as a way of maintaining emotional balance. The physical activity taking place—in both the right and left hemispheres—opens the way to verbal processing and integration in the left hemisphere. In my own practice I have found that vigorous physical movement—swordplay or boxing—works differently than drawing or game playing with a highly defended child. During physical activity, things can be said and heard that are otherwise off the table. The importance of such work is that it allows segregated experiences to be integrated with and modified by the entirety of remembered experience.

Put another way, nonverbal activity can allow verbal thought that would otherwise not occur. A common instance of this is the experience of being able to think better when one is walking. Another common experience, between parent and child, is to be able to talk about guarded subjects while walking, or driving in a car. Less obvious is the circumstance—incredible to parents but true for many anxious children—of being able to concentrate *better* on their homework when the TV is on, although they are not watching it. I suspect that the presence of sound and movement that are unformulated (not attended to) facilitates the verbal processes required by the homework.

The use of movement or sound to integrate dissociated verbal and nonverbal experiences is central to eye movement desensitization and reprocessing (EMDR). This treatment uses movement, touch, or sound carried on simultaneously with focused recall to desensitize and reintegrate dissociated experience in traumatized patients. As I emphasized in Chapter 3, language attenuates feeling. Practitioners of EMDR believe that their technique integrates experiences segregated in the right brain with language and memory in the left. In consequence, those experiences are more accurately perceived and emotionally less disabling. Bessel van der Kolk, a distinguished expert on post-traumatic stress disorder (PTSD), has done imaging that supports this under-standing of EMDR. It may be that this therapeutic technique holds promise for some bipolar children who are traumatized by life's ordi-nary circumstances.

# PART III

## Treatment

# CHAPTER TWELVE

# Psychotherapy

Treatment of bipolar disorder in a child needs to make use of many different resources and several different kinds of trained professionals.

## TYPES OF THERAPISTS

### CHILD PSYCHIATRISTS

Psychiatrists are medical doctors (M.D.) who have undergone training in all areas of medicine before specializing in the diagnosis and treatment of psychiatric illness. Child psychiatrists have received additional training in the treatment of psychiatric disorders in children. Child psychiatrists also have studied child development and its interaction with psychiatric illness. Some psychiatrists get additional training in psychotherapy, play therapy, or child psychoanalysis; some undergo additional training in psychopharmacology; some do both. Additional training gives them particular expertise. It is appropriate to ask a psychiatrist what training he or she has had in psychotherapy or psychopharmacology beyond initial training as a psychiatrist. Always ask a psychiatrist to describe his or her experience in diagnosing and treating children with bipolar disorder.

## CHILD PSYCHOLOGISTS

Child psychologists (Ph.D. or Psy.D.) have undergone training in the diagnosis and treatment of psychiatric disorders. Although psychologists do not have training in other areas of medicine, they are trained in areas in which M.D.'s are not, for example, administering and interpreting psychological testing. Psychologists are important members of the team that treats patients in psychiatric hospitals and in private practice. The education psychologists undertake beyond their Ph.D. can vary: some receive training in psychotherapy, play therapy, or psychoanalysis; some study psychological and neuropsychological testing; some do both. As with a psychiatrist, be sure to ask a psychologist about any training and experience acquired after his or her degree.

## PSYCHIATRIC SOCIAL WORKERS

Psychiatric social workers (M.S.W., C.S.W., or D.S.W.) have training in the diagnosis and treatment of psychiatric disorders and in psychology. They are also trained to appreciate and work with the environmental factors affecting mental disorders. Social workers are also an important part of the team treating psychiatric patients in a hospital or in private practice. Like psychologists and psychiatrists, clinical social workers may be specially trained in psychotherapy, play therapy, and psychoanalysis. Similar to a psychiatrist or psychologist, a social worker's expertise as a therapist depends on the training he or she pursues after obtaining a degree.

## SUBSTANCE ABUSE COUNSELORS

Treatment of substance abuse requires special expertise. Many skilled therapists (myself among them) need to consult when severe substance abuse is a factor in a patient's treatment. The highest level of certification in this area is Certified Addiction Professional or Counselor (CAP or CAC). These are professionals who, together with psychiatrists, psychologists, and social workers, diagnose and treat substance abuse in individual and group settings. They have special training and experience in working with the problems that accompany substance abuse—physical danger, denial, relapse, social isolation, problems with self-regulation, chronic dishonesty, boundary violations. They themselves have sometimes recovered from substance abuse, know the dangers of these disorders, and use this knowledge to help other people. Many mental health professionals benefit in their ability to work with mental illness from the experience they have had in working with their own problems. Such experience is a tremendous asset.

## OCCUPATIONAL THERAPISTS

When subtle sensory or physical disabilities accompany bipolar disorder, as they often do, an occupational therapist may be needed for both diagnosis and treatment. These professionals work to remediate problems affecting visual or auditory processing, heightened sensory awareness, and problems with fine- and gross-motor coordination. Because a young child's central nervous system is particularly adaptive, the sooner such treatment is begun, the more effective it can be.

# FORMS OF PSYCHOTHERAPY

A child with bipolar disorder requires different kinds of treatment at different stages of development for different problems. Appropriate medication addresses biological problems; appropriate psychotherapy treats the individual and the family with those problems.

## INDIVIDUAL THERAPY

There are a number of different types of individual therapy, which are used for different problems and at different ages.

**COGNITIVE-BEHAVIORAL THERAPY (CBT)**   This kind of therapy has developed into a powerful tool in treating many disorders in recent years. Cognitive-behavioral therapy helps identify unexamined ideas that can contribute to (or help change) problematic behaviors; it also devises strategies (behavioral plans) to modify behavior. CBT can be effective with patients who are unable to use other forms of therapy; it can also sometimes be more direct and economical. CBT is used with problems like oppositional behavior, bed-wetting or soiling, obsessive-compulsive symptoms, post-traumatic stress disorder, and borderline personality disorder. CBT can also be combined with other forms of therapy.

**INSIGHT ORIENTED THERAPY**   This is talk therapy, the common kind of treatment used for many different purposes. It can help identify unexamined or deeply buried experiences that affect a child's behavior or mood; peculiarities or frightening parts of a child's inner life can be explored and validated. In the protected environment maintained by the therapist, a child can take on developmental problems that have not been solved. In talking, a therapist can help a child approach problems that are too sensitive to handle directly with parents or other adults. Through the child's relationship with the therapist, damaged parts of a child's relationship with his parents—mistrust, overdependence, poor self-esteem—can be repaired. Problems with identity, intimacy, and sexuality can be approached. Talk therapy is normally used with adults and adolescents.

**PLAY THERAPY**   Children normally use play to master or dramatically express their emotional life. As in a dream (or in art), play can also reach otherwise inexpressible thoughts and feelings. In the protected let's-pretend world of play, a child can dramatically enact forbidden anger, terrifying loss, or disturbing fantasies. In games, a child can learn to risk aggression, play by the rules (often first by not observing them), tolerate and enjoy competition, and acquire skills bit by bit rather than in fantasy.

Activities in play therapy become healing because they are observed and facilitated by the therapist. A child's need to be seen and his fear of being seen meet in play—in an act that enlarges and strengthens the child's sense of himself. The presence of a special adult who pays careful attention to, participates in, and guides a child's play allows the child to express, sometimes change, and become comfortable with thoughts and feelings that have been disabling.

## Group Therapy

The corrective force in group therapy is the interaction between the members of the group and the connection each member makes to the group. The group is experienced by each member as a separate presence, distinct from the presence of any individual member. The problems many bipolar children have in the peer group make group therapy a crucial resource in their treatment. Indeed, problems that come up in the peer group cannot be effectively addressed in individual or in family therapy. Unfortunately, an appropriate group is often difficult to find, because group therapy for children is a seriously undervalued and, consequently, underused form of treatment.

**SOCIAL SKILLS GROUP** This is probably the most commonly available group for younger children (eight to twelve). This form of group therapy takes a cognitive-behavioral approach, identifying problematic behaviors and modeling desirable behaviors and skills. There is a strong directive adult presence in this group, along with practical interaction with peers.

**ACTIVITY-GROUP THERAPY** This type of group is less frequently encountered but is probably the most effective kind of treatment for children who have difficulty entering the peer group. Unlike the social skills group, there is no direct instruction and the therapist's presence is much less prominent, although it is crucial in a different way. The forces for change and development in this type of group therapy are nonverbal: the desire of children to be with other children (social hunger), the interactions among the members (which include aggression, competition, cooperation, and dysfunctional behaviors), and the allegiance the members form to the group. The action of the group itself instructs its members in the management of aggression in a hands-on way by exposing them to it, encouraging them to play with aggression—deal it out, fend it off, and put a spin on it—helping them get a feel for limiting their own aggression and setting limits with that of their peers. Leadership in an activity group is assumed by one of the members, who is tacitly recognized, obeyed, and emulated by the other members. The therapist's role is to facilitate the group's play, contain it within a physical boundary, and ensure safety. As the group culture matures, however, these functions are gradually assumed by the group members and especially by its leader. Because it works nonverbally, an activity group is accessible to children with a wide variety of diagnoses and verbal capacities. It is far more powerful than talk for children age eight to twelve.

**ADOLESCENT GROUP THERAPY** As children move into adolescence, their earlier preoccupation with aggression is replaced by an interest in and a need for emotional and sexual intimacy. At the same time, adolescents develop a new capacity for abstract thinking and consequently an increased capacity for verbal expression and interaction. These changes make groups that are verbally oriented (psychoanalytic or cognitive) more effective for adolescents. Difficulty with peer relationships continues to be the most compelling reason for group therapy with an adolescent, but by this age the developmental goal is intimacy rather than managing aggression. The two types of group are similar, however, in an important way: the school-age child needs to learn to confront and manage aggression with peers; the adolescent needs to learn to manage verbal confrontation and interaction with peers. With both ages, the process of confrontation and resolution—the back-and-forth process of the group—is therapeutic. The increased interaction between boys and girls in adolescence makes a mixed group appropriate, providing an additional kind of confrontation.

Consumption disorders, which carry with them difficulties managing intimacy, need specially composed groups (groups for eating disorders, drug abuse, or alcohol abuse), but these groups all take advantage of the same forces: dynamic confrontation by peers, articulation of thoughts and feelings, and acknowledgment or validation of particular adolescent concerns. Social anxiety, a need to belong, and a longing for intimacy are key problems with adolescents suffering from consumption disorders; the action of a group is particularly effective in helping these difficulties.

In a verbally based group led by a therapist, things work differently than in an activity group. Members attach both to the therapist and to the group, and the therapeutic process works to get the adolescent to talk. As with the activity group, however, the therapeutic agent is the adolescent's interaction with the members and with the group as a whole, including confrontation by other members, articulation of problems, and acknowledgment from the group. It is the adolescent's desire to be part of the group that allows her to tolerate the therapeutic process of confrontation and articulation.

The intense self-consciousness and sense of inadequacy adolescents suffer—particularly adolescents who are struggling socially—makes it crucial for them to have their concerns acknowledged *by peers*. Acknowledgment is particularly important at an age when, if one is socially isolated, the sense of deformity can be overwhelming. A group gives its members such acknowledgment. What is more, this acknowledgment can come without active participation, by simply listening to and observing the problems faced by other members and the ways they work with them. In addition to the holding environment the group and the therapist provide, this acknowledgment by peers is an important part of the therapeutic process. Such acknowledgment is not available in individual treatment.

## FAMILY THERAPY

Like individual therapy, family therapy can serve a number of functions: parental counseling can educate a family about bipolar disorder and its treatment; it can help parents manage difficult circumstances (such as limit setting with a severely oppositional child or offering appropriate support to a child struggling with a particular problem); it can foster better cooperation between parents; it can serve as a safe place where damaged relationships between family members can be repaired, where untreated family members (who need treatment) can be identified, and where family secrets can be talked about. The family members who attend sessions vary with the task at hand and the age of the afflicted child. Parental counseling may be limited to the parents or parental figures; problems with wider family function often require all members—during such sessions younger children often talk about things older family members don't notice or cannot approach. They provide valuable perceptions of what goes on in the family. In most cases it is best that the therapist who treats the child also conducts the family therapy. There are times, however, when an adolescent's treatment needs to be separated from family work. In such cases, separate therapists should work with the adolescent and with the family as a whole.

## Why Therapy Works

### Therapy Expands Consciousness

*Consciousness* gives us choice. It puts disturbing thoughts and feelings in front of us rather than allowing them to remain hidden. Whether exposing unexamined ideas, as in cognitive therapy, or expressing deeply buried feelings, as in talk therapy or play therapy, an enlargement of consciousness gives us more flexibility in our behavior.

### Therapy Helps Us Practice Acts That at First Are Impossible

The behavioral plans in cognitive therapy and the free-ranging discussion of talk therapy both help a person do things that at first are undoable. Therapy increases our ability to act effectively because it establishes new neural pathways, allowing us to make connections be-tween desire and action, between one experience and another, or be-tween feelings and the words to express them. Therapy can help a person trapped in a state of agony move beyond it or see that the painful state does not have to be permanent. Therapy makes connec-tions between one part of the brain and another (thought with action, feeling with language, the deep brain with various parts of the cortex, and one part of the cortex with another). Learning also creates such connections, but therapy is a special kind of learning.

## THERAPY DECREASES FEELINGS THAT LIMIT OUR ABILITY TO ACT OR TO MAKE CHOICES

Our central nervous system can accommodate unmanageable feelings. For example, when we first get into a hot tub, the water is uncomfort-ably hot, but within a moment or two it begins to feel comfortable and pleasant. Our nerves have adjusted (accommodated) to the tem-perature. If we pull back from the hot tub too soon, however, we do not adjust to the temperature. If the water is too hot, we are not able to adjust—we get burned.

Similarly, therapy can help a person accommodate to experiences and perform acts that otherwise would be (or have been) overwhelming. The therapist uses his or her skill to keep the exposure within tolerable limits and help a person not pull back from the discomfort of the process. Ac-commodation happens by connecting deeper parts of the brain (in-volved with raw emotion) with the cortex (the part that observes, acts, and talks). However, the cortex is also a part of our brain that *inhibits* overwhelming feeling. So by talking about uncomfortable things, or by doing them, we moderate feelings that had previously been intolerable.

## THERAPY CAN VALIDATE FEELINGS THAT WERE THOUGHT TO BE UNACCEPTABLE OR WEIRD

Our thoughts and feelings need to be echoed or confirmed. The words *conscience* (from the Latin *con scio*) or *acknowledge* (from the Greek *ak nous*) both mean to "know next to." This *knowing next to* is crucial to mental health; it confers integrity or wholeness. A therapist knows about important things *next to* the child; accompanies the child into unmanageable or terrifying situations, internally or externally; and is present as the child does things that once were impossible. Because the therapist is also aware of the peculiar symptoms children have, he or she can explain those symptoms and keep children from feeling weird or ashamed. A therapist also knows about the confusing or frightening appearance of unconscious ideas and can explain and validate their presence to a child. This *knowing next to* is healing and empowering.

Therapy connects (or strengthens the connection between) different parts of the brain. When a feeling is put into words, a connection is made between deeper, more primitive, parts of the brain and the cortex—the most evolved part of the brain where language resides. When a sequestered experience is expressed in play or in words, two parts of the brain that were kept separate from each other (in a way that was causing pain or disability) are connected. These new connections confer integrity and wholeness to the person.

## Choosing an Approach

The kind of therapy used depends on the problem being addressed and what is causing the problem. Most therapists use different kinds of therapy for different parts of the treatment. Here are some examples.

*An eight-year-old boy is wetting the bed* because he has an inherited type of bed-wetting (connected with extremely deep sleep). Parents need to understand that their child is not defiant or seriously immature. The child may need reassurance, and a plan may need to be worked out about how to limit the problem (this may include fluid restriction just before bed, a pad and bell, or a medication to decrease filling of the bladder, especially on sleepovers). These are cognitive-behavioral approaches.

If, however, it is discovered that the child's bed-wetting is a result of extreme anxiety or sexual abuse, individual play therapy may be needed to identify the sources of anxiety or, in the case of abuse, to help the child uncover what happened and begin to deal with its effects. Family therapy may be needed to address family dysfunction causing the problem or to support parents who are overwhelmed by what has happened to their child.

*An eight-year-old boy has severe oppositional behavior.* It is important to determine if the behavior occurs at home or outside the home. Parents may need help in understanding how to set appropriate limits; a behavioral plan may need to be drawn up; coordination may need to be established with the child's school. These are all cognitive-behavioral approaches.

If these approaches are not working and the oppositional behavior is driven by an unstable or irritable mood, medication may be needed before any form of treatment will be effective. If parents are in severe conflict with one another, family therapy may be needed. If the child has suffered serious problems in his relationship with a parent because of extended conflict or ongoing family problems (a divorce, depression or substance abuse in a parent), individual play therapy and family therapy may be needed to repair basic trust, self-esteem, and the relationship between child and parent. In the case of a hostile divorce, a group for children involved in divorce may also be helpful. If the oppositional behavior has seriously affected the child's peer relationships, group therapy may be needed.

*A thirteen-year-old girl develops anorexia.* A psychiatric evaluation needs to be done to determine if there is a contributing mood disorder, sexual trauma, or personality disorder and if the child is in medical danger. An internist who specializes in adolescent medicine should be consulted. If the psychiatrist is comfortable taking charge of the treatment, he or she will do a family assessment as well, because eating disorders are usually tied into a family problem. Individual therapy should be begun with a therapist experienced in treating eating disorders. If there are significant problems with peer relationships, adolescent group therapy may be necessary. Family therapy will most likely be needed to help parents understand how to help their child, and, if necessary, to address problems within the family that are contributing to the problem.

*A sixteen-year-old girl, in individual psychotherapeutic treatment for several years, has failed to improve and is having increasing difficulties at home, in school, and with friends.* A conference needs to be held with the child's therapist (and psychiatrist if one is involved) to get a sense of why things are getting worse. A second opinion from another psychiatrist is needed. This psychiatrist need not be someone who would assume treatment. Sometimes it is best to see a highly experienced psychiatrist who will give a second opinion and provide a referral if needed.

## STAGES OF RECOVERY

In evaluating your child's treatment, it is important to understand that recovery from bipolar disorder takes place in stages. These stages are defined by the kind of problems they address.

### MOOD STABILITY

Initial stabilization of mood may take from two to six months. It may not be complete at first but progress from year to year. The task may require several classes of medication: a mood stabilizer, a major tranquilizer, a minor tranquilizer, and, when tolerated, an antidepressant and a medication for ADD. The number of medications used is less significant than the doses and combinations. It is safer and more effective to use a combination of medications at lower doses than one or two medications at higher doses or with an incomplete response.

As recovery continues, there will be changes in mood from season to season and year to year, but the episodes will be less severe.

Medications usually need to be adjusted during an episode and at the change of some seasons.

Over time, a goal will be to have a child or adolescent take more and more responsibility for communicating with the psychiatrist to alert him or her of changes or of side effects from medications.

## Judgment

A person's judgment is affected by mood changes in bipolar disorder and the developmental impact of the condition. Judgment takes a longer time to be restored than mood. With a first severe manic episode in an adolescent or an adult, judgment may take six months to a year to return to its previous capacity. In a child, the development of judgment will lag behind that of peers. Psychotherapy, the reestablishment of developmental progress, and repair of the psychosocial base are important to the restoration of judgment.

## The Psychosocial Base

Self-esteem, family relationships, peer relationships, and academic or professional function are damaged by bipolar disorder. The restoration of these parts of a person's life can take one to two years or more. The process is more gradual in a child and in someone who has recurrent disabling episodes. It is crucial for a therapist to help a patient and family see that progress made in this part of the treatment, although it is made over years, is the base of true stability.

# Problems in Therapy

Sometimes therapy is not effective. Problems can arise from a number of directions.

## A Parent Knowingly or Unknowingly Undermines Therapy

Children work with a therapist with a parent's approval. Their ability to feel safe with the therapist and their ability to express themselves freely depends on the parent's permission to do so. When a parent objects to a treatment or consistently interferes with it—for example, by voicing opposition to the treatment in front of the child, by not bringing a child regularly, or by always having someone else bring the child—the child gets the message that cooperating with the treatment is unnecessary or against the parent's wishes.

## A Child Resists Treatment Despite a Parent's Cooperation

No one begins therapy, and no parent brings his or her child into therapy, because it would be a good idea or interesting. A person agrees to therapy only because she is in unbearable pain, is about to lose something she doesn't want to lose, or someone else makes her do it. Therapy is uncomfortable, painful, and hard work that a person has to pay for. Therapy enters into areas of our thoughts and feelings that normally are kept private and protected from even our own view. For these reasons, as a therapist works, a child will *resist* his or her efforts.

A child can resist therapy by refusing to come, refusing to talk or play, exhibiting boredom or disconnection with the work, cooperating superficially but remaining more deeply guarded or defiant, or lying. Resistance is normal, and a skilled therapist learns to work with it. At times, however, a child completely refuses to cooperate over a long period of time, or the child acts in a dangerous or persistently defiant way outside of the treatment. When this happens, a competent therapist tells a parent and the child that the treatment is not working and that a different one is needed: another therapist, another type of treatment (group or family rather than individual, or specific treatment for substance abuse), or another level of treatment. The therapist should then help with an appropriate referral.

## A Therapist Mismanages the Treatment

Not every therapist is right for every child, every family, or every disorder. Sometimes a therapist consistently approaches a child in a way that prevents the child from feeling safe or trusting; sometimes a therapist lacks the skill to help the child move through his resistance; sometimes a therapist fails to establish a working relationship with the child's parents. Ideally, the therapist acknowledges such a difficulty and offers to refer the family to someone else, but if this does not happen, it is important for you to bring up concerns about or objections to the treatment. *The best assurance that a treatment will go well is the child's and the parents' ability to effectively complain when things do not feel right.* If complaints are not answered, you need to consider working with another therapist.

## RESOURCES

Because bipolar disorder affects a child's mind as well as her mood, affects development, and affects the parents and the family, it needs to be treated psychotherapeutically as well as pharmacologically. Finding your way among the different treatments and the professionals who practice them can be confusing and upsetting. You should expect and ask for help in this process—from a pediatrician, a psychiatrist, an educator, and other parents who have experience. Available resources vary from place to place, and you may need to travel for an expert opinion regarding one or another facet of your child's treatment. *Find knowledgeable people who pay attention to you and your child, over time.* In most cases there needs to be more than one person helping you. It is important that these people communicate with each other, but you are the center of the team, holding it together with your attention, your questions, and your knowledge of your child.

### INITIAL EVALUATION

The suggestion that your child may suffer from bipolar disorder may come from a pediatrician or neurologist, a therapist, an educator, another parent, or your own experience with the disorder. The evaluation of that suggestion needs to be done by a child psychiatrist experienced in the evaluation and treatment of bipolar disorder in children. There are several ways to find such a person:

· If you live in a metropolitan area with one or more university hospitals, there are specialists nearby. Someone in your network of acquaintances may be experienced enough to give you a referral. A referral from someone you know often includes knowledge of the psychiatrist that goes beyond credentials and hospital affiliation.

· If no one in your network can help you—or the suggestions you receive prove inadequate—the Internet is the quickest way to find people who have experience and the names of accomplished psychiatrists. Here are some useful Web sites:

- · Child and Adolescent Bipolar Foundation: bpkids.org
- · American Academy of Child and Adolescent Psychiatry: aacap.org
- · Depression and Bipolar Support Alliance (DBSA): dbsalliance.org
- · Juvenile Bipolar Research Foundation: bpchildresearch.org

· You can contact the Department of Child Psychiatry at a major university hospital. Even if you do not see someone at that center, you can find someone to make a competent referral. These hospitals have leading clinicians in child bipolar disorder:

*East Coast*

Massachusetts General Hospital
Pediatric Psychopharmacology Unit
55 Fruit St.
Boston, MA 02114
(617) 726-2725

Division of Child and Adolescent Psychiatry
State University of New York

Stony Brook, NY 11794
(631) 632-8850


Children's Hospital of Philadelphia
Department of Child and Adolescent Psychiatry
34th St. and Civic Center Blvd.
Philadelphia, PA 19104
(215) 590-7573


Virginia Treatment Center for Children
Division of Child and Adolescent Psychiatry
515 N. 10th St.
Richmond, VA 23298
(804) 828-3129


*Midwest*


Rush-Presbyterian-St. Luke's Medical Center
1653 W. Congress Parkway
Chicago, IL 60612
(312) 942-5592


Pediatric Bipolar Program
Children's Hospital
Medical Center of Cincinnati
3333 Burnet Ave.
Cincinnati, OH 45229
(513) 558-0956


Stanley Research Center
Case Western Reserve University
Cleveland, OH 44106
(216) 844-3881

Washington University
Child Psychiatry Clinic
Children's Hospital
St. Louis, MO 63110
(314) 286-1740

*West Coast*

Pediatric Mood Disorders Clinic
Stanford School of Medicine
401 Quarry Rd.
Stanford, CA 94305
(650) 723-5511

Adolescent Mood Disorders Program
UCLA Neuropsychiatric Institute
Los Angeles, CA 90024
(310) 825-5730

In contacting one of these departments, a psychiatrist or pediatrician you work with may be able to make the contact more easily. Doctors have an easier time getting to speak to doctors.

## FINDING A THERAPIST

· As with finding a psychiatrist, a referral from someone you know may be based on more direct information about the clinician.

· The Web sites listed above can also serve as referral sources for therapists. In addition, consult
  · American Group Psychotherapy Association: agp.org
  · American Association for Marriage and Family Therapy: aamft.org

## Support Groups

Joining a local support group is one of the best ways to learn about nearby clinicians, medications, resources, problems, and solutions other families have found, and to make the kind of personal contacts that are most important over the long haul. The Child and Adolescent Bipolar Foundation (bpkids.org) is an excellent source for locating one near you.

## Online Blogs

Online discussions about bipolar disorder are a source of information about other people's experiences. Although they can contain misinformation, they can also provide a view of bipolar disorder and its treatments not available in published material. I use them to learn about side effects people have with medications that I may not have seen or heard about from colleagues.

## Reading

*For a Popular Audience*

*The Bipolar Child: The Definitive and Reassuring Guide to Childhood's Most Misunderstood Disorder* by Demitri Papolos, M.D. and Janice Papolos (2002). Dr. Papolos provides a wealth of detailed information about diagnosis, scientific understanding, and resources needed at various stages of treatment of bipolar disorder in children.

*Surviving Manic Depression: A Manual on Bipolar Disorder for Patients, Families and Providers* by E. Fuller Torrey, M.D. and Michael Knable, D.O. (2002). A comprehensive source of information—scientific, clinical, and practical. Dr. Torrey is a leading authority and an excellent writer.

*Acquainted with the Night: A Parent's Quest to Understand Depression and Bipolar Disorder in His Children* by Paul Raeburn (2004). An account of the author's harrowing struggle to understand the disorder that afflicted his two children (a boy and girl) very differently and that fractured his family. Raeburn's account of his experiences contains information about resources in a context that unmistakably defines their value.

*An Unquiet Mind: A Memoir of Mood and Madness* by Kay Redfield Jamison (1995). A brilliant writer, psychologist, and psychiatrist, and an international authority on bipolar disorder, Dr. Jamison gives an account of her struggle to recognize, master, and accept pharmacologic treatment for bipolar disorder. An unmatched account of this disease from someone who knows it personally and scientifically.

*Night Falls Fast: Understanding Suicide* by Kay Redfield Jamison (1999). Dr. Jamison looks at the histories and the psychological states of people who commit suicide. She uses her personal and clinical experience and her understanding to portray this problem and the measures that are needed to contend with it.

*Scientific Work*

*Bipolar Disorder in Childhood and Early Adolescence* edited by Barbara Geller, M.D. (2003). Dr. Geller is a leading physician and scientist in the field of bipolar disorder in children. Her book is the most recent and highly regarded scientific account.

*The Dissociative Mind* by Elizabeth F. Howell (2005). Dr. Howell's detailed study of dissociation as it occurs along the spectrum from normalcy to severe trauma explains an area of psychology that is just beginning to be understood. Her book provides an important and different way of looking at the mental states found in many different disorders.

# CHAPTER THIRTEEN

# Conclusion

*Bipolar Disorder at the Beginning of the*
*Twenty-First Century*

## WHERE HAVE WE BEEN? WHERE ARE WE NOW? WHERE ARE WE GOING?

Today bipolar disorder can be treated readily and effectively. To most parents, however, the diagnosis of bipolar disorder is frightening and mysterious, but it can be treated like any other manageable illness—asthma or epilepsy for instance. However, treatment should begin early, be continued consistently, and be preventative as well as symptomatic. The good news is that the biological treatment of bipolar disorder is advancing faster than any other area in psychiatry. New medications are not only being developed but the underlying causes of bipolar disorder are also being identified. More precise observation of the brain's activity will help to make meaningful distinctions between one form of the disorder and another and explain some of the accompanying problems, such as ADD or dyslexia. These developments will also help us understand more precisely what medicines to use and when.

It will also be necessary, however, to understand the impact this disorder has on a child's development. The developmental problems children with bipolar disorder suffer are every bit as disabling as the biological ones. Wider understanding of these problems will help parents and clinicians work more effectively, preventing developmental failure as well as exacerbations of the illness.

The biggest problem is getting the right care to the children and families who need it. Delivering that care will be made possible by greater recognition and understanding of this disorder, its biology, and its effects on development. In the last century, infectious diseases came to be understood, effective treatments and preventative strategies were found, and these measures were implemented. The near eradication of polio and smallpox are among the more stunning results of these efforts. A similar improvement in the understanding and treatment of depression and bipolar disorder is now taking place. Indeed, many people who would have been consigned to lives of emptiness and suffering have already been restored to normalcy or better.

However, our ability to treat bipolar disorder today is limited in important ways by attitudes formed in the recent past. It is, after all, only about sixty years since the discovery of lithium as a treatment for bipolar disorder, forty years since antidepressants were introduced, and twenty years since the anticonvulsant mood stabilizers began to be used in bipolar disorder. It is only in the last five years that the distinction between bipolar disorder and ADD/ADHD has become clearer. The description and recognition of bipolar disorder in children are still emerging. The complexities of treating this disorder in children and adults are also just beginning to be worked out.

As this marvelous biological evolution takes place, it is important not to discard tools that have worked in the past. There has been an unfortunate tendency during this biological enlightenment to minimize the importance of psychotherapeutic help—the detailed and painstaking work that is needed to understand the mind of a person with bipolar disorder. There are those—distinguished psychiatrists among them—who dismiss psychotherapy as a cumbersome and expensive treatment that has been superseded by medication. Although psychotherapy cannot quell the more severe biological storms, it provides the tools we need to work with the developmental problems those biological disruptions bring about.

It is also true that because effective treatment is so recent, psychiatry still labors under the shadow of a time when there were no medical treatments for mental illness, and the afflicted were managed with confinement. One of the obstacles to changing the current state of care is a profound but largely unacknowledged fear of mental illness and a consequent denial of its presence. This fear also leads to a persistent confusion between the person suffering from an illness and the illness itself. In psychiatry, unlike most other areas of medicine, the problems we treat come very close to who a person is. Reaching the person caught in the illness is usually our first task. Making the distinction between the illness and the person is much more difficult, however, for people outside psychiatry, including other physicians and even people suffering from a psychiatric condition. Consequently, a bipolar child frequently is regarded as bad, delinquent, disruptive, or foolish. Confusion of a person with the illness causes people to shun the person rather than solve the problem.

Understanding the person with bipolar disorder is also a political problem. The insurance industry is permitted to treat psychiatric illness as a nonmedical condition. Consequently, appropriate treatment—when it is available—is beyond the reach of many families. Too many clinicians have no way around the limits set by managed care, and these limitations have affected the training of clinicians as well as their ability to offer care. Sophisticated psychopharmacologists are hard to find; pharmacologists skilled in treating children are even more difficult to find. Frequent psychotherapy, competent family therapy, and especially group therapy are also largely unavailable. It is rare for a child to be seen more than once a week by a therapist, rarer yet for a child to be offered group therapy. The political and economic forces that have fostered managed care have not only curtailed the availability of care, they also have changed the accepted standard of care, even among those clinicians who are not subject to such management. Consequently, even when resources are not a problem, it can still take years before a child is properly diagnosed and appropriate treatment is prescribed. At present, most children with bipolar disorder—one estimate puts it at four out of five—go undiagnosed and untreated.

In other words, scientific difficulties are not the only reasons for the undertreatment of mental illness in general and bipolar disorder in particular. Because effective treatments are so recent, mental illness inspires helplessness not just in the people who suffer it but also in the people around them, the people making decisions affecting their care. One way of managing helplessness about mental illness is to turn your back on the problem. A related strategy is to conclude that mental illness can't really be treated, so spending resources on its treatment is extravagant. This turns out to be a convenient logic for permitting insurance companies to offer more limited benefits for psychiatric than for medical care.

Mental illness and injury are in many ways invisible. We see no tumors or physical deformities in these patients; there are no blood tests to validate the presence of most mental conditions. Present techniques of imaging can only barely discern the changes that go on in the brain. Suffering that is invisible is easily ignored not only at the personal level but also on a wide social scale. Refusal to acknowledge an illness is maddening to people suffering from it.

The practice of confining mental patients—excluding them from the community—became widespread during the eighteenth century, the Age of Reason. The need to see people as rational and in control led inevitably to a denial and abhorrence of the irrational parts of our nature. Our own culture worships attractiveness, power, and fame. In such a culture, acknowledging mental illness—in oneself or one's family—carries an unspoken penalty, engendering feelings of uneasiness and suspicion.

Many people, including powerful politicians, struggle with their own emotional problems and don't want to be reminded of their difficulties or have them exposed. In many cases it is socially safer to suffer an untreated mental problem than to acknowledge it and seek treatment. The vague unexamined idea that mental illness is contagious, although rationally absurd, is widespread. Denial of mental illness is a social force as well as an individual evasion. Consequently, the enormous presence of mental illness in our society is denied, its real cost is minimized, the people suffering from it are isolated, and the need for treatment is evaded. This is a particularly destructive approach when it concerns children.

It takes courage to acknowledge the presence of bipolar disorder, in ourselves and in our children. Without acknowledgment, however, there can be no understanding or commitment to treatment—on the part of the culture or on the part of people and families suffering from the illness. Courage is not the absence of fear but the ability to do the right thing in the presence of fear. We have much less reason today to be afraid of the biology of bipolar disorder. There is still reason to be concerned about the fear and ignorance people have about this condition and to be concerned about the unwillingness of our society to help rather than shun children suffering with it. Change will need to come from both within and from outside the group of people who suffer from and who treat bipolar disorder. Denial needs to be confronted publicly as well as privately. Clinicians and their patients need to be informed about children's needs, but so must society at large.

I am confident that the science and clinical art *potentially* available for children with bipolar disorder will improve at an increasing rate— they certainly have in the past ten years. Our challenge is to get that treatment to the children who need it. Part of that task is to pay for the treatment they need. This is not a clinical but a political problem. To begin with, psychiatric illness must be acknowledged to be a medical illness. But, as this book has argued, it will also be necessary to go beyond the biology to the person. The crucial importance of psychotherapeutic treatment must also be acknowledged. Families need to be as free to seek psychotherapeutic help as they are to seek medicines. There must be a commitment not just to managing the symptoms but also to understanding the mind of the bipolar child.

# Common Medications
## *A Reference Guide*

The pharmacologic treatment of bipolar disorder is progressing at a faster rate than any other area in psychiatry. New drugs are being developed each year, and our knowledge of those already in use is growing rapidly. Indeed, our current understanding of bipolar disorder has in large measure developed from our growing experience with various medications. In a sense, medicines have served as biological probes to help us understand the nature of this disorder at a molecular level, as it affects specific neurotransmitters and their interactions between regions of the brain. Our ability to safely treat this disorder in children, and thereby improve its course over their lifetimes, is developing with great speed.

Pharmacologic treatment of bipolar disorder has two goals: to relieve symptoms and to prevent recurrent episodes of depression or mania. It is usually necessary to use a combination of drugs to achieve these goals. Some drugs stabilize mood, others treat depression, some are for anxiety, and others calm manic symptoms. The number of medications used is less important than finding the proper dosing and the right combination.

Finding the right combinations and dosages is as much an art as it is a science. Different amounts of medication may be needed depending on whether treatment is for an acute episode or to prevent a recurrence.

Because many people experience seasonal changes in their mood, it is often necessary to vary the combinations of medicines throughout the year. It is also important to bear in mind that any medicine can have different, even opposite, effects on different people with similar symptoms. There is no way to tell, simply on the basis of symptoms, how a person will respond to a particular drug.

## CHILDREN ARE SPECIAL CASES

The pharmacologic treatment of bipolar disorder in children is an extremely delicate task. The effect of medicines on children is uncertain because their central nervous system is still developing. There is very little experimental information about how medications affect children as compared to adults both immediately and over time. The long-term effects of some of the medications used to treat bipolar disorder in children—the anticonvulsant mood stabilizers—are better known because they have been used to treat epilepsy in children for a longer period of time.

It is also true that a mood disorder that begins in childhood is usually a more serious illness than one that begins later on in life. Studies indicate that antidepressants do not work as well in children as in adults. I suspect that this is because depression seen in children is most likely bipolar depression, and antidepressants are problematic in the treatment of bipolar disorder in adults as well as children. Similarly, the higher incidence of suicide in children treated with antidepressants could be explained by the fact that depression beginning in childhood is most commonly bipolar depression, that bipolar disorder in childhood is harder to recognize, and consequently the inappropriate use of an antidepressant in a child is more frequent.

Despite the uncertainty about the effects of medicines on children, we do know that the risk of the untreated illness is much higher than that of the medications used in its treatment. Moreover, in most cases, for psychotherapeutic treatment to be effective, pharmacologic treatment must be in place.

# CRUCIAL TERMS

**Dependence** is a common occurrence. A diabetic may depend on a drug to control blood sugar, a person with epilepsy may depend on one or several medications to prevent seizures, and someone with bipolar disorder may depend on one or more medications to control various symptoms. Dependence does not mean physiological dependence, tolerance, or addiction. Dependence on a medication is not related to a person's character or to the properties of the medication but simply to the person's medical condition.

**Physiological dependence** occurs when the nervous system, or one or more organs, adapts to the presence of a medication. The biochemistry of the human body consists of numerous chemical equilibriums, or balances. Certain medications shift the set point of these equilibriums so that, when the medication is *suddenly* withdrawn, the equilibrium is upset and a person experiences withdrawal symptoms. The symptoms of withdrawal vary depending on the properties of the medicine. For example, withdrawal from a benzodiazepine starts out as anxiety and progresses to rapid heartbeat, increased or decreased blood pressure, tremulousness, and confusion. Withdrawal symptoms from a short-acting antidepressant can be dizziness, muscle aches, nausea, and fatigue. Benzodiazepines, steroids, anticonvulsants, and some antidepressants all bring about physiological dependence. Medications that have this property are not necessarily mood altering, although they may be.

**Tolerance** results when the effect of a medicine diminishes and the dose must be increased to maintain efficacy. Tolerance can develop to one of a medicine's effects but not to others. For example, you may become tolerant to the hypnotic (sleep-inducing) effect of a benzodiazepine: after a week or so of constant use it doesn't make you drowsy anymore, but it continues to have its full effect of relieving anxiety. Similarly, the sedating effects of anticonvulsants like Tegretol, Trileptal, and Depakote fade after a period of time, but the anticonvulsant properties do not give way to tolerance: at a therapeutic blood level you continue to receive anticonvulsant protection for an unlimited period of time.

**Addiction** is a set of behaviors connected with the use of a substance and is characterized by use of that substance—cocaine, opiates, tobacco—to alter consciousness (to get high) in a way that threatens personal, interpersonal, or occupational function (marriage, friendships, job, health). Addiction *always* involves lying and dishonesty. Tolerance to the mood-altering characteristics of particular drugs develops over time. For example, after a period of time cocaine loses its euphoric effect and merely causes anxiety or irritability; after continued use opiates no longer produce euphoria and their relief of pain diminishes. Some abused substances—opiates, benzodiazepines, tobacco, caffeine, marijuana—also induce physiological dependence; abrupt discontinuation causes withdrawal symptoms.

It is true that some people are at particular risk for addiction when using certain medications, but the medications themselves are not addictive. Addiction is a pattern of behavior seen in a person, not the property of a medication. *It is possible to depend on a medication that has properties of physiologic dependence and tolerance without being addicted to that medication.*

## MANY MEDICINES FOR A COMPLEX DISORDER

The range of symptoms occurring in bipolar disorder include elevations and depressions of mood (including mania; hypomania; melancholic, atypical, and psychotic depressions), chronic pervasive anxiety, panic attacks, irritability, and sleep disturbance. Treatment of these different symptoms often requires several classes of medication:

· one or more mood stabilizers
· an antidepressant
· a minor tranquilizer
· a major tranquilizer or antipsychotic

Effective treatment usually entails the use of several of these drugs in combination, which may vary from one time to another.

## MOOD STABILIZERS

If you think of bipolar disorder as a spring suspended from two points, like a stretched-out Slinky bouncing up and down, mood stabilizers keep the spring from bouncing too much; they limit the ups and downs. To put it another way, they put in a floor to protect against depression and a ceiling to guard against mania or agitation.

Lithium was the first mood stabilizer discovered (in the middle of the twentieth century). With its discovery, many patients, previously considered untreatable, recovered. In the 1980s, when the anticonvulsant carbamazepine began to be used in the treatment of bipolar disorder, another group of patients, who had been unresponsive to lithium, also recovered. Since the introduction of carbamazepine, four or five other anticonvulsants have come into use as mood stabilizers.

### LITHIUM

Exactly how lithium helps moderate bipolar disorder is still not fully understood, but the medicine is known to slow the activity of neurons that become overactive—without affecting their function when they are normally active. Lithium can also enhance the effects of other medications used to treat bipolar disorder.

Lithium is *the* most effective of all medications for bipolar I, and when used skillfully it has minimal side effects. Because it is used to treat severe bipolar I disorder, lithium is thought of as a strong medication. When appropriately used, however, a person may not even be aware of its presence. Long-term studies have shown that patients (including children) who respond to lithium are well advised to remain on it without interruption.

When used alone, lithium must be given in a dose that will reach a known therapeutic concentration in the blood. A higher level is required to treat acute mania than to maintain protection when a person's mood is stable. When used by itself, lithium works by limiting the cells' capacity to become overactive. It takes a week or more for this effect to develop, and the effect remains for a week or more when use is interrupted. Because people eliminate lithium from their bodies at different speeds, doses vary from person to person: initially, blood levels should be measured weekly until the appropriate dose is determined. It is also possible to correlate saliva levels of lithium with therapeutic blood levels, thereby avoiding frequent blood drawing in a child.

Lithium is also combined with mood stabilizers, antidepressants, and major tranquilizers to increase their effectiveness. When used in this way, lithium begins to take effect more quickly and usually can be used at a lower dose.

## GETTING A BLOOD LEVEL

For several medications—lithium, Tegretol, Depakote, Lamictal—therapeutic blood levels have been established, and in using these medications a psychiatrist may order a drug level. Levels of medications are usually measured at their low point, twelve hours following an evening dose (and before a morning dose if there is one). The timing of the evening dose can be moved, however, to make the morning drawing more convenient—for example, from 6 P.M. to 8 or even to 10:00 P.M.

**LITHIUM DOSING** Lithium works inside the cells, inside the central nervous system (CNS). There is a barrier between the blood and the central nervous system, called the blood-brain barrier, which protects the CNS from large, potentially destructive molecules found in the blood. Lithium can pass through the blood-brain barrier, but only via specific cellular channels. This means that lithium gets to the CNS more slowly than into the blood; it also leaves the CNS more slowly than it leaves the blood.

The fact that lithium leaves the blood more rapidly than it does the CNS can be useful in managing its side effects. A single large dose of lithium will reach therapeutic levels in the CNS but will be cleared from the blood long before it leaves the CNS. This means that after an initial loading period, the drug can be taken once a day, or once every two days: the level in the CNS is adequate, while the blood level is quite low between doses. Consequently, there are fewer effects on peripheral organs, such as weight gain, increased urination, or gastrointestinal discomfort. When lithium is given at night, the most pronounced effects on peripheral organs occur during sleep. Once-a-day dosing is also more convenient.

In some children, a high dose of lithium at night causes bedwetting, and a single dose in the morning causes gastrointestinal distress. For them, lithium is better given several times a day to decrease the peak blood levels and the side effects on the body.

**LITHIUM'S SIDE EFFECTS** The difference between a therapeutic and a toxic level of lithium can be quite small, especially when it's being used to treat acute mania. For this reason, it's important to distinguish the side effects of lithium that may occur when the drug is at a therapeutic level and those that occur with a toxic level. When administered properly, lithium's side effects are mild and completely reversible when the medication is discontinued or the dose is lowered. The one exception occurs only with long-term use of lithium—fifteen to twenty years. After this length of time, the ordinary effects of aging make the task of eliminating lithium more difficult, and a loss of kidney function can occur. There is otherwise no evidence that lithium damages the brain or other peripheral organs.

There is recent research showing that lithium has a *protective* effect on the brain: patients receiving long-term lithium treatment had a higher rate of cell regeneration in the brain than normal subjects not treated with lithium. There is also a study showing that children with bipolar disorder treated with lithium do not experience the decrease in brain volume that is seen in children with bipolar disorder who are untreated.

When taken at a therapeutic dose, the *possible* side effects of lithium include

· Mild nausea and a sensation of abdominal bloating, usually temporary.

· Increased thirst and urination. This is a dose-related and reversible side effect caused by a decrease in the kidneys' ability to concentrate urine. Although this is usually a mild effect, it can be particularly troubling to younger children whose bladder control is tenuous, causing them to wet their bed at night. This problem can sometimes be avoided by giving them their lithium in the morning. If this doesn't work, certain water pills (diuretics) can be given to moderate this side effect. A synthetic antidiuretic hormone delivered via a nasal spray just before sleep is also effective and safe.

· Decreased thyroid function, possibly causing mood instability or fatigue. This is also a reversible side effect and is rare in children. Because it can begin subtly, however, thyroid function should be tested every six months. If there is a decrease in thyroid function, thyroid supplementation is a simple remedy and lithium treatment need not be discontinued.

· Acne, or aggravation of existing acne, in adolescents.

· Weight gain, the severity of which varies depending on a child's metabolism.

· A mild, fine tremor. (In children who already have difficulties with fine-motor coordination or graphomotor skills, the tremor may cause problems with handwriting.)

· Mild problems with concentration. These difficulties can aggravate symptoms of ADD. In some children, lithium can block the beneficial effects of stimulants. In patients who are hypomanic, however, concentration may actually improve with lithium.

· A mild decrease in fine-motor coordination. This is usually a subtle effect and most important in children who are competitive athletes.

· Limitations in peak athletic performance, without affecting normal activities. This, again, is a side effect most troublesome in competitive athletes.

## SIGNS OF LITHIUM TOXICITY

· severe nausea
· diarrhea
· vomiting
· an increased, coarse tremor
· drowsiness
· confusion

**GUIDELINES WHEN USING LITHIUM**   Lithium is a salt that closely resembles sodium. The kidneys carefully monitor sodium, which regulates the amount of water in the body (hydration). Your sodium level falls if you lose large amounts of body fluids, for example, through excessive perspiration, diarrhea, or vomiting. As the body's level of sodium drops, the kidneys retain lithium *as if it were sodium,* causing an increase in the lithium level, although the dose is unchanged.

During the summer, or when exercising strenuously, a child or adolescent on lithium must be careful to replace salt lost in perspiration. This can be done with salt tablets, or by making sure there is adequate salt in the child's diet. There is no danger of taking too much salt, for excess sodium is simply excreted by the kidneys. Salt replacement is particularly important in a child attending summer camp.

If a child develops diarrhea or vomiting while on lithium, it may not be possible to distinguish early lithium toxicity from an illness, and even if it is an illness, the loss of fluids will increase the child's lithium level. When a child on lithium develops diarrhea or vomiting—for any reason—lithium should be discontinued until these symptoms are gone. The positive effects of lithium are not lost if it is stopped for a few days. When vomiting or diarrhea have passed, lithium can be safely restarted. *When in doubt, discontinue the lithium and contact the child's psychiatrist.*

Almost none of the medications given to children and adolescents interact with lithium. The most common that do are nonsteroidal anti-inflammatory drugs (NSAIDs) such as aspirin, ibuprofen, and naproxen (Aleve). These medications slightly decrease the kidneys' ability to eliminate lithium, and with *prolonged* use increase lithium levels. One or two doses of an NSAID will not have a significant effect. If any of these drugs must be used for a prolonged period of time, the dose of lithium should be lowered during that time but need not be discontinued. In children with asthma, aminophylline or theophylline can lower lithium levels. These medications are taken on a constant basis like lithium, so the dose of lithium needs to be adjusted in their presence.

An important difference between lithium and the other mood stabilizers—all of which are anticonvulsants—is that lithium can *lower* the seizure threshold. Lithium should not be used in children with epilepsy or an irritable spot in the brain. This is important to remember, because there is sometimes a subtle overlap between bipolar disorder and epilepsy. This overlap is more frequent in bipolar II than bipolar I.

Because of its effects on concentration, coordination, and urination, and its tendency to aggravate acne, lithium can be more problematic in children and adolescents than in adults. On the other hand, children tend to tolerate higher doses of lithium without side effects.

When it suits the needs of a child, lithium provides considerable safety in bipolar disorder both in treating symptoms and in preventing future episodes. In a compelling circumstance, lithium can be discontinued abruptly without any negative *physical* effects. When there is a choice, however, it is not advisable to stop lithium (or most psychiatric medications) abruptly. Studies have shown that recurrence of episodes of depression or mania are much less likely when lithium is gradually discontinued over the course of several months.

## ANTICONVULSANT MOOD STABILIZERS

The reason anticonvulsants work in bipolar disorder is that both epilepsy and bipolar disorder consist in a periodic overactivity of the CNS. Anticonvulsants are designed to prevent overactivity of neurons without affecting their normal function. In the same way that anticonvulsants protect against seizures, they also protect against the mania, anxiety, irritability, and agitation seen in bipolar disorder. Unfortunately, most do not protect against depressive episodes. Anticonvulsants, sometimes in combination with lithium and sometimes alone, are more effective than lithium alone in bipolar II disorder.

Anticonvulsants as a class cause physiologic dependence—they should not be stopped abruptly unless absolutely necessary.

*Anticonvulsants Commonly Used as Mood Stabilizers*

- carbamazepine (Tegretol, Atretol, others)
- oxcarbamazepine (Trileptal)
- valproic acid (Depakote)
- lamotrigine, Lamictal
- gabapentin (Neurontin)
- topiramate (Topamax)
- zonisamide (Zonegran)
- levetiracetam (Keppra)

**CARBAMAZEPINE (TEGRETOL, ATRETOL) AND OXCARBAMAZEPINE (TRILEPTAL)** Carbamazepine was the first anticonvulsant to be used widely to treat bipolar disorder, and it has been particularly effective in helping with symptoms of irritability, aggression, anxiety, and insomnia. There are long-term studies suggesting that carbamazepine can prevent recurrent episodes of mania and depression. The drug has been effective in treating bipolar I patients who are not helped by lithium alone. I use it particularly for a highly anxious, irritable, or impulsive child who does not have depressive symptoms.

Carbamazepine can be used alone or with a small dose of lithium. Combination with other mood stabilizers is possible, but its interactions with other medications—to treat bipolar disorder or other medical problems—can be complex. The interaction between carbamazepine and Depakote is particularly problematic, which is also true of its interaction with fluoxetine (Prozac). These medicines can be used together, however, by an experienced physician. Carbamazepine raises levels of macrolide antibiotics (erythromycin, Biaxin, Zithromax) and there is a risk of nausea if the combination is not used carefully. Carbamazepine decreases levels of oral contraceptives, causing a risk of pregnancy if the dose of the contraceptive is not increased.

The most serious (rare but unpredictable) side effect seen with carbamazepine is a sudden drop in the white blood cell or the platelet count. A normal blood count before your child begins using carbamazepine, or even after he has been using it for a period of time, does not ensure that he will not develop this problem. Because they cannot predict a problem, repeated blood counts are not done with carbamazepine. If there are signs of a drop in the white count (an infection that does not go away) or a drop in the platelet count (a petechial rash, i.e., pinpoints of red on the skin), the medicine is discontinued and a blood count is done.

A more frequent but less dangerous difficulty with carbamazepine is a drug rash. The most common rash has small, raised, red bumps that are close together, usually on the chest, back, or abdomen; they may appear on the face or scalp. The rash usually itches. If the dose is lowered, the rash frequently clears up in about five days. The dose can then be raised safely. In the meantime, topical or oral Benadryl will relieve the itching.

Tegretol can also, very rarely, cause a disturbance in the body's regulation of fluids, causing a lowering of the level of sodium—Syndrome of Inappropriate Antidiuretic Hormone (SIADH). Symptoms of SIADH are water retention, loss of appetite, nausea, or vomiting. When this occurs, the drug must be discontinued.

Despite these potential difficulties, carbamazepine can cause an enormous improvement in some bipolar patients. For the right person it offers a release from intolerable irritability and anxiety; it can also help with sleep. Usually it is not accompanied by weight gain or problems with concentration or memory.

Oxcarbamazepine (Trileptal) is a slightly modified form of carbamazepine that has fewer side effects and fewer interactions with other medications. In most cases, the drugs are comparable in efficacy, so the decreased risk of toxicity with oxcarbamazepine provides a significant advantage.

Another advantage of oxcarbamazepine over carbamazepine is that it does not have complex interactions with SSRIs such as fluoxetine (Prozac), mood stabilizers such as valproic acid (Depakote), and antibiotics like erythromycin and Biaxin. Oxcarbamazepine can be combined safely with these medications. Caution should still be taken in combination with oral contraceptives. Oxcarbamazepine is also less likely to cause a decrease in the white blood cell or platelet count, and poses less of a risk of liver toxicity. Like carbamazepine, it usually does not cause weight gain. Oxcarbamazepine is, however, significantly more expensive than carbamazepine.

Both of these medicines are particularly valuable in anxious, irritable, or aggressive children. In some children, their efficacy can be enhanced by the addition of lithium or another mood stabilizer. Both medicines need to be introduced gradually, however, so that they do not cause sedation, dizziness, or nausea. For this reason, they are less useful in the treatment of acute mania. Two studies show that carbamazepine is effective in depression. However, I have seen both carbamazepine and oxcarbamazepine bring on or aggravate symptoms of depression and irritability. In general, these medications work better as a *ceiling* (against hyperarousal) than as a *floor* (to prevent or treat depression).

Carbamazepine is usually begun at a dose of 100 mg and raised by 100 mg every five to seven days until a desired response is achieved. Doses may go as high as 1200 mg. Carbamazepine increases its own clearance by the liver, so doses may need to be raised once or twice after an initial therapeutic level is reached. In many patients, there is a significant difference in the absorbability of generic carbamazepine as compared to the brand-name Tegretol; switching between the two may require adjustment of the dose. Oxcarbamazepine is begun at 150–300 mg and is raised by 150 mg every five to seven days. The dose may go as high as 1800 mg.

Although there are recognized therapeutic blood levels for both these medications *when used to treat epilepsy*, these levels do not necessarily predict response or an appropriate dose in the treatment of bipolar disorder. The psychiatrist's experience and vigilance as the dose is raised—together with the report of the child and parent—is a better guide.

## DEALING WITH A DRUG RASH

*Always notify the prescribing physician of any rash.*

Many medications can cause a rash. The most common rash has small raised, red bumps. The bumps are close together and usually found on the chest, back, or abdomen, although they may also appear on the face or scalp.

Less common, but more dangerous, is an urticarial rash or hives, because hives can form in the throat, obstructing breathing. If an urticarial rash arises, the medicine that caused it must be stopped. If the rash appears to be spreading or getting worse, an injection of epinephrine may be needed; this can be obtained quickly at an emergency room.

When a medicine is difficult to replace, is important at present, or may be in the future, the more common raised red rash can often be managed by reducing the dose of the medication to the lowest possible dose and waiting until the rash goes away. The itching that accompanies the rash can be relieved with an antihistamine applied topically or taken by mouth. *This should always be done under the supervision of a physician experienced with the procedure.*

*If the medication causing a rash is discontinued entirely, it cannot be taken again without great risk.* When a medicine is stopped in the midst of a rash, the immune system is alerted to its presence; it has produced T-helper cells and will react strongly when the medicine is reintroduced. If the medication is *lowered* and the rash clears up, the immune system has adapted to the presence of the medication—it has produced T-suppressor cells—and the dose of the medicine can be raised or the medication can be used in the future. The immune system has a memory for these two opposite circumstances, and the passage of time does not affect this.

**VALPROIC ACID (DEPAKOTE)** Depakote was the second anticonvulsant to be widely used in bipolar disorder. Like lithium, it can be particularly effective in calming mania in bipolar I and is also effective in some bipolar II patients. Unlike lithium, Depakote works quickly. Depakote—unlike Trileptal or carbamazepine—can be increased rapidly to therapeutic levels. For this reason, Depakote is frequently used in hospitals to treat acutely ill patients. (An incidental additional effect of Depakote is an ability to prevent migraine headaches.)

When used over the long term, however, Depakote can have troublesome side effects, the most common of which is prominent weight gain. This occurs in as many as 50 percent of patients and can trigger the development of insulin resistance and the metabolic syndrome, a cascade of metabolic interactions leading to obesity and type II diabetes. There are also some reports of an association between the long-

term use of Depakote and the occurrence of polycystic ovaries, especially in women treated with this medication from the time of puberty.
When possible, a different mood stabilizer should be considered when
a patient is stabilized. Other possible side effects include nausea,
tremor, and sedation.

There are recognized therapeutic blood levels for the use of Depakote in bipolar disorder, and an excessive dose is usually not dangerous, although it is uncomfortable. Rarely, serious liver toxicity can
occur with Depakote. Thus, liver function tests should be performed
prior to use and periodically thereafter.

Depakote has complex interactions with carbamazepine and significantly raises levels of lamotrigine (Lamictal). It does not affect levels of
oral contraceptives.

**LAMOTRIGINE (LAMICTAL)**   Lamotrigine has been used to treat bipolar
disorder for about eight years. Recent studies document its effectiveness
with bipolar I, bipolar depression, and dysthymia (mild chronic depression). I have also found it useful in treating premenstrual mood changes.
Lamotrigine is particularly useful because of its ability to treat both
symptoms of arousal in bipolar II (irritability, anxiety, hypomania) and
depressive episodes.

As with all mood stabilizers, lamotrigine can be effective in one patient and ineffective or even agitating in another. When it is appropriate, however, it can be used on a long-term basis with practically no
side effects—without weight gain, cognitive, or gastrointestinal effects,
and without interfering with sexual function.

One serious danger with lamotrigine is a rare, but potentially fatal,
autoimmune reaction—called Steven's Johnson syndrome—which involves the skin, mucous membranes, and internal organs. The risk of
this reaction is greatest when lamotrigine is first begun or when the
dose is raised quickly. In the vast majority of cases, once the immune
system adjusts to the drug's presence, it can be used safely. The risk, although it is small to begin with, is decreased further if the medication
is introduced at a low dose (5 mg) and gradually increased (every five to

seven days) in 5 mg increments for the first six weeks of use. Steven's Johnson syndrome, when it occurs, comes on gradually (usually starting with a skin rash or sores on the mucous membranes); its progress can be prevented by discontinuing the medication.

A benign skin rash may occur when lamotrigine is begun. Since this is a valuable medication, the benefits of which are not matched by other mood stabilizers, I do not necessarily discontinue lamotrigine when a rash appears. I examine the rash, and if it appears to be a common drug rash, I lower the dose and wait to see if the rash clears up. If, however, a person has had a persistent rash, hives, or signs of the onset of Steven's Johnson syndrome (e.g., sores on the mucous membranes) lamotrigine must be stopped and cannot be started again.

Because lamotrigine needs to be introduced gradually, caution must be exercised if it is begun in a hospital. Currently most psychiatric hospital stays are about two weeks. This is not a sufficient time to safely reach a therapeutic dose of lamotrigine. Rushing the introduction of this medicine can cause the onset of Steven's Johnson syndrome, preventing a child from ever using it in the future. I have seen two children develop early signs of Steven's Johnson syndrome when started too quickly on lamotrigine while hospitalized.

There is a wide range of effective doses with lamotrigine. I have seen efficacy between 10 mg twice a day and 200 mg three times a day; in children, the average dose is between 25 mg and 100 mg twice a day. For each person there is a window within which the drug is effective: lower doses are ineffective, higher doses cause prohibitive side effects or increased mood instability. By starting at a low dose and increasing slowly, the range within which a patient responds can be seen more clearly. As in the case of other mood stabilizers, the effectiveness of lamotrigine can sometimes be augmented by the addition of lithium or of another mood stabilizer.

Lamotrigine has few interactions with other medications used in combination with it. An important exception is Depakote, which can *double* levels of Lamictal, significantly increasing the risk of an autoimmune reaction to Lamictal. When the two are to be used together,

Lamictal must be added more gradually than when started alone or with another medication. As with any of the mood stabilizers, lamotrigine should not be abruptly discontinued when it can be safely tapered.

One of the actions of Lamictal is to reduce levels of glutamate, a widely distributed CNS stimulant. We know that excessive levels of glutamate cause irritability and can eventually cause cell death. There is good reason to believe that lamotrigine, because it acts to reduce levels of glutamate, has a long-term effect of protecting the brain from excessive stimulation, in addition to its protection against symptoms of bipolar disorder.

## RILUZOLE (RILUTEK)

Riluzole is just beginning to be used in the treatment of bipolar disorder. Riluzole is not an anticonvulsant. I mention it for two reasons: riluzole, like lamotrigine, works to decrease levels of glutamate. (It has been effective and safe with some patients who have had an autoimmune response—including Steven's Johnson syndrome—to lamotrigine.) What is particularly interesting, however, is that riluzole has been demonstrated to be neuroprotective against the toxic effects of glutamate. For this reason, riluzole is indicated for the treatment of amyotrophic lateral sclerosis (ALS) or Lou Gehrig's disease. (In that condition, areas of neural damage are found to have high levels of glutamate.) It is possible that in some bipolar patients, lamotrigine and riluzole go beyond treating symptoms to promoting healing of troubled areas of the CNS. If this proves true over time—it is still very early in their use—these medicines are in an exciting new class by themselves.

## GABAPENTIN (NEURONTIN)

Like lamotrigine, gabapentin has antidepressant as well as mood-stabilizing effects. It has the additional advantage of being able to be started rapidly: the dose can be increased safely and its effects are seen within hours, so that a trial of this medication can be made quickly.

There is a wide range of doses within which gabapentin is effective for different patients: anywhere from 100 mg twice a day to 800 mg four times a day. Gabapentin also has almost no interactions with other medications. Like lamotrigine, gabapentin can be effective for one patient and agitating or sedating for another.

Gabapentin has several other coincidental beneficial effects: it can be used to relieve chronic pain and migraine headaches, decrease craving for alcohol, and relieve restless leg syndrome. On the other hand, gabapentin can increase appetite and promote weight gain, although this effect is not as marked as with Depakote and some other medications. Another drawback with gabapentin is its short duration of action: often it requires dosing three to four times a day.

## Topiramate (Topamax)

Among mood stabilizers, topiramate has the unusual effect of *decreasing* appetite. Because many medications used to treat bipolar disorder promote weight gain, topiramate can be a valuable tool for offsetting this effect. Topiramate resembles Trileptal in its properties as a mood stabilizer, being a better ceiling than a floor. It does not have prominent antidepressant properties but usually relieves anxiety, irritability, and hypomania. Topiramate has also begun to be used by addiction specialists to decrease craving for alcohol, and (like Depakote and Neurontin) is used in the treatment of migraines.

Topiramate is begun at a dose of 15 or 25 mg once a day and increased by 25 mg once a week. Effective doses in bipolar disorder are usually lower than those used for epilepsy, commonly between 25 and 50 mg twice a day.

Topiramate has several side effects that can be particularly troublesome. The drug can cause cognitive difficulties in some people (problems with memory and word retrieval) and severe difficulties in some children. This medication can cause kidney stones if a person is not well hydrated; it is important to drink plenty of water while on it. Topiramate has also been associated with visual changes and increased pressure in the eye (glaucoma). Any visual disturbances, eye pain, or headaches occurring while on the drug need to be evaluated by an ophthalmologist.

In some patients, topiramate can cause an unpleasant tingling in hands or feet, which usually passes. An excessive dose of topiramate causes fatigue and sedation.

## ZONISAMIDE (ZONEGRAN)

Zonisamide, like topiramate, is unusual in its ability to decrease appetite. Because its use as a mood stabilizer is recent, information about its efficacy and drawbacks is anecdotal. Unlike topiramate, zonisamide does not have negative effects on memory or word retrieval. In some patients I have treated, zonisamide had an antidepressant effect. The usual dose is 100 mg two times per day. Like most of the mood stabilizers, it can be sedating in some patients and activating in others. Like topiramate, it can cause kidney stones, so it is important to drink plenty of water on this medication. Eye problems including glaucoma have been reported, although infrequently.

Topiramate and zonisamide both cause changes in the acidity of blood. In preadolescent children, these changes, when severe, can affect bone development. If they are an important medication for your child, periodic blood tests are advisable.

## LEVETIRACETAM (KEPPRA)

Levetiracetam is the most recently approved antiepileptic drug available and it has been studied by the NIMH (National Institute of Mental Health) as a treatment for bipolar illness. Levetiracetam is thought to have a unique mechanism of action that does not affect most excitatory and inhibitory neurotransmitter systems. Because it is able to stop the development and completion of amygdala-kindled seizures, it may be effective in limiting the emotional explosions (coming from the amygdala) seen in bipolar disorder. Levetiracetam is a derivative of the memory-enhancing agent piracetam and may have cognitive advantages. It is not metabolized by the liver and thus has fewer interactions with other medications. As with almost all other medications used to treat bipolar disorder, levetiracetam can in some people cause undesirable changes in mood: agitation, hostility, apathy, or depression.

Dosing is begun at 250 mg and increased by 250 mg every three to five days. Maximum doses range from 1000–3000 mg per day in epilepsy. There is no established dose or blood level in bipolar disorder, but lower doses are often used. Commonly reported side effects (often dose related) are as follows: dizziness; loss of energy or strength; unusual drowsiness or sleepiness; muscle pain or weakness; cough; dry or sore throat; hoarseness; runny nose; tender, swollen glands in neck; difficulty swallowing; changes in voice. I have also seen weight gain.

## ANTIDEPRESSANTS

Depression is more difficult to treat in children than in adults, and in bipolar disorder it is one of the hardest symptoms to treat. All antidepressants have a risk of precipitating mania, promoting rapid cycling between mania and depression, or inducing a mixed state of arousal together with depression. The difficulties encountered in treating depression in children stem from several factors:

· Most children who are depressed are bipolar, neglected, or traumatized, and sometimes a combination of all three.

· Neglect and trauma in a child are always part of complex family problems and require much more than medication.

· A child's central nervous system may respond unpredictably to medicines used to treat depression.

· Depression in a child who has not been traumatized or neglected is most likely to be bipolar depression and needs to be
treated as part of a more complicated condition. In a child with
bipolar disorder, the use of an antidepressant should be accompanied by mood stabilization.

Recently there has been increased concern about suicide in children
treated with antidepressants. Nonetheless, untreated depressed children
run a higher risk of suicide than do depressed children who are treated.
An untreated depression in a child can have other serious consequences:
academic problems; problems observing limits; problems with parents,
siblings, and peers. It is frequently necessary to use an antidepressant
(in combination with a mood stabilizer and sometimes a major tranquilizer) in a depressed bipolar child. Most often the medication can be
used briefly and at lower doses. When an antidepressant is continued
on a regular basis, the dose needs to be reassessed with each change in
season.

**SELECTIVE SEROTONIN REUPTAKE INHIBITORS (SSRIS)** Selective
serotonin reuptake inhibitors (SSRIs) such as fluoxetine (Prozac) are the most
widely prescribed antidepressants, because of their efficacy and lack of lethal
side effects, as compared to tricyclic antidepressants and monoamine oxidase
inhibitors (MAOIs). (The uses of these other drugs are discussed below.)

SSRIs work by increasing the amount and the duration of serotonin
in a synapse (the transmitting site between nerves). Serotonin is known
to play a role in relieving depression and anxiety; it is also known to interact with the neurotransmitters norepinephrine and dopamine. Clinically, stimulation of norepinephrine and dopamine can in some cases
enhance the antidepressant effects of serotonin.

Typically, a bipolar patient reacts quickly and to relatively low doses
of these medicines. (In contrast, an obsessive-compulsive patient reacts
gradually and to relatively high doses.) The bipolar patient's response
can be temporary, however, and there is a temptation to increase the
dose. Augmentation with another medicine is usually a better strategy,
because higher doses of an SSRI can cause agitation or mania. In other

cases, raising the dose leads to tolerance (a loss of effectiveness) and to progressively higher doses, each of which ultimately becomes ineffective. More is not necessarily better.

Any antidepressant that increases concentrations of serotonin should not be taken with MAOIs. Combination of an SSRI with an MAOI can cause serotonin syndrome—a combination of physical and mental symptoms that can be lethal if not treated promptly. (Details of serotonin syndrome are given in the Glossary.)

The differences among the various SSRIs consist in the effects they have on other neurotransmitters (such as dopamine, norepinephrine, and histamine), in the different periods of time they remain in the bloodstream after a single dose (their half-life), and in their interactions with other medications. Because of these differences, certain SSRIs can be desirable in different patients. SSRIs can also have markedly different side effects in different patients, or in combination with different medications. My description of these medicines, then, is generally true, but their effects can vary for any particular patient.

## SSRIs AND THE SEASONS

In patients who have seasonal depressions, it is often advisable to lower the dose or discontinue the medication in the spring or summer months. Exercise caution in the spring, however, because that is the most unstable period for some people with bipolar disorder. In general, unless patients are manic, it is always advisable to move slowly in manipulating their mood and, consequently, in adjusting the dose of these medications.

**SIDE EFFECTS OF SSRIs** SSRIs can aggravate bipolar disorder by

· precipitating a manic state
· causing increased impulsivity and aggressiveness in a depressed person

· increasing the risk for suicide or assaultive behavior
· elevating anxiety and bringing on panic attacks
· inducing rapid cycling

When used cautiously—combined with a mood stabilizer or a major tranquilizer in low doses—SSRIs play an important role in the treatment of bipolar disorder. Depression continues to be one of the more difficult aspects of bipolar disorder to treat.

SSRIs are the drug of choice for treatment of panic disorder, but many bipolar patients with panic attacks cannot tolerate them. There are complicated interactions between serotonin and other neurotransmitters known to affect bipolar disorder. My observation is that SSRIs increase anxiety in bipolar patients with panic disorder.

SSRIs promote weight gain with extended use, although this effect may not be evident in the first several months of use. Indeed, many patients initially experience a reduced appetite. SSRIs probably cause weight gain by affecting both satiety and the metabolism of fat cells. Their effects are less potent, however, than those of the major tranquilizers and of tricyclic antidepressants. SSRIs all cause negative effects on sexual function: delayed ejaculation in men, decreased sensation in women, and decreased sexual appetite in both men and women.

FLUOXETINE (PROZAC) Fluoxetine, the first SSRI to be approved, remains one of the most useful. It is used for depression, anxiety, obsessive-compulsive disorder, social anxiety disorder, panic disorder, bulimia, and (in some people) prevention of migraines. It is widely effective, and its long half-life makes it easy to discontinue and makes the effect of missing a dose less dramatic. It has been the most widely studied of the SSRIs, so we know the most about its long-term side effects.

At low doses, fluoxetine affects both serotonin and norepinephrine reuptake; at higher doses its serotonin reuptake becomes predominate. Fluoxetine has an active metabolite—what it turns into after going once through the liver—called norfluoxetine. Whereas fluoxetine has a half-life of about three and a half days, norfluoxetine has a half-life of two weeks. It takes about five half-lives for a drug to reach a steady state in the body. This means that it takes about ten weeks for fluoxetine to reach a maximum level and ten weeks for it to leave the body. The long half-life of fluoxetine/norfluoxetine can be an advantage because they leave the CNS gradually, giving the brain time to adjust to the change.

In some people, fluoxetine can cause akathisia, a side effect that can be particularly uncomfortable and can cause increased anxiety. This is a dose-dependent side effect, and failure to recognize it can put a patient at increased risk for impulsive and self-destructive, even suicidal, behavior. Like all SSRIs, fluoxetine has negative effects on sexual function: delayed ejaculation in men, decreased sensation in women, and decreased sexual appetite in both men and women.

Fluoxetine has complex interactions with many other medications, both those used psychiatrically and in general medical practice. When used in combination with other medications, it is important to have your physician or pharmacist check for interactions. Among the more dangerous is serotonin syndrome, caused by the combination of fluoxetine with an MAOI. Fluoxetine can be used safely, however, with over-the-counter antihistamines, decongestants, and cold remedies. Fluoxetine inhibits the metabolism of alcohol, so that a single drink can have the effect of two or three, including a rise in the blood-alcohol level.

**SERTRALINE (ZOLOFT)** Sertraline was the second SSRI to become available and has been widely studied. It can be more stimulating than fluoxetine and in some patients is more effective. It is widely used for depression, anxiety, obsessive-compulsive symptoms, social anxiety disorder, and panic disorder. It also has fewer interactions with other medications than fluoxetine.

In addition to its serotonin reuptake, sertraline increases the activity of dopamine, which can be a distinct advantage in patients with ADD, but it can cause intolerable side effects in others. Sertraline has a half-life of sixty to one hundred hours, long enough to avoid withdrawal symptoms seen with shorter-acting SSRIs. Like fluoxetine, sertraline can cause akathisia and agitation. Initially, sertraline tends to promote weight loss. With extended use, however, it can cause weight gain. Also, as with fluoxetine, sertraline has negative effects on sexual function: delayed ejaculation in men, decreased sensation in women, and decreased sexual appetite in both men and women. Like all drugs that increase the activity of serotonin, sertraline cannot be used in combination with an MAOI. Sertraline also inhibits the metabolism of alcohol, causing higher blood levels with lower consumption.

**PAROXETINE (PAXIL)** Paroxetine, like the other SSRIs, is widely used for depression, anxiety, obsessive-compulsive symptoms, social anxiety disorder, and panic disorder. Because it is the most calming of the SSRIs it is sometimes chosen for an especially anxious patient or one for whom other SSRIs are too stimulating.

Paroxetine owes its calming property to its antihistaminic and serotinergic activity. It is almost five times more potent than sertraline and sixteen times more potent than fluoxetine as a serotonin reuptake inhibitor. Its antihistaminic profile, not shared by other SSRIs, also has a calming effect. These same properties—its potency as an SSRI and its antihistaminic activity—also account for paroxetine being the most potent SSRI in promoting weight gain. Paroxetine is unlikely to cause akathisia, but it can be overstimulating in some bipolar patients. Because of its effects on serotonin, paroxetine has negative effects on sexual function: delayed ejaculation in men, decreased sensation in women, and decreased sexual appetite in both men and women. Like fluoxetine, paroxetine interacts with other medications and consultation is important when adding an additional medication. Like all drugs that increase the activity of serotonin, paroxetine cannot be used in combination with an MAOI. The same caution with respect to alcohol—an increase in blood levels and the effects of alcohol—applies with paroxetine as with fluoxetine and sertraline.

Paroxetine has a short half-life (twelve to fourteen hours), which can cause two difficulties. A missed dose can result in both a loss of efficacy and the beginnings of withdrawal within a day or so. When paroxetine is discontinued, some patients experience uncomfortable but not dangerous withdrawal symptoms—nausea, dizziness, muscle aches, headache—which can last from five to ten days. Recently, an extended-release preparation of paroxetine has become available, which may have fewer side effects than the original preparation. Withdrawal symptoms are still seen with the extended-release preparation, however.

**FLUVOXAMINE (LUVOX)** Fluvoxamine, like the other SSRIs, is used for depression, anxiety, obsessive-compulsive symptoms, social anxiety disorder, and panic disorder. Fluvoxamine is regarded as one of the best medicines for the treatment of OCD and is less stimulating than other SSRIs, which makes it a good choice (together with mood stabilization) for a child suffering from both bipolar disorder and OCD. It is more potent than fluoxetine in blocking serotonin reuptake but is significantly less potent than sertraline and paroxetine. Fluvoxamine has relatively weak effects on norepinephrine and virtually no effect on dopamine, which accounts for it being more tolerable for people who find other SSRIs too stimulating. Fluvoxamine has a relatively short duration of action and for this reason can cause a withdrawal syndrome. It has the same side effects from serotonin reuptake as other SSRIs: sexual dysfunction and long-term weight gain. Like all drugs that increase the activity of serotonin, fluvoxamine cannot be used in combination with an MAOI.

**CITALOPRAM (CELEXA) AND ESCITALOPRAM (LEXIPRO)** Citalopram has the distinction of being the only pure SSRI. Consequently, it lacks some of the side effects and some of the benefits of other SSRIs. Like the other SSRIs, citalopram is widely used for depression, anxiety, obsessive-compulsive symptoms, social anxiety disorder, and panic disorder.

A modified preparation of citalopram, called escitalopram (Lexipro), may have fewer side effects than citalopram. Molecules exist in two forms that are mirror images of each other, called left (l) and right (r) isomers. Although they have the same chemical formula, the biological activity of these isomers can be quite different. (The makers of citalopram observed that the antidepressant and antianxiety properties of citalopram came from the l-isomer. The r-isomer was associated with a number of undesirable side effects.) Escitalopram is a preparation of the pure l-isomer. Consequently, it is expected to have fewer side effects (and is also more potent) than citalopram. For some patients, especially those with concurrent obsessive-compulsive disorder, this is a distinct advantage with respect to both tolerability and efficacy.

In some bipolar patients, however, increased potency may be a disadvantage, because a more powerful effect causes a more pronounced change in the CNS equilibrium and, consequently, increased oscillation of mood. Citalopram and escitalopram share the side effects attributable to serotonin reuptake: possible aggravation of bipolar disorder, sexual dysfunction, long-term weight gain, and a withdrawal syndrome in some people coming off the drug. Like all drugs that increase the activity of serotonin, citalopram and escitalopram cannot be used in combination with an MAOI.

**VENLAFAXINE (EFFEXOR)** Venlafaxine has a two-pronged attack on depression, increasing levels of both serotonin and norepinephrine. This may be the reason venlafaxine is more effective in some patients than standard SSRIs; in some cases it also works sooner.

At lower doses, venlafaxine behaves like an SSRI; at higher doses, it inhibits the reuptake of both serotonin and norepinephrine. For this reason, venlafaxine is called a norepinephrine-serotonin reuptake inhibitor (NSRI). Possibly, because of its dual activity, venlafaxine can be a more potent antidepressant than the SSRIs and may be effective when they are not. I have found this to be true at lower doses as well as higher ones. Probably because of its activity on norepinephrine, venlafaxine does not promote weight gain as strongly as the SSRIs. This drug is also sometimes used in the prevention of migraines.

Venlafaxine shares some of the side effects of SSRIs, but it has more prominent side effects of gastrointestinal distress and in some people can cause problems with concentration. Venlafaxine has been associated with a mild increase in blood pressure, although this is rarely a problem in children. Venlafaxine has an even shorter half-life than paroxetine (seven hours) and can have uncomfortable withdrawal symptoms: headache, fatigue, muscle aches, which can last as long as two weeks or more. Because of its short half-life, the extended-release preparation of venlafaxine is preferable. Like other antidepressants, venlafaxine can be overstimulating in some bipolar patients, particularly in the absence of a mood stabilizer. Because venlafaxine is more potent than other antidepressants, it is necessary to be more careful about overstimulation. Venlafaxine shares the side effects attributable to serotonin reuptake: possible aggravation of bipolar disorder, sexual dysfunction, and possible long-term weight gain. The potential for weight gain is less, however, because of venlafaxine's effects on norepinephrine. Like all drugs that increase the activity of serotonin, venlafaxine cannot be used in combination with an MAOI.

**DULOXETINE HCL (CYMBALTA)** Newly indicated by the FDA (2004) for treatment of depression, duloxetine is a norepinephrine-serotonin reuptake inhibitor (NSRI) like venlafaxine. As an NSRI duloxetine has a more vigorous action in treating depression than the SSRIs; it also has less propensity to cause weight gain. Doses range from 40–60 mg.

Duloxetine shares the side effects attributable to serotonin reuptake inhibitors: possible aggravation of bipolar disorder, sexual dysfunction, and possible long-term weight gain. The potential for weight gain is less, however, because of duloxetine's effects on norepinephrine. Duloxetine has a longer half-life than venlafaxine (twelve hours as compare to seven), putting it in the same range as paroxetine (Paxil). It does, however, have a potential to cause a similar withdrawal syndrome when discontinued. Because it is the newest of the antidepressants, its uses and side effects are not as well known.

Like all drugs that increase the activity of serotonin, duloxetine cannot be used in combination with an MAOI.

## DIRECT SEROTINERGIC MEDICINES (AGONISTS)

These drugs act directly on serotonin receptors rather than indirectly by increasing levels of serotonin, like the SSRIs. This slightly different mode of action eliminates some of the side effects of SSRIs, most notably sexual dysfunction. They are less potent antidepressants, but for just this reason may be tolerated by some patients who cannot use SSRIs. They are used for both depression and for anxiety.

**TRAZODONE (DESYREL)** Trazodone has been used for both depression and anxiety, including panic disorder. Although less potent than the SSRIs, trazodone is more sedating, which has led to its common use (at a lower dose) as a sedative in depressed patients with a sleep disturbance. This use has grown because trazodone does not have a potential for abuse. In a bipolar patient, however, its use as a sedative may be unwise, given the capacity for *any* antidepressant to cause activation over time. I also have encountered many patients who find that trazodone's sedation carries through unpleasantly into the next day. An unusual side effect of trazodone in males is a sustained and painful erection. Trazodone also has interactions with some other medications that complicates its use. Like all drugs that increase the activity of serotonin, trazodone cannot be used in combination with an MAOI.

**MIRTAZAPINE (REMERON)** Mirtazapine is a potent antidepressant that acts quickly and is quite calming. It increases the direct effects of serotonin, norepinephrine, and dopamine, which accounts for its potency. In addition, it has potent antihistaminic properties, which cause it to be sedating (so it is usually given at night) and to promote weight gain. Its specificity for a narrow range of serotonin receptors and its direct action on serotonin gives it freedom from sexual side effects. Like all drugs that increase the activity of serotonin, mirtazapine cannot be used in combination with an MAOI.

## Monoamine Oxidase Inhibitors (MAOIs)

Although not commonly used because of their side effects, MAOIs are probably the most powerful antidepressants; they also have powerful antianxiety effects. They are highly effective in depression and panic disorder. In a few cases, bipolar depressions respond to no other medicines but these. Their power as antidepressants probably results from their capacity to increase the level of all three neurotransmitters known to be involved in depression: serotonin, norepinephrine, and dopamine.

One reason these drugs are so rarely used, especially in children, is that they require patients to avoid certain foods. Aged cheeses, smoked meats (salami, bacon, ham), or soy sauce (basically aged protein) can cause a dangerous elevation of blood pressure and heart rate. A similar but more severe reaction occurs with over-the-counter decongestants (e.g., pseudoephedrine). Many of the warnings not to take with antidepressants seen on over-the-counter cold medications or diet pills refer only to MAOIs.

It is also important to add that *MAOIs cannot be used in combination with* **any** *of the serotinergic antidepressants.* The combination can cause a potentially fatal condition called a serotonin syndrome.

MAOIs have side effects even when used with a proper diet: they can cause a drop in blood pressure when standing up (orthostatic hypotension); phenelzine (Nardil) can be troublesomely sedating and strongly stimulates weight gain; tranylcypromine (Parnate) is less sedating and tends not to cause weight gain, but it can cause jitteriness, difficulty with urination, and sometimes intolerance to cold.

## Nonserotinergic Antidepressants

Although the serotinergic antidepressants have ushered in a new era in the treatment of depression and anxiety, their side effects (weight gain and sexual dysfunction being the most troublesome) and the tendency of many patients after a time to lose their response to these medicines leaves a need for drugs that are specific to other neurotransmitters, especially norepinephrine and dopamine. These nonserotinergic antidepressants are also frequently used in combination with serotinergic medicines.

**BUPROPION (WELLBUTRIN)** Bupropion is a stimulating antidepressant with significantly fewer side effects than the SSRIs. It can be good for the slowed-down, listless depressions often seen in bipolar disorder, especially in seasonal winter swings. It can be used alone or in combination with other medications.

Bupropion increases the activity of norepinephrine and (to a lesser extent) dopamine. It can be an effective antidepressant by itself and lacks many of the side effects of the serotinergic medicines. Its noradrenergic activity can decrease appetite, and its dopaminergic activity can reduce craving for substances such as nicotine or carbohydrates. Indeed, it is marketed as an aid to people wanting to quit smoking. Because of its effects on dopamine and norepinephrine, bupropion has been used in some cases to treat ADD, but its efficacy is not comparable to that of stimulants. Bupropion's major drawback is that it does not act to decrease anxiety—and in some people aggravates anxiety or irritability. Bupropion is frequently used, however, together with serotinergic medicines to complement their efficacy in depression.

In many bipolar patients, bupropion causes marked irritability and, like any antidepressant, it can precipitate mania. In combination with a mood stabilizer and a medication that decreases anxiety, bupropion is, however, a very useful adjunct. Bupropion can increase the risk of seizure. In most cases this increased risk is minimal, but in certain conditions that also lower the seizure threshold—bulimia or severe alcohol abuse—bupropion can pose a more serious risk. This risk is markedly reduced when it is used with an anticonvulsant mood stabilizer.

## Tricyclic Antidepressants (Imipramine, Desipramine, Amitriptyline)

Tricyclics were the first medicines found to have antidepressant properties. They are no longer widely used because they have side effects not found with SSRIs and other more recently developed antidepressants. Nonetheless, some people who do not respond to other antidepressants do respond to a tricyclic, either alone or in combination with an SSRI. Imipramine and desipramine were once also commonly used in some children with ADD/ADHD.

Imipramine and desipramine mainly increase levels of norepinephrine; amitriptyline also has significant effects on serotonin. The most serious side effect of tricyclics is their ability to promote cardiac arrhythmias, especially in overdose. There have also been cases of sudden cardiac death in children treated with desipramine at a normal therapeutic dose. More commonly, and less dangerously, tricyclics cause sedation, dry mouth, constipation, and weight gain. Because they were the first of the antidepressants and were in use for a long time, tricyclics have been widely studied. Like all other antidepressants, they have been found to be less effective in children than in adults.

## Modafinil (Provigil)

Modafinil is indicated—approved to be advertised for—narcolepsy, a disorder consisting of marked sleepiness and sudden attacks of falling asleep. Its invigorating property has led to its being used as an adjunct to antidepressants. Like any medicine that augments an antidepressant, modafinil can aggravate bipolar disorder, especially in the absence of a mood stabilizer.

Modafinil's mechanism of action is not fully understood, although it has been found in one study, like stimulants, to have a euphoric effect. Also like stimulants it has some potential for abuse.

## Sulpiride

Sulpiride is an unusual drug not commonly used in this country. At higher doses it acts as a major tranquilizer; at lower doses it works as an antidepressant. I mention it because sulpiride is effective in some bipolar patients who cannot use standard antidepressants. Sulpiride usually does not cause the arousal that is commonly seen with antidepressants in bipolar disorder and has a lower risk for kindling mania. When it is used as an antidepressant (at a low dose), sulpiride also has few side effects: it can, however, cause weight gain, and it raises prolactin levels.

Sulpiride is widely used in Europe and has been shown to be as effective as amitriptyline (a widely studied tricyclic antidepressant). Unfortunately, sulpiride is not available in this country because it is not approved by the Food and Drug Administration. Nor is it likely that sulpiride will be approved by the FDA, because it is so inexpensive it is not worth a pharmaceutical company's investment to pay for the necessary trials. Consequently, in the United States, sulpiride is used by very few psychiatrists, and only when other antidepressants are not effective.

## FDA APPROVAL: INDICATIONS AND OFF-LABEL USE OF DRUGS

The term *indicated* when applied to a medication refers to its approval by the FDA *to be advertised* for use in a certain medical condition in a certain population: for example, fluoxetine is indicated for depression in adults, although not in children. The process by which a medication receives this designation requires several experimental trials of the drug's effectiveness in a particular set of patients. The expense of these trials is borne by the pharmaceutical company hoping to market a medicine. When a drug is approved by the FDA, the pharmaceutical company is approved to advertise it for a certain medical condition. The FDA does not have the authority to limit a physician's prescription of that drug for another use, or in another population.

This distinction is particularly important when it comes to prescriptions for children. A pharmaceutical company's pursuit of FDA approval is market driven: when there is no economic incentive to advertise a drug for a particular use, pharmaceutical companies usually do not pursue an indication and do not fund research trials for the drug. This is the case for most psychiatric drugs used with children and many used with adults. For example, only two of the mood stabilizers used to treat bipolar disorder, lithium and lamotrigine, are indicated for that purpose, and neither is indicated—in bipolar disorder—for children. Lamotrigine *is* indicated for a particular kind of seizure disorder in children.

When a physician prescribes a drug for a purpose not indicated by the FDA, it is termed an *off-label* use of the medication. This is not only perfectly legitimate, it is a necessary practice in child psychiatry. It is a good thing that the FDA monitors the marketing of medicines, but FDA approval has economic and political dimensions as well as a medical purpose. It is necessary for physicians to treat patients with medicines that are not FDA approved for a particular condition.

## MINOR TRANQUILIZERS

Benzodiazepines, referred to as minor tranquilizers, act quickly and have minimal side effects but are not good mood stabilizers or antimanic medicines. These drugs also do not cause weight gain, are relatively safe if an overdose occurs, and have no gastrointestinal or cardiac side effects. Their principal side effects are sedation, a slowing of reflexes (in high doses or in elderly patients, memory loss), and in some cases, more commonly with children, decreased inhibition, which appears in movement as agitation, or mentally as hallucinations.

Benzodiazepines have four different properties: they decrease anxiety (anxiolytic), they induce sleep (hypnotic), they reduce the likelihood of a seizure (anticonvulsant), and they relax muscles (antispasmodic). Of these four properties, only their ability to induce drowsiness decreases with extended use; the other properties do not diminish over time. This means that in the treatment of anxiety, including panic attacks, increasing doses are not needed over time. In fact, as anxiety is controlled, the dose can often be lowered.

Some forms of anxiety experienced in bipolar disorder are responsive *only* to benzodiazepines. In a bipolar patient with panic disorder, benzodiazepines may be the only effective medications. This is important because untreated panic attacks can aggravate bipolar disorder and bring on depression and even psychotic symptoms. In some children with bipolar disorder, benzodiazepines can also be useful for anxiety that occurs in certain situations: for example, in school refusal, with certain medical procedures, or in the evening when the cortisol level drops. Failure to treat the anxiety in these situations can be disabling, but the use of a major tranquilizer may be unduly sedating, unnecessarily long acting, and in some cases ineffective.

Benzodiazepines are also useful in treating insomnia. In many patients increasing doses are not required—they retain their efficacy indefinitely. The duration of their action can also be varied to meet different needs: initial insomnia, middle of the night awakening, early morning awakening, and early morning panic attacks. Benzodiazepines are not effective, however, when a sleep disturbance is due to incipient mania or to bipolar agitation. In these situations a major tranquilizer, sometimes combined with a mood stabilizer, must be used.

Benzodiazepines also affect the architecture of sleep: they decrease REM sleep (during which dreams occur) and stage-three and -four sleep. This means they can be used to prevent nightmares and to treat sleep disturbances that occur in stage-four sleep, such as night terrors or sleepwalking.

Two properties of benzodiazepines distinguish the different types of this medication: potency (their strength milligram for milligram) and duration of action (how long they remain in the blood). The high-potency benzodiazepines alprazolam (Xanax), lorazepam (Ativan), clonazepam (Klonopin), and triazolam (Halcion) are used in doses from 0.125 mg to about 2 mg; the low-potency benzodiazepines diazepam (Valium) and temazepam (Restoril) are commonly used in doses from 2 to 30 mg. Shorter-acting benzodiazepines are useful for acute or short episodes of anxiety; longer-acting ones are better for chronic anxiety not treated by a mood stabilizer or antidepressant or for sleep disturbances that carry through the night.

When benzodiazepines are used episodically they do not cause physiological dependence; when they are used consistently, which is sometimes necessary, physiological dependence develops in a week to ten days. Once physiological dependence has developed, if it is necessary to discontinue a benzodiazepine, it should be tapered gradually in intervals of a week or more. However, *the continued use of a benzodiazepine at a regular dose in a prescribed way is not addiction* any more than the continued use of a mood stabilizer or an antidepressant is an addiction.

Benzodiazepines are controlled substances in some states because a small number of people abuse them. The vast majority of patients are not in this category. As with stimulants, the appropriate use of a benzodiazepine can *reduce* the risk of substance abuse in many patients and allows certain patients to function at a higher level. Like any other medication, their use with children needs to be carefully supervised.

Although rarely needed in younger children for this purpose, benzodiazepines prevent withdrawal from alcohol (a life-threatening medical emergency) and so are regularly used in detoxification. In this case, the benzodiazepine is started at a relatively high dose and gradually tapered. It is worth remembering that with any substance that induces physiological dependence—a benzodiazepine, an antidepressant, an anticonvulsant, nicotine, or caffeine—it takes the CNS five to ten days to adjust to a decrease in the dose. While withdrawal with most substances is uncomfortable but not dangerous, in the case of a benzodiazepine, as with a steroid, withdrawal can be dangerous and needs to be conducted gradually—at intervals of five to ten days and longer if the patient has been on the medication for an extended period of time. There is no advantage to withdrawing a patient more quickly.

## ALPRAZOLAM (XANAX)

Alprazolam is useful in the acute treatment of a panic attack, in situational anxiety, and for insomnia characterized by middle of the night awakening. It is a high-potency, short-acting benzodiazepine with a half-life of four to six hours. It is usually dosed between 0.25 and 2 mg. When it is used for chronic anxiety, alprazolam needs to be taken four to six times a day, unless a controlled-release preparation is used.

## CLONAZEPAM (KLONOPIN)

In contrast to alprazolam, clonazepam leaves the CNS more gradually and less noticeably than other benzodiazepines. It is useful when sustained relief from anxiety is needed.

Clonazepam is a high-potency, long-acting benzodiazepine. Its half-life is twenty to forty hours, and its potency is about twice that of alprazolam. Clonazepam is useful in bipolar disorder to treat anxiety that remains after mood stabilization is achieved. Clonazepam is also useful when bipolar disorder is accompanied by severe social anxiety or in a patient with severe panic disorder because it can provide sustained protection.

Unlike other benzodiazepines, clonazepam increases levels of serotonin in the brain. In some cases this is helpful; in some cases it causes side effects not present with other benzodiazepines. I have treated patients who become depressed with clonazepam but not with other benzodiazepines. Clonazepam, despite its high potency, is not very effective for insomnia.

## Lorazepam (Ativan)

Lorazepam has an intermediate length of action (a half-life of ten to twenty hours) and a potency of about half that of alprazolam. Its usefulness, like that of other benzodiazepines, can vary with the situation. It does not leave the system as quickly as alprazolam, which is an advantage when it is being used over a long period of time. It is less desirable in situations of acute anxiety lasting for a brief period of time.

## Triazolam (Halcion)

Triazolam is most useful in getting a person to sleep without causing drowsiness in the morning. Triazolam is high in potency and brief in its activity, having a half-life of one and a half to four hours. For this reason it is most useful for people who have difficulty falling asleep but once asleep remain asleep. In some children and adults, however, the high potency of triazolam can bring on hallucinations, nightmares, or disorientation. Because of its short duration of action it is also not useful for middle of the night awakening and early morning awakening.

## Temazepam (Restoril)

Temazepam is a longer-acting, low-potency benzodiazepine. Usual doses are 15–30 mg; in some adult bipolar patients, as much as 60 mg may be needed, but I have never required that dose in a child. In some children it causes grogginess in the morning.

Temazepam is a good choice for people who have difficulty sleeping through the night. It is more useful in inducing and sustaining sleep than in treating daytime anxiety.

## Diazepam (Valium)

Valium acts more quickly than any other benzodiazepine and is effective for a very long time. The first benzodiazepine to be used, diazepam is also one of the best recognized. In some situations, however, it is less useful than other medicines for two reasons. Because it is highly fat soluble, it is quickly absorbed but then quickly leaves the bloodstream, disappearing into fatty tissue. This means that when first used, effects quickly peak and then drop off; with continued use the drug gradually accumulates in fatty tissue and the blood level remains more constant. Diazepam also turns into a number of other active substances (active metabolites) that take a long time to be eliminated from the bloodstream. The positive side of these properties is that diazepam leaves the system gradually and withdrawal symptoms can take as long as a week or two to appear.

## Ramelteon (Rozerem)

Ramelteon is a brand-new medication designed to bring on sleep by stimulating melatonin receptors. This drug is of interest both because it can induce sleep and because it may reset a dislocated sleep cycle. Ramelteon is significantly more potent than melatonin and may be an important new tool in addressing some of the sleep disturbances seen in bipolar disorder. I have found it to be useful—both to induce sleep and to bring back an advanced sleep cycle—in a fragile bipolar child who could not tolerate benzodiazepines and who became unduly sedated with a major tranquilizer. Ramelteon does not have a potential for abuse and may also be useful in those few patients who are at risk to abuse a benzodiazepine.

## Benzodiazepines and Addiction

Benzodiazepines have an undeservedly bad reputation because they can cause physiological dependence and tolerance, and are abused by a small number of people. Confusion among dependence, physiological dependence, tolerance, and addiction has caused many physicians to completely avoid their use. In some children, benzodiazepines can increase agitation. It is worth bearing in mind, however, that several of the other medications widely used in bipolar disorder—some SSRIs and most anticonvulsants—also cause physiological dependence and can cause agitation in some children. Stimulants used to treat ADD are also abused by a small number of people, and a common over-the-counter antihistamine like Benadryl can cause tolerance and agitation in some bipolar children.

It is also true that chronic untreated anxiety, especially social anxiety, motivates the abuse of more toxic substances such as marijuana and alcohol. Even when substance abuse does not occur, the anxiety itself is more toxic to the CNS and to the cardiovascular system than a benzodiazepine.

## MAJOR TRANQUILIZERS (ANTIPSYCHOTICS)

The term *antipsychotic* is something of a misnomer for major tranquilizers. Although they are used to treat psychosis, they are also important in the treatment of severe anxiety, mania, rapid cycling, and in some cases depression. In bipolar disorder, major tranquilizers are used to treat psychotic symptoms occurring in both mania and in depression, but they are also important medications in quelling mania, hypomania, and agitation, and they can treat an otherwise intractable sleep disturbance. The intense anxiety—including, at times, psychotic symptoms—seen in bipolar disorder, and especially in mania, can require quick intervention to prevent rapid deterioration or to control intolerable anxiety and dangerous behavior. Major tranquilizers are the best medications for this purpose. In patients whose agitation does not respond fully to mood stabilizers, a major tranquilizer may be needed on a long-term basis.

When chlorpromazine (Thorazine), haloperidol (Haldol), fluphenazine (Prolixin), and perphenazine (Trilafon) were first introduced, they were considered miracle drugs because they relieved symptoms that had never before been treatable. After years of use, however, we grew concerned over their neurological side effects. Some of these side effects, like pseudoparkinsonism, tremor, akathisia, and dystonia (see the box below), arose immediately, while others, such as tardive dyskinesia and tardive dystonia, emerged over the long term. The current generation of atypical antipsychotics was developed in an effort—largely successful—to avoid these neurological side effects.

In some cases of severe bipolar disorder, especially mania and mixed states, atypical medications are not effective, and a first-generation major tranquilizer is necessary. (I have had particularly good results with perphenazine.) The first-generation medications are, however, usually accompanied by neurological side effects that must also be treated. The most common medications used are diphenhydramine (Benadryl) and benztropine (Cogentin). In cases of pseudoparkinsonism (discussed below), amantadine (Symmetrel) can be effective and has fewer side effects.

## NEUROLOGICAL SIDE EFFECTS SEEN WITH MAJOR TRANQUILIZERS

**Akathisia.** This is an uncomfortable feeling of restlessness experienced as an inability to remain still. It is usually felt in large muscle groups, such as in the arms and legs. People experiencing this symptom may say they feel like they are going to jump out of their skin. Akathisia can add to a person's anxiety, agitation, or impulsivity, and it can be mistaken for mere anxiety. Atypical medicines *can* cause akathisia.

**Dystonia.** This is a sustained spasm in the neck, throat, arms, or legs that comes on at the time (within an hour) a major tranquilizer is taken. It can be readily and safely treated with Benadryl or benztropine (Cogentin). This symptom is rarely seen with the atypical medicines.

**Pseudoparkinsonism.** This is a reversible set of side effects seen with medicines—like the major tranquilizers—that block dopamine. These symptoms appear right away and are dose related. The syndrome consists of rigidity of the arms and legs, giving the person a robotic, slowed movement; a decrease in facial expression; and a tremor of the arms and legs. Commonly seen with higher-potency first-generation major tranquilizers—haloperidol, fluphenazine, perphenazine— pseudoparkinsonism can also be treated with benztropine or amantadine, but the treatment with these drugs must continue while the major tranquilizer is in use. These symptoms are rarely seen with atypical medicines such as aripiprazole, clozapine, olanzapine, risperidone, quietapine, and ziprasidone.

**Tardive dyskinesia.** A dyskinesia is an abnormal movement. Tardive dyskinesia is a syndrome of involuntary writhing movements that can involve the mouth and throat, the arms or legs, or the body's trunk. It can be accompanied by dystonia in these regions. These movements and contractions can be painful as well as disfiguring.

This condition is called tardive because it is tardy and comes on later in the use of major tranquilizers. It can appear while a person is on the drug, or as he or she is discontinuing it. It can occur in patients who have been on these drugs for an extended period of time, as well as in some who have been treated for as briefly as six months. The risk for this difficulty is not dose related. It occurs somewhat more often in women than men, and is more likely to strike people with mood disorders than those with schizophrenia. Children who have preexisting neurological conditions—epilepsy, problems with sensory integration, pervasive developmental disorder—are also at higher risk. Tardive dyskinesia can be masked by increasing the dose of a major tranquilizer; it becomes more evident as the dose is lowered. In many cases, the condition resolves after the person has been off major tranquilizers for a period of time, which can vary from weeks to months. Occasionally, the condition is permanent. *The risk for this condition with the atypical major tranquilizers—with the exception of risperidone (Risperdal)—is thought to be extremely low.*

Neuroleptic malignant syndrome (NMS) is a rare and potentially lethal set of symptoms seen with major tranquilizers. Symptoms of NMS are muscle rigidity, fever, sweating, confusion, and instability of pulse and blood pressure. The cause of NMS is not precisely understood, but it is known to occur more frequently when a person is overheated or during hot weather. NMS also occurs more frequently when a major tranquilizer is combined with lithium. Although the condition is rare, it requires emergency hospitalization. The condition is rarer yet with the atypical agents, although it has been reported.

## CLOZAPINE (CLOZARIL)

The first of the atypical major tranquilizers, clozapine is still the most effective. It's also free of the risk of long- and short-term neurological effects. However, clozapine can cause an unpredictable, fatal drop in the number of white blood cells. Consequently, this medication requires weekly blood testing to ensure safety. Clozapine can also cause sedation and prominent weight gain. Despite its troublesome side effects, clozapine can be effective—both in schizophrenia and in some cases of bipolar disorder—when nothing else works.

A number of newer atypical major tranquilizers—risperidone (Risperdal), olanzapine (Zyprexa), quietapine (Seroquel), ziprasidone (Geodon), and aripiprazole (Abilify)—have been developed in an effort to capture the benefits of clozapine while avoiding its serious side effects. These medications are all safe with regard to the blood disorder associated with clozapine. With the exception of risperidone, they also appear to be safe with regard to the long- and short-term neurological side effects seen with first-generation medicines. Risperidone also has a much lower risk for tardive dyskinesia than the original major tranquilizers, although cases have been reported with its use.

Each of the atypical major tranquilizers has some unique qualities, but they all share the characteristic of selectively quieting the part of the brain that generates mania and psychosis while having minimal effects in the part of the brain responsible for the movement disorders just described.

## Using the Major Tranquilizers

As with other classes of psychiatric medications, these medications all have slightly different properties and, consequently, have varying effects on different people. As a class, however, they are particularly good in treating the acute agitation seen in mania and the agitated irritability seen in many children with bipolar II disorder. *They sometimes work when no combination of mood stabilizers is effective.* For some patients, they are also the only medications that can correct a sleep disturbance caused by bipolar disorder. In addition, antidepressant effects have been reported in some patients with olanzapine (Zyprexa), ziprasidone (Geodon), and aripiprazole (Abilify).

Because of their ability to simultaneously treat symptoms that are otherwise difficult to control, such as agitation and depression, some psychiatrists have begun to recommend atypical major tranquilizers as first-line medicines and as medicines to be used alone in the treatment of bipolar disorder.

## Side Effects of Major Tranquilizers

Although the atypical major tranquilizers appear to be safe with regard to long-term neurological effects, they are comparatively new: we do not have information about their long-term neurological effects on either adults or children. One effect we do know about—weight gain—can be medically and socially problematic for a child. In some children, and at some doses, these medications can also be sedating or reduce alertness. On the other hand, there are cases in which an atypical major tranquilizer not only treats symptoms that antidepressants and mood stabilizers can't relieve but also has fewer side effects than these other medicines. The anticonvulsant mood stabilizers and lithium have been used with children and adults over a longer period of time, so more is known about their effects and their safety in the long term.

As with any other medications that have antidepressant activity, the major tranquilizers that have antidepressant effects in some children can at times trigger agitation and kindle mania in others. Akathisia can be seen with aripiprazole. Weight gain can be marked with aripiprazole, olanzapine, and risperidone, and moderate in some patients taking quietapine. Of more concern is the fact that weight gain caused by these newer medications can foster insulin resistance and type II diabetes.

## METABOLIC SIDE EFFECTS SEEN WITH MAJOR TRANQUILIZERS

**Weight gain.** All the major tranquilizers can cause weight gain by interfering with satiety, making users feel constantly hungry. They also separately affect the metabolism of carbohydrates, leading in some cases to insulin resistance and type II diabetes.

Insulin resistance is an impaired response to the hormone insulin: the result is that active muscle cells cannot take up blood sugar (glucose) as easily as they should, resulting in high blood sugar and chronically higher insulin levels. Higher insulin levels inhibit fat cells from giving up their energy stores to allow weight loss. As the amount of body fat increases, insulin resistance worsens. As weight gain progresses, children find it more difficult to be physically active, and physical inactivity magnifies the problem.

Insulin resistance is also associated with higher levels of fats (cholesterol and triglycerides) in the blood, as well as an increase in inflammatory hormones thought to play a role in hardening and blocking arteries and increased blood pressure. As this vicious cycle proceeds, the body cannot keep up with the need for insulin, resulting in type II diabetes. (Type II diabetes used to be called adult-onset diabetes, but this condition is appearing more and more in children.) Another concern regarding weight gain in children has to do with the *number* rather than the size of fat cells. During periods of active growth, high levels of growth hormone increase the number of fat cells as well as their size, leading to hypercellular obesity. Obesity of this type is especially hard to reverse.

Clozapine and olanzapine promote weight gain most potently, followed by risperidone, and then by quietapine and aripiprazole. Ziprasidone may be weight neutral.

**Elevated prolactin levels.** The release of the hormone prolactin from the pituitary gland is actively inhibited by dopamine. The major tranquilizers, which inhibit dopamine, can increase prolactin secretion. Prolactin stimulates the development of mammary glands and milk production. It also plays a role in reproduction and reproductive behavior. In adolescents, elevated prolactin can cause excessive development of breast tissue (more disturbing in boys than girls); elevated prolactin in an adolescent can also impair bone formation. Elevated prolactin in women can inhibit the menstrual cycle (amenorrhea). Men with elevated prolactin typically develop reduced secretion of sex hormones, with decreased sex drive, decreased sperm production, and impotence. Men can also develop breast enlargement but less commonly produce milk.

Elevated prolactin levels are seen regularly with the use of first-generation major tranquilizers. Dose-related increases in prolactin occur with risperidone, whereas olanzapine and ziprasidone cause only mild and transient increases of this hormone. Clozapine and quietapine cause the least change in secretion of prolactin.

## STIMULANTS AND OTHER DRUGS USED TO TREAT ADD/ADHD

The various medications used to treat ADD/ADHD increase attention, sustain motivation, and inhibit impulsivity. They differ from each other in how quickly they act, how long their effects last, whether they need to be taken daily, and how effective they are for different people.

Problems with hyperactivity, attention, and sustained motivation commonly affect children with bipolar disorder. In many cases these difficulties have a distinctly different character from ADD/ADHD seen in other children. Nonetheless, children with bipolar disorder can benefit from the same medications used with other children. However, all drugs used to treat ADHD or ADD can cause mania or mood instability in some bipolar patients. What is more, this effect may come on gradually (weeks or months), while the drug's effect on thinking, motivation, and impulsivity is rapid (hours). Some bipolar children cannot tolerate these medicines; others tolerate them in the presence of a mood stabilizer. In general, their use should be avoided or minimized when possible. For some children, however, they can make an important difference at home, in school, in sports, and in the peer group. The decision about whether to use them needs to be made on an individual basis.

The stimulants—methylphenidate (Ritalin, Concerta) and amphetamines (Adderall, Dexedrine)—act quickly (in a half hour to an hour) and don't need to be taken every day to be effective. In their short-acting forms, they can be used like reading glasses in situations that require their use but not at other times. Both methylphenidate and amphetamines are available in sustained-release preparations to avoid double dosing during a schoolday.

These medicines can decrease hyperactivity as well as improve attention and motivation, which makes them useful in two ways in ADHD. On the other hand, their effects on movement can interfere with peak athletic performance. For some children, this can be an important consideration or a reason to use a medicine that can be discontinued at times of athletic competition.

## Balancing the Dual Effects of Stimulants

The effects of stimulants on thinking can vary from their effects on motor activity. If the dose of a stimulant is adjusted simply to decrease excessive movement, at a certain point restlessness may be reduced at the expense of a child's ability to think. Control of hyperactivity and impulsive behavior in some cases results in a child feeling spaced out. Even children who are not hyperactive sometimes tell me that they can focus better with the drugs but are less spontaneous, less themselves.

The two neurotransmitters targeted in the treatment of ADHD or ADD are norepinephrine and dopamine. Dopamine and norepinephrine have distinct effects on movement and concentration. A medicine that is more active in stimulating norepinephrine may have side effects not present in one that stimulates only dopamine. In some children, however, a drug that has more powerful effects on norepinephrine works better than one that affects only dopamine. No one medicine is better for all children. Trials of different medicines may be needed.

## METHYLPHENIDATE (RITALIN, CONCERTA, METADATE)

Methylphenidate is the most frequently used stimulant in ADD. It works quickly and in many children treats the whole range of symptoms—attention, motivation, and impulsivity. It is available in long-acting as well as simple preparations and does not need to be taken daily.

Methylphenidate stimulates arousal in the brain stem and inhibition in the prefrontal cortex by increasing the activity of both norepinephrine and dopamine. In its regular form, methylphenidate reaches its peak activity in about two hours; the different sustained-release forms are active for an average of five to eight hours. There is no known therapeutic dose or blood level for methylphenidate. Although the initial dose is most often correlated to a child's weight, children of the same weight may respond to different doses. Extended-release preparations—Concerta, Metadate, Ritalin-SR—are available to avoid repeated dosing during school hours. Their rate of onset and duration of activity differ. It may be necessary to try more than one to find the best fit.

Methylphenidate can both increase attention and decrease excessive movement. When the dose is too high, however, a child can feel dazed and disconnected. As with all medications used to treat ADD, there is a risk that it will cause agitation or a slow kindling of mania in a bipolar child or adult. Common side effects include dry mouth, loss of appetite, difficulty sleeping, and rapid heartbeat. Because of its effects on dopamine, tics or an aggravation of a tic disorder such as Tourette's disorder also is seen. Take caution when a child requires an escalating dose, or develops a rebound reaction (intense irritability or agitation beginning when the medicine wears off), agitation, a pronounced loss of appetite, or a sleep disturbance, which are all signs of overstimulation of the deep brain. Because of its euphoric effect, methylphenidate has a potential for abuse.

## Dextroamphetamine (Dexedrine)

Dextroamphetamine is quick acting but short in its duration of activity. It affects levels of both dopamine and norepinephrine but acts more powerfully on dopamine.

Like methylphenidate, dextroamphetamine stimulates arousal in the brain stem and inhibition in the prefrontal cortex, producing beneficial effects of sustained motivation, increased ability to concentrate, and decreased impulsivity. Dextroamphetamine works both to increase the amount of dopamine that is released from a neuron and to inhibit its reuptake after release, giving it a stronger effect on dopamine than on norepinephrine. Some people feel wired or on edge with amphetamines; others find this class of drug to be more effective than methylphenidate. Because amphetamines have a less pronounced effect on norepinephrine, some patients tolerate them better than methylphenidate. In its regular form, dextroamphetamine takes approximately three hours to reach its maximal concentration; its sustained-release form takes eight hours.

As with methylphenidate, dextroamphetamine has the potential to induce mania, irritability, or agitation in a bipolar patient. Consequently, be alert when a child requires an increasing dose or develops a rebound reaction, agitation, pronounced loss of appetite, or a sleep disturbance (all signs of overstimulation in the deep brain). Because it is especially potent in increasing levels of dopamine, this medicine is more likely to aggravate tics in vulnerable children. Common side effects are similar to those of methylphenidate, including dry mouth, loss of appetite, difficulty sleeping, and rapid heartbeat.

The related medicine Adderall combines several amphetamine salts to produce similar effects over an extended period of time, reaching its peak concentrations in eight hours, coming on quickly but leaving more gradually.

Because of their euphoric effects, amphetamines have a potential for abuse; in most states they are controlled substances.

## ATOMOXETINE (STRATTERA)

Atomoxetine is not a stimulant but it increases the activity of norepinephrine (by inhibiting its reuptake) and so treats some of the same symptoms as the stimulants. In some children it does not have the undesirable effects of stimulants—insomnia, decreased appetite, increased anxiety, aggravation of tics—and does not have a potential for abuse. Atomoxetine must be taken daily and takes effect gradually over the course of two to four weeks.

Atomoxetine may be a useful alternative in children who have difficulty with tics or other abnormal movements induced by stimulants, a sleep disturbance induced by stimulants, or a potential to abuse stimulants. Its efficacy as compared to stimulants has not yet been thoroughly examined. As with any a new drug, its long-term side effects are not yet known, but there have been two recent reports of liver toxicity. It is therefore necessary periodically to check liver function in a child taking this medication.

In my experience, this medicine also has a potential to cause mania, agitation, or irritability in some bipolar patients, but it is safe and effective in some who cannot tolerate stimulants. Atomoxetine can also have significant interactions with other medications, increasing blood levels of drugs eliminated through the same pathway in the liver: some SSRIs and some antibiotics, for example. In some children atomoxetine has a sedating effect and needs to be taken at night.

## MODAFINIL (PROVIGIL)

Modafinil has been indicated by the FDA for use in narcolepsy, a disorder causing excessive daytime sleepiness. Recently, however, it has been tried as an alternative drug in the treatment of ADD. It has a more limited area of activity in the brain than stimulants and has only weak effects on dopamine, making it safer for children suffering from tics. Its mechanism of action is controversial, but there is some evidence that it stimulates the activity of norepinephrine, but in a more limited way than atomoxetine (Strattera) and methylphenidate. Anecdotal reports of its effectiveness in ADD are mixed. In two cases I have found it to promote irritability in a bipolar patient; in others it has been quite effective. There is also some interest in it to augment the treatment of depression.

## CLONIDINE (CATAPRES)

Clonidine is used for impulsivity—more for ADHD than for ADD— and is used also for children with tics that are aggravated by stimulants. Originally developed as an antihypertensive, clonidine has been used with some hyperactive children, including bipolar children, to decrease hyperactivity or to induce sleep. Clonidine does not have a potential to induce mania but it is quite sedating and can in some cases cause depression; it does not improve attention or sustained motivation. Sudden discontinuation of clonidine causes rebound hypertension, so it needs to be tapered.

# NONPHARMACOLOGIC MEASURES

## MELATONIN

Melatonin is a hormone that is released from the pineal region in the brain. It is known, among other things, to help regulate our sleep cycle and can be used as a natural way to help a child fall asleep. Many bipolar children have a dislocation—a delay or an advance—of the normal cycle of sleep and wakefulness. Melatonin given at bedtime (in a dose of 3–6 mg) sometimes not only helps a child fall asleep but also helps to reset that cycle.

## THERAPEUTIC LIGHT BOXES

These specially made lamps or panels of light have a particular (high) intensity. The light is of a normal frequency—it does not contain ultraviolet light. The lamp achieves its therapeutic benefit from its high intensity. The intensity of light is measured in lux. The light in a well-lit room is about 500 lux. It takes light of at least 3,000 lux to affect the neural pathway that stops the release of melatonin. Most therapeutic lights are designed to produce 10,000 lux at a distance of about one foot.

When used at the appropriate time of day, a light box can relieve depression related to the loss of light in the winter. Light of this intensity can, like melatonin, be used to reset the sleep cycle, but light has an opposite effect, helping a child wake up in the morning or remain alert in the evening.

High-intensity light should not be used indiscriminately: it can be beneficial when used at the right time but can worsen difficulties when used at the wrong time or in excessive amounts. The proper timing for the use of light depends on the position of a person's sleep cycle—how advanced or retarded it is.

## THE SLEEP-WAKE CYCLE

Falling asleep and waking up are not simply a matter of being tired or being rested. We have a daily hormonal cycle that regulates when we fall asleep and when we awaken. Normally melatonin is released for about twelve hours in the evening, causing us to want to go to sleep; it shuts off in the morning and we awaken. (We have ways of getting around this cycle by keeping ourselves up at night or awakening ourselves earlier with an alarm in the morning.) In most people this cycle is slightly more or less than twenty-four hours. As a result, if the cycle is not continually reset, it drifts forward (in those whose cycle is more than twenty-four hours) or backward (in those whose cycle is less than twenty-four hours). What resets the cycle is daylight coming through our eyes. Daylight shuts off melatonin and resets the cycle.

If the cycle drifts forward, a person falls asleep later and later and awakens later and later. When the cycle drifts backward, a person falls asleep earlier and earlier and wakes up earlier and earlier. Some people, including some children, experience a dislocation of their sleep cycle, especially in the fall and winter because their exposure to daylight is curtailed as the days shorten. For many people with bipolar disorder, this problem is accompanied by a seasonal depression. Seasonal depression can be treated, to some extent, with light. Therapeutic light boxes provide light at a particular intensity that can relieve seasonal depression. A person who tends to stay up late and wake up late needs light in the morning; a person who tends to go to bed early and get up early needs light in the afternoon or early evening.

## Fish Oil

You may have heard that fish is brain food. It seems that what makes fish beneficial to the brain is the composition of fish oil. Several well-regarded studies have shown significant long-term benefits in people with bipolar disorder (and other psychiatric conditions) from supplemental fish oil.

The membranes of neurons are composed of various fats, among them alpha-3 omega fatty acids. The receptors in a neuron are proteins that have one end outside the cell and the other inside the cell. For these receptors to function at their best, the cell membrane needs to have a certain balance of fluidity and rigidity. The fatty acids in fish oil help maintain that balance. There is no consensus about the right dose of fish oil: one study done with adult bipolar patients showed marked benefits using 10 g per day; another distinguished scientist has found 1–2 g to be more effective than 4 g in depressed patients. Excessive amounts of any fatty nutrient pose some risk, however. Nutrition is one of the areas in which the treatment of bipolar disorder is rapidly progressing and better and better information is likely to be available soon.

## Exercise

Exercise improves mood for numerous reasons and more are being discovered. There is no controversy, however, about the importance of exercise in helping maintain and restore mood stability. The exercise doesn't always have to be vigorous. Movement can improve thinking, quell obsessive preoccupations, resolve anger, oppose the listlessness of depression, or calm an agitated state. Exercise also counteracts the weight gain caused by many medications.

## Special Diets

Bipolar disorder is not caused by what we eat, but the mood stability of some children with bipolar disorder can be affected by their diet. Unstable blood sugar definitely affects mood, especially in a bipolar child. Some children with bipolar disorder are sensitive to other nutritional factors, for example the presence of wheat in their diet. I am not an expert on nutrition, but I have seen dietary changes help some children.

## Acupuncture and Acupressure

I have found acupuncture (which uses delicate needles) and acupressure (a manual technique) helpful in the treatment of anxiety and depression in bipolar patients, especially ones who do not respond sufficiently to medication. I have found it to be safe even when its effects are limited.

.   .   .

There is a complicated—some would say bewildering—set of medications used to treat bipolar disorder in children. These medicines give us
a flexible and comprehensive set of tools to work with, and treatment
can be tailored to an individual child's needs and to that child's different
needs at different times. The many medications used simultaneously to
treat bipolar disorder can, however, make it hard for a psychiatrist,
much less a parent, to keep track of what each medicine is doing. Over
time, medications can be added until the various effects of the combination can't be sorted out. This is not necessarily a bad situation; a good
pharmacologist can be like a good cook—knowing how to blend subtle
combinations to get the right effect, an effect that is *recognized* more
than it is understood.

It is crucial, however, that a parent understand, to some extent, what
each medication is supposed to do and what its risks may be, alone or in
combination with other medications. This means that a psychiatrist
should teach you about the medicines being used, and you need to demand clear explanations and repetitions of those explanations when
necessary. There is no such thing as a foolish question; there can be
foolish hesitation to ask. It is also wise to fill all prescriptions at the
same pharmacy so the pharmacist can screen for potentially bad interactions.

The rapid progress in the development of medications is a cause for
great optimism, as is the rapidly developing understanding of the
brain. It is unlikely that bipolar disorder will be cured; it is likely that it
will be better and better understood and more precisely controlled. As I
have stressed, however, proper treatment will always include a treatment of the person as well as of the brain. Especially in psychiatry and
especially with children, medications are given in the context of a relationship that must be developed and maintained.

As children mature, they should become more and more partners in
their own care. This means they should know about the medications
they take, the doses, the timing, and the side effects. They should begin

to recognize important symptoms as they appear and know when to bring them to someone's attention. Their choices should become more and more important, especially their choice to take control of their thoughts and feelings. In order to do this, their complaints need to be encouraged and heard. I often say that a child's job is to complain—about anything—and my job is to listen.

# How to Fight Weight Gain
# in Children

Childhood obesity has become increasingly widespread, bringing with it an epidemic of type II diabetes—also known as adult on-set diabetes—in children. Overweight children have increased in number for several reasons. The enormous hold television and computer games have on children, especially those who are socially isolated, has resulted in excessive amounts of sedentary play. At the same time, the increasing number of households in which there is a single parent, or in which both parents work full-time, has led to a more frequent consumption of fast foods. When the metabolic influences of psychiatric medications are added to increasing amounts of sedentary play and greater reliance on fast foods, the risk for obesity in a child with bipolar disorder becomes formidable.

## BEYOND WEIGHT: CARBOHYDRATES AND EMOTIONAL SOOTHING

Controlling weight in a child with bipolar disorder is complicated by several connections between carbohydrate metabolism and brain chemistry that predispose a child with anxiety or depression to overeat. Anxiety frequently appears in the guise of a vague abdominal discomfort that can be mistaken for hunger. (I treated one person with bipolar disorder whose whole family would get what they called "the feeling," a vague abdominal discomfort.) There is also a specific connection between carbohydrate metabolism and the brain's regulation of anxiety. Ingesting carbohydrates increases levels of serotonin in the brain and in the gut. Serotonin plays a crucial role in regulating mood, anxiety, and impulsivity; it also modulates eating patterns, affecting both satiety and the desire for carbohydrates. Put simply, the chronic anxiety seen in bipolar disorder can lead to compulsive carbohydrate consumption as people try to calm their anxiety and lift their mood.

Depression is also affected by carbohydrates. Three kinds of depression commonly seen in bipolar disorder—atypical depression, seasonal affective disorder, and premenstrual dysphoric disorder—are accompanied by carbohydrate craving. When a child eats something high in carbohydrates—especially sugar—his blood sugar (glucose) rises rapidly. The effects of a sugar high are initially pleasurable: brain metabolism speeds up and serotonin levels rise; anxiety and depression are relieved. (Some children become hyper or silly.) However, the body responds to a surge in blood sugar by releasing large amounts of insulin to direct this sugar into body cells. The surge of insulin then causes blood sugar to fall off rapidly. Because the brain's activity is directly dependent on blood sugar, and because levels of blood sugar affect levels of serotonin, the drop in blood sugar has an emotional as well as a metabolic impact. Depression, anxiety, irritability, impulsivity, and problems concentrating all increase, accompanied by an intense craving for carbohydrates. This craving brings on another round of carbohydrate bingeing, high blood sugar, mood elevation, a drop in blood sugar, mood instability, and further carbohydrate craving.

## CARBOHYDRATES, INSULIN RESISTANCE, AND THE BIPOLAR CHILD

At the same time that an increased consumption of carbohydrates skews emotional and behavioral control, it also upsets the body's metabolism. An elevated insulin level prompted by excessive carbohydrates causes more blood sugar to flow into fat cells, leading to increased production of fat. This is especially troubling during infancy and adolescence, when levels of growth hormone are high. The combination of a stimulation of fat production and large amounts of growth hormone leads to an increased *number* of fat cells—not just larger fat cells, but more of them—and a decrease in the production of protein and muscular tissue. The ratio of fat to lean body mass goes up. Then, because fat cells have a lower metabolic rate than muscle cells, the overall metabolic rate drops. Despite constant craving for carbohydrates, the body uses less and less energy. Consequently, more and more glucose is devoted to the production of fat.

As the size and number of fat cells increase, a condition known as insulin resistance develops: cells have more difficulty taking up glucose in response to insulin; the pancreas responds by producing more insulin; increased insulin then aggravates the metabolic problem. Eventually the pancreas cannot keep up with the demand for insulin, resulting in chronically high blood sugar, or diabetes.

Insulin resistance is also accompanied by an increase in fats in the blood and the release of certain inflammatory proteins: inflammation damages the walls of arteries, which then accumulate fatty deposits. These deposits later calcify, causing hardening and narrowing of arteries (arteriosclerosis) and high blood pressure. Insulin resistance also contributes to the neurological and visual problems that come later on with diabetes.

Before developing high blood sugar, a vulnerable child experiences unstable blood sugar with episodes of low blood sugar (hypoglycemia) and becomes irritable, tearful, impulsive, or inattentive if she doesn't eat frequently. She also craves carbohydrates more than most children. Consequently, the child has a high risk of both mood instability and obesity—both of which complicate the course of a child with bipolar disorder. Because anxiety, irritability, depression, and impulsivity are aggravated, there is a higher risk of social isolation. The task of self-regulation, already problematic, becomes more difficult. When this metabolic pattern occurs in an adolescent, especially an adolescent girl, the stage is set for an eating disorder.

In families with a history of adult onset diabetes, early cardiovascular disease, or obesity, this metabolic tendency is often inherited. It is not surprising, then, that among bipolar patients with such a family history there is also a high rate of eating disorders and alcohol abuse; both conditions consist of abnormal carbohydrate consumption and an unsuccessful attempt to control mood and anxiety.

## DIET AND EXERCISE

A diet with proportionately more protein and fiber moderates both glucose and insulin levels and improves mental alertness throughout the day. Adjust the ratio of protein to carbohydrates—more protein earlier in the day. Protein stimulates the release of a hormone called glucagon, which has an opposite effect from insulin: glucagon directs blood sugar into muscle cells more than into fat cells; it also directs it into the liver to be converted into glycogen, a substance the body uses to maintain stable blood sugar. Consequently, muscles develop, blood sugar is more stable, and the release of insulin is moderated. Protein early in the day gets the body off in the right direction. By contrast, carbs early in the day start the cycle of ups and downs in blood sugar. Children with a breakfast high in carbohydrates—sugared cereal, pancakes with syrup—bottom out by midmorning, have difficulty concentrating, and crave more carbs at lunchtime. Studies show that children who have protein for breakfast consume fewer carbs at lunch.

Next, increase fiber in your child's diet. Fiber—found in vegetables, most raw fruits, and whole grains—slows the absorption of carbohydrates, preventing surges in blood sugar and promoting more moderate insulin levels. For breakfast have whole wheat toast—hold the jelly. Whole-grain cereals, especially oatmeal, are good. Melon, grapefruit, and berries (particularly strawberries and blueberries), are also great. If possible, substitute grapefruit juice for orange juice or apple juice, which have no fiber and are high in sugar. A fresh apple is fine, however. Include some vegetables or raw fruit with lunch.

Exercise—because it stabilizes blood sugar, promotes the release of endorphins, and increases levels of norepinephrine—alleviates anxiety and elevates mood. What is more, exercise has been found to increase blood levels of phenylethylamine, a neuroactive compound known to have an antidepressant effect.

Metabolically, exercise stimulates the release of both glucagon and growth hormone, while slowing the release of insulin. Consequently, exercise not only burns calories, it also stabilizes insulin and glucose levels, while promoting the development of muscle and the break-down of fat. There is another benefit: muscle tissue—even at rest—has a higher metabolic rate than fatty tissue, so building more muscle promotes further consumption of energy and the break-down of fat. As the metabolic balance shifts, cravings for carbs also decrease.

## DIETARY FAT

Gram for gram, fat contains many more calories than carbs, but it requires carbohydrates to turn fat into sugar and into *your* fat. So the most potent sources of weight gain are foods that com-bine fat with carbohydrates—ice cream, a cheeseburger, french fries, almost any fast food. Alas, these are the most tempting for a child.

Low-carb, high-fat diets—most notably the Atkins approach—take advantage of the fact that the body requires carbohydrates to break down fat. So when fat is eaten without carbohydrates, the body has to give up calories to digest it. That's why, when eaten without carbs, fat can be satisfying without causing weight gain.

There is a problem when this approach is carried too far. It is very hard for an adult to eliminate carbohydrates so completely that fat cannot be turned into sugar. Even if a person does successfully restrict carbohydrates, the body takes calories to break down fat from protein, that is, from lean body mass. What is more, animal fat—contained in meat and dairy products—can contain hormones or other fat-soluble substances that have their own dangers.

There are good fats, however. Olive oil, peanut oil, and fish oil all have beneficial effects. When these fats are eaten separate from carbs, they can be satisfying and healthful. Try olive oil instead of butter on vegetables, or a snack of peanut butter alone—a brand without added sugar.

## CONQUERING OBESITY

How, then, can this metabolic theory and the relationship between anxiety and carbohydrates be translated into practical measures? To begin with, understand that weight gain is a psychotherapeutic as well as a medical problem. Before approaching the problem with your child, discuss the situation with his therapist so you can learn how to help your child with the powerful emotional currents surrounding eating and obesity. Beyond the metabolic connection between carbohydrates and anxiety, the psychological connection between eating and safety is among the earliest and most powerful of associations. Your child needs the full protection of his relationship with you to give up this source of emotional comfort. If your child is already overweight, in addition to a metabolic balance working against him and a loss of feeling emotionally nourished, there will be problems with self-esteem.

## Limiting Medications That Promote Weight Gain

Adjusting medications can be one of the simplest measures to take, although your child's particular needs may impose certain limits. First, make sure you are informed by your child's psychiatrist about any medications that promote weight gain, as well as the possible alternatives. Ask the psychiatrist about medicines that may *decrease* appetite: topiramate (Topamax) or zonisamide (Zonegran) are mood stabilizers that have this property; ziprasidone (Geodon) is a major tranquilizer that may also help with weight loss. Metformin (Glucophage) can be a helpful addition for children above the age of ten. This medication, when carbohydrates are moderated, can stabilize blood sugar and lower insulin levels, helping with weight loss.

## Modifying the Diet

The next step in controlling weight is dietary modification, which can be particularly difficult with a child. Setting an example is crucial: our children frequently don't do what we tell them, but they almost always do what we do. With a boy, this is especially true in relation to his father. Setting an example often is a challenge, however: a child who suffers from obesity usually has at least one parent who shares the problem, from whom he probably inherited his metabolic tendency.

The goal is to cut down on sugar, cereals (especially sugared cereals), bread, pasta, and potatoes and to increase vegetables and other sources of fiber. Consumption of fat must be reduced, especially the fat-carbohydrate combination found in french fries, potato chips, ice cream, and most fast foods.

· Find snacks that are low in sugar, such as nuts or peanut butter (without added sugar), raw carrots, apples, pears, berries.

· Preparing bite-sized portions of these snacks in advance makes them more available and more palatable. These choices are difficult to encourage outside the house, but at home in the afternoon or the evening you have more control.

· Consider low-carb, high-protein drinks. They are filling and change the ratio of protein to carbohydrates.

· Whey protein can be added to muffins, pancakes, or waffles to increase the ratio of protein to carbohydrates. Flavored whey protein can also be mixed with skim milk to make an evening shake that quickly increases serotonin levels without markedly increasing insulin levels.

· Make sure your child drinks plenty of fluids, because thirst or dehydration can be misinterpreted as hunger. Encourage your child to drink more water.

· Limit the consumption of soda, however; it contains enormous amounts of sugar. Fruit juices are also surprisingly full of sugar. Try cutting juices with seltzer as a more healthful alternative to soda.

· There are safe nutritional supplements—for example, encapsulated fiber and conjugated linoleic acid—that can help shift the metabolic balance in your child's favor. (Avoid supplements containing ephedrine, ma huang, guarana, or caffeine, all of which can cause anxiety and a worsening of bipolar disorder.)

Most of these measures require active parenting—not just setting limits—and work (food preparation, shopping, supervision of eating) that falls principally on a mother. This makes a father's participation all the more important, because there is a risk for a child to identify the unpleasantness of dieting with his mother. This is particularly true because children associate food, or the lack of it, with their mothers, and because mothers are emotionally highly invested in feeding their child. Dad must join closely with Mom in this work because bipolar children are more likely to split between their parents, making one the good and the other the bad parent.

# CHOCOLATE

Chocolate contains small quantities of anandamide, a cannabinoid (the active ingredient in marijuana, THC, is a cannabinoid) found naturally in the brain. Although you would have to consume several pounds of chocolate before noticing significant psychoactive effects, the amount in normal portions of chocolate still may influence brain chemistry. Chocolate contains two structural cousins of anandamide—N-oleoylethanolamine and N-linoleoylethanolamine—both of which slow the metabolism of anandamide. Some researchers have speculated that these two substances promote and prolong the feeling of well-being induced by the anandamide in chocolate. Chocolate also contains tryptophan, an amino acid that promotes the production of serotonin. Enhanced serotonin typically diminishes anxiety.

Acute monthly cravings for chocolate among premenstrual women are also partly explained by its rich magnesium content. (A deficiency of magnesium exacerbates premenstrual symptoms.) Drugs that increase available serotonin are also known to relieve premenstrual symptoms. One study reported that 91 percent of chocolate cravings associated with the menstrual cycle occurred between ovulation and the start of menstruation. In another study, chocolate cravings were acknowledged by 15 percent of men and 40 percent of women. Cravings are usually most intense in the late afternoon and early evening, when cortisol drops and anxiety increases.

One implication of these findings is that children (and adults) with bipolar disorder, and especially adolescent girls, are likely to crave chocolate. However, many of the psychoactive properties of chocolate are independent of its sugar content, so unsweetened or slightly sweetened forms of chocolate can satisfy these cravings without jolting blood sugar. The better preparations tell you the amount of chocolate used. So look for 70–95 percent cocoa on the label.

## Burning Off the Pounds

Increasing your child's physical activity helps burn weight away, reduces anxiety, and improves mood. Look for ways to increase walking. Particularly in the suburbs, where almost all traveling is done in a car, you may have to invent an occasion for walking. Take an evening walk—when cortisol levels drop—and see the stars. Take a regular weekend hike. Have your child spend less time watching television and playing computer games. Involve him in outdoor activities, especially in the winter when skiing, skating, and hiking are active alternatives to staying inside. These activities provide sunlight as well as exercise and are a great remedy for cabin fever, an older name for SAD.

Some children do not have the personality to play team sports, so they need activities that can be pursued alone or in parallel with peers—such as running, skiing, swimming, hiking, and climbing. Here again, active parenting is required. It is necessary for you to accompany and encourage your child, even when you don't actually share in the activity. As with dietary changes, what you do is more important than what you say. The upside is that you and your child will spend more time together and deepen your relationship.

## Seeking Outside Aid

A camp that specializes in weight loss can be helpful to a child struggling with obesity, if she can tolerate the developmental challenge. If a child is willing to accept it, such a setting relieves some of the shame that invariably accompanies being overweight, a shame that is particularly intense in the peer group. Camp activities also increase her sense of physical competence, helping to give her an appetite for exercise and sports. For those in better physical condition, there are camps that encourage backpacking, rock climbing, and kayaking, combined with counseling that helps children improve their peer relationships. Scouting is an established and inexpensive way to do this year-round. Participation in scouting requires, however, a degree of social facility that some children with bipolar disorder cannot manage.

**agonist.** A medication that activates the receptors of a particular neurotransmitter, intensifying the effects of that transmitter. For example,
trazodone is a serotonin agonist—it mimics the action of serotonin,
stimulating serotonin receptors.

**akathisia.** An uncomfortable feeling of restlessness experienced as an
inability to remain still. It is usually felt in large muscle groups, such
as in the arms and legs. People experiencing this symptom may say
they feel like they are going to jump out of their skin. Akathisia can
add to a person's anxiety, agitation, or impulsivity, and it can be mistaken for mere anxiety.

**antagonist.** A medication that inhibits or blocks the receptors for a specific neurotransmitter. For example, major tranquilizers are dopamine antagonists; they block the action of dopamine.

**delusion.** An irrational idea that is believed to be true. For example, a
depressed person can have delusions that he is being persecuted by
someone, a persecutory delusion; a manic person can believe she is all-
powerful, a grandiose delusion. A delusion is a psychotic symptom.

**half-life.** The time it takes for half of a drug, once it has been absorbed
into the bloodstream, to be eliminated from the body. For example,
the half-life of alprazolam (Xanax) is four to six hours. Because
drugs are eliminated gradually from the CNS and the body, it is easier

and more revealing to describe their duration of action in terms of their half-life. It requires calculus to determine how long it takes for alprazolam to be completely removed, but its effects are substantially reduced by the time it is half gone.

**metabolism.** The biochemical process by which one compound or several compounds are transformed into another. The metabolism of a drug is the process by which it is transformed into an inactive compound that can be eliminated from the body, usually by the liver or the kidneys.

**metabolite.** When a drug passes through the liver, it is metabolized or turned into another substance, which is usually inactive and more easily eliminated. This is the body's way of removing and deactivating biologically active substances in the blood. This substance, the product of metabolism, is called a metabolite. For example, alcohol is metabolized by the liver first into acetaldehyde and then into acetone. Acetone is a substance that does not affect the CNS and is easily eliminated. In some cases metabolites are active or can have important side effects in the body. For example, fluoxetine (an SSRI) is metabolized into norfluoxetine, a substance that also acts on serotonin. Norfluoxetine is a therapeutically active metabolite. But when alcohol is metabolized into acetaldehyde, acetaldehyde causes dizziness, nausea, and vomiting; it is also an active metabolite, but one that is toxic.

**mourning.** The emotional process through which a loss—of a person, a valued idea of the self, or a valued idea of someone else—is accepted. The process includes denial, anger, and depression as necessary preliminaries to acceptance. Mourning is particularly difficult—and therefore crucially important—in bipolar disorder because the intrinsic psychological symptoms of the condition (denial, grandiosity, mania, contempt, rage) are all defenses against loss. With both patients and family, the psychotherapy of bipolar disorder *must* include helping patients mourn the illness.

**neurotransmitters.** Small molecules, made inside neurons, that are released into a synapse and bind to receptors on the adjacent neuron, with the effect of either stimulating or inhibiting that neuron. Serotonin, norepinephrine, dopamine, and acetylcholine are well-known and clinically important neurotransmitters.

**nightmares.** Disturbing dreams that have an extended narrative content and occur during REM sleep. The dreamer may awaken from nightmares and usually has a memory of the dream content.

**night terrors.** Episodes in which a sleeping child becomes agitated, thrashes around physically, and may cry out. If the parent attempts to awaken and comfort the child, he becomes more agitated and is difficult to awaken. Upon awakening, the child often has no memory of what was so disturbing. If he does remember something, it is usually a scene rather than an extended narrative. These events occur in stage-four sleep, the stage in which sleepwalking or talking in one's sleep occurs. Night terrors are not dreams in that they do not occur in REM sleep, during which there is a relative lack of physical movement.

**psychosis.** A state of anxiety during which a person loses the ability to distinguish between internal mental events and external ones. Simply, the person cannot tell what is real and what is not. Psychotic symptoms may include hearing voices, seeing things, or having wildly irrational thoughts that are believed to be true (delusions); they can have a depressive, grandiose, or bizarre quality. In the case of hallucinations, in order to be psychotic, the person must also believe that they are true or coming from outside her mind. Psychotic symptoms may accompany severe depression, mania, or schizophrenia; they can also be brought on by drugs or drastic changes in a person's metabolism. They are symptoms and do not by themselves confirm a particular diagnosis.

**reuptake inhibitor.** A medication or chemical that acts on the presynaptic neuron (the nerve that comes before the synapse and releases a neurotransmitter into the synapse). This agent inhibits that neuron's ability to reabsorb the neurotransmitter it has released. As a result, the duration and strength of the signal given to the postsynaptic neuron are amplified. For example, a selective serotonin reuptake inhibitor (SSRI) acts on a neuron that releases serotonin in such a way that its reuptake of serotonin is inhibited, increasing the effect of serotonin on the postsynaptic neuron.

**serotonin syndrome.** A dangerous combination of physical and mental symptoms brought on by excessive release of serotonin in the brain: euphoria, drowsiness, sustained rapid eye movement, overreaction of the reflexes, rapid muscle contraction and relaxation in the ankle causing abnormal movements of the foot, clumsiness, restlessness, feeling drunk and dizzy, muscle contraction and relaxation in the jaw, sweating, intoxication, muscle twitching, rigidity, high body temperature, mental status changes, shivering, diarrhea, loss of consciousness, and possibly death. Serotonin syndrome is generally caused by a combination of two or more drugs, one of which is often an SSRI. The most frequent combination causing this condition is the combination of an MAOI (monoamine oxidase inhibitor) with SSRIs or other drugs that have a powerful effect on serotonin, e.g., clomipramine (Anafranil), trazodone (Desyrel), mirtazapine (Remeron).

**synapse.** The space between two neurons into which one neuron—the presynaptic neuron—releases a neurotransmitter such as serotonin, dopamine, norepinephrine, GABA, or glutamate. The neurotransmitter crosses the synapse and either stimulates or inhibits the postsynaptic neuron.

**thought disorder.** A term used to refer to various disturbances in the logical coherence of a person's thought. For example, a loose connection between one idea and another, associations on the basis of sound rather than sense, illogical jumps from one thought to the next, getting lost in the details of a subject, racing thoughts, or a sudden loss of thought. Like psychosis, a thought disorder can be seen with different psychiatric conditions and is not by itself diagnostic of any one.

Gregory T. Lombardo, M.D., Ph.D., is a psychiatrist practicing in New York, specializing in evaluating and treating children and adults pharmacologically and psychotherapeutically. He is board certified in child, adolescent, and adult psychiatry, and is a diplomate of the American Society of Clinical Psychopharmacology. Prior to his work as a psychiatrist, he taught at the college and secondary school levels. He has a doctorate in literature and is a Shakespearean scholar.